CONTEMPORARY POLITICAL STUDIES SERIES

Series Editor: John Benyon, University of Leicester

Published

DAVID BROUGHTON
Public Opinion and Political Polling in Britain

JANE BURNHAM and ROBERT PYPER
Britain's Modernised Civil Service

CLYDE CHITTY
Education Policy in Britain: 2nd edn

MICHAEL CONNOLLY
Politics and Policy Making in Northern Ireland

DAVID DENVER
Elections and Voters in Britain: 2nd edn

JUSTIN FISHER
British Political Parties

ROBERT GARNER
Environmental Politics: Britain, Europe and the Global Environment: 2nd edn

ANDREW GEDDES
The European Union and British Politics

WYN GRANT
Pressure Groups and British Politics

WYN GRANT
Economic Policy in Britain

DEREK HEATER and GEOFFREY BERRIDGE
Introduction to International Politics

DILYS M. HILL
Urban Policy and Politics in Britain

RAYMOND KUHN
Politics and the Media in Britain

ROBERT LEACH: 2nd edn
Political Ideology in Britain

ROBERT LEACH and JANIE PERCY-SMITH
Local Governance in Britain

PETER MADGWICK
British Government: The Central Executive Territory

ANDREW MASSEY and ROBERT PYPER
Public Management and Modernisation in Britain

PHILIP NORTON
Parliament and British Politics

MALCOLM PUNNETT
Selecting the Party Leader

Forthcoming

CHARLIE JEFFERY
Devolution and UK Politics

Contemporary Political Studies Series

Series Standing Order ISBN 978–0230–54350–8 hardback
Series Standing Order ISBN 978–0230–54351–5 paperback

(outside North America only)

You can receive future titles in this series as they are published by placing a standing order. Please contact your bookseller or, in case of difficulty, write to us at the address below with your name and address, the title of the series and one of the ISBNs quoted above.

Customer Services Department, Macmillan Distribution Ltd
Houndmills, Basingstoke, Hampshire RG21 6XS, England

Political Ideology in Britain

Second Edition

Robert Leach

First edition 2002 (reprinted four times)
Second edition 2009

Published by
PALGRAVE MACMILLAN

Palgrave Macmillan in the UK is an imprint of Macmillan Publishers Limited, registered in England, company number 785998, of Houndmills, Basingstoke, Hampshire RG21 6XS.

Palgrave Macmillan in the US is a division of St Martin's Press LLC, 175 Fifth Avenue, New York, NY 10010.

Palgrave Macmillan is the global academic imprint of the above companies and has companies and representatives throughout the world.

Palgrave® and Macmillan® are registered trademarks in the United States, the United Kingdom, Europe and other countries.

ISBN-13: 978–0–230–58472–3   hardback
ISBN-10: 0–230–58472–1   hardback
ISBN-13: 978–0–230–58473–0   paperback
ISBN-10: 0–230–58473–X   paperback

This book is printed on paper suitable for recycling and made from fully managed and sustained forest sources. Logging, pulping and manufacturing processes are expected to conform to the environmental regulations of the country of origin.

A catalogue record for this book is available from the British Library.

A catalog record for this book is available from the Library of Congress.

10   9   8   7   6   5   4   3   2   1
18   17   16   15   14   13   12   11   10   09

Printed and bound in China

Contents

List of Figures, Tables and Boxes

Preface

This is the fully revised and updated second edition of *Political Ideology in Britain*, originally published by Palgrave Macmillan in 2002, although that book followed two editions of an earlier title, *British Political Ideologies* (1991, 1996). This is effectively the fourth version of a book that has had a wide readership over the years.

There are now several good books on political ideologies. This one focuses on ideology in British politics. Political ideologies are not pure political theory, but emerge from and interact with the practice of politics. Ostensibly broader accounts of ideologies often involve either an implicit bias towards a limited number of western political systems, or very generalized accounts of political ideas in the abstract, and not illustrated with examples of their application. Relating ideologies to politics in a particular country helps to capture the interplay between political ideas and practice. It also incidentally aims to serve the requirements of specific university undergraduate courses relating to British politics, as well as relevant advanced level units for schools and colleges.

Yet the approach is far from insular. Distinctive British variants of ideologies are compared with international currents of thought and set against wider political developments, including globalization, the world environmental crisis and international relations. Key concepts of specific ideologies are explored in this wider context before the evolution of relevant political ideas and movements are examined in Britain. The sometimes considerable differences between the interpretation and experience of political creeds such as liberalism, conservatism and socialism in Britain and in other countries are fully discussed.

What is different in this new edition? There have been major developments in British politics and political ideas since the 2002 edition, which was published after 9/11 but before the Iraq war and the experience of terrorist attacks on London in 2005 and Glasgow airport in 2007. Since 2002 the major three British political parties have all changed their leaders, the Conservatives and Liberal Democrats twice, with some considerable implications for party policy and ideology. More important perhaps have been developments in the wider world that have inevitably impacted on Britain. These include a dramatic expansion of the European Union, growing realization of the impact of climate change, concerns over new international conflicts, new genocides and new waves of asylum-seekers. However, and above all, it has been the dramatic and largely unanticipated crisis in the world banking system in 2008 and the following global economic recession that have sharply challenged some prevailing ideological assumptions. The impact of all these far-reaching developments is explored.

Beyond such essential updating there has been some restructuring of material. In 2002 I included separate chapters on the New Right and New Labour in addition to chapters on Conservatism and Socialism. This had some advantages, but risked exaggerating the transformation of ideologies and downplaying elements of continuity in the thinking in both major parties. The New Right is now history, and the Conservative party in some respects has moved on, while New Labour is no longer novel. I toyed with an alternative division, but ultimately decided it was preferable to revert to fuller substantive chapters on 'Conservatism' and 'Socialism', from their origins to the present. I have also devoted a separate chapter to 'multiculturalism', formerly rather uncomfortably bracketed with racism and fascism. This allows a rather broader discussion of the concept, relating it to other aspects of culture besides 'race', including religion, age and class. Beyond all this I have generally expanded my analysis and discussion of specific political concepts. I considered a separate glossary of terms, but decided that key concepts were more appropriately explored in the context of relevant chapters.

Finally, I have to express my thanks to Stephen Wenham and Steven Kennedy at Palgrave Macmillan, as well as to some anonymous reviewers, who have contributed some invaluable advice, some general, others highly specific. I also thank Keith Povey (with the help of Nancy Richardson) for carefully editing my text. Finally, and as usual, my greatest debt is to my wife Judith.

ROBERT LEACH

1

Introduction: Ideology in British Politics

Political ideas and ideologies

Serious study of political ideas goes back at least as far as Greece of the fifth and fourth centuries BC when thinkers such as Socrates, Plato and Aristotle speculated about the best system of government and the meaning of terms like 'justice', 'equality' and 'freedom'. The modern study of political theory or political philosophy has focussed on the writings of major political thinkers and the key concepts and theories that they examined. The study of political ideologies, such as liberalism, conservatism and socialism, draws on this very old study of ideas but is of more recent origin. The term 'ideology' is itself problematic and contested (see below) but for the present may be loosely defined as 'any system of ideas and norms directing political and social action' (Flew, 1979, p. 150). The key words here are 'system' and 'action'. An ideology involves firstly an interconnected set of ideas that form a perspective on the world. Secondly, ideologies have implications for political behaviour – they are 'action-oriented.'

Most of the political ideologies which influence the way we think and act today have developed relatively recently, over the last two hundred or so years, shaped directly or indirectly by the eighteenth-century enlightenment, industrialisation and the American and French revolutions, although influenced by older ideas. Thus, while conservative habits of thought are perhaps as old as humanity, conservatism as a coherent political perspective was only articulated more systematically in response to radical political doctrines which sought to change the world, such as liberalism and socialism. Some ideologies, including fascism and green thinking, were essentially products of the twentieth century, although again their core ideas developed out of, and in opposition to, mainstream political thinking from the enlightenment onwards.

This book explores these ideologies both in general terms and with particular reference to British politics. Yet before we proceed to a more detailed examination of specific ideologies, it is important to discuss some general issues surrounding the study of political ideologies. Thus this opening chapter explores the nature of political ideology and its relationship with power and interests. It examines key elements of ideologies and their conventional classification on a left–right scale. It looks at the different levels at which ideologies are held and expressed. It concludes with a brief introductory discussion on the role of ideology and pragmatism in British politics.

Ideas, power and interests

How important are political ideas? Ideas, it might be urged, are the lifeblood of politics. There is nothing so powerful as an idea whose time has come. Thus the ideas expressed in the American Declaration of Independence or the French revolutionary slogan 'Liberty, Equality, Fraternity' transformed the world. The Communist Manifesto of Marx and Engels inspired a revolution in Russia and an economic and political system that once shaped the lives and work of a third of the globe. More recently the rediscovery of the idea of the free market has stimulated political and economic change over the western, former Communist and third worlds.

From another perspective, politics is essentially about power and interests rather than ideas. As Thrasymachus in Plato's *Republic* (Cornford, 1945, p. 18) argues, 'just or right means nothing but what is to the interest of the stronger party.' Ideas of what is right involve rationalisations of interest. Those in power are well-placed to ensure that the ideas which are widely accepted are those that are in accordance with their own interest, or, as Karl Marx put it much later, 'The ruling ideas of every age are the ideas of the ruling class.'

Marx was concerned with the source of ideas. How and why do ideas originate? One of his targets was idealism, the philosophical approach derived ultimately from Plato but featuring especially Kant and Hegel, that suggested that ideas are the ultimate reality, and the motive force in human history. Against this, Marx presented his own materialist conception of history in which ideas derive from the material circumstances of humanity. 'Life is not determined by consciousness, but consciousness by life' (Marx, ed. McLellan, 1977, p. 164). Our experience of the world shapes our outlook, not the other way round. Thus ideas reflect social and economic circumstances. Marx, moreover, saw society as deeply divided, so that the moral and political ideas expressed at any time reflect conflicting class interests.

Such an approach provides insights into the mainstream ideologies of the western world. Thus traditional conservatism may be linked with landed interests, liberalism with financial and industrial capital, and socialism with the industrial working class. Conservatives, liberals and many non-Marxist socialists would deny that that their political convictions reflected such specific class interests, but claim instead that they have a universal relevance, and draw support across classes. Nevertheless, analysis of the membership, electoral support and policies of political parties associated with these ideologies suggest some significant, if not overwhelming, connections with class interests.

Relating political ideas to material interests is certainly a fruitful approach, whether ideologies are linked exclusively to economic classes in the Marxist sense, or associated more broadly with other interests in society, such as those based on gender, religion, nation or ethnicity. It does make sense to ask who is putting forward particular doctrines and why, and whose interests they serve. Answers to such questions can be very illuminating. Even so, there are ideologies such as environmentalism (or green thinking) which are less easily equated with specific interests within human society. Moreover, while ideologies may be strongly associated with material interests, this does not necessarily entail that they are simply rationalisations of interest, and have no intrinsic validity.

Marx himself generally employed the term 'ideology' in a pejorative (or negative) sense, and identified ideology with illusion. The prevailing ideas in any society, he suggested, will reflect the existing power structure, the current pattern of domination and subordination, partly because those with economic and political power will be well-placed to control the dissemination and legitimation of ideas, through, for example, education and the mass media. It follows that subordinate classes will not necessarily recognise the real basis of society, nor their own exploitation, but will hold a distorted, mistaken view of reality. Marx commonly used the term 'ideology' to describe this distorted view that a social class, such as the industrial proletariat, might have of its own position in society as a whole. Much of the prevailing wisdom of his day, such as the ideas of the classical economists, Smith, Malthus and Ricardo, Marx regarded as ideological rather than scientific. Their theories served the interests of capitalism. By contrast, Marx thought his own method provided a powerful tool for penetrating below the surface and understanding the real economic and social forces which shape change. Thus, Marxism was science rather than ideology.

This identification of ideology with illusion and distortion and what Engels later called 'false consciousness' (McLellan, 1995, p. 20) is of course highly pejorative. However, Marx sometimes used the term in a more neutral sense, and later Marxists, such as Lenin, Gramsci and Lukács assumed a need to promote a working-class socialist ideology to counter the dominant ruling-class ideology.

Ideology as dogmatism – the 'end of ideology'

Some modern, particularly American, social scientists have also, like Marx, employed the term ideology in a highly pejorative way, but in a quite opposite sense to his. Thus non-Marxist economists, sociologists and political scientists emphasised the need for detached, value-free, rigorous empirical research – which they saw as the essence of the social science method. Marxist analysis was regarded, by contrast, as dogmatic, unscientific and 'ideological'. Ideology was identified particularly with closed 'totalitarian' systems of thought, under which heading they included both fascism and Marxist-inspired communism. Ideology was the enemy of western pluralist democracy. The future lay with non-ideological thinking, pragmatism rather than ideology. Preconceived ideas and all-embracing theories were useless or positively dangerous.

Just as many Marxists did not think their own political ideas were 'ideological', so these western political thinkers did not consider that the liberal pluralist or conservative ideas they held were ideological either. An ideology was the political outlook of someone else. The liberal pluralist ideas on which post-war western society rested were scientific and non-ideological. Thus the triumph of pluralist liberal democracy involved the 'end of ideology' (Bell, 1960, Freeden 2003, pp. 35–9). More recently, in an echo of Bell's thesis, the fall of the Berlin Wall and Soviet communism marked the victory of liberal capitalism and, according to Francis Fukuyama (1992) the 'end of history'.

Ideological conflict and consensus

Meanwhile, in Britain and western Europe ideological conflict apparently gave way to an ideological consensus (or agreement) in the post-Second World War era. In Britain it appeared that leading Labour and Conservative politicians increasingly shared the same assumptions, and often the same remedies. The term 'Butskellism' was coined (from the names of Labour and Conservative Chancellors, Gaitskell and Butler) to describe the similar approach of both major parties to economic management. There was widespread acceptance across the party divide of the social welfare ideas of William Beveridge and the economic theories of John Maynard Keynes, and this was accordingly described as the Keynes–Beveridge consensus (Kavanagh, 1990, pp. 34–60). Over western Europe generally there was a similar 'social democratic' consensus around the welfare state and managed capitalism (Judt, 2005, pp. 360–73).

The extent of ideological consensus in the post-Second World War era has arguably been exaggerated. However, a widely prevailing consensus does not necessarily imply the 'end of ideology' in Bell's sense. Rather it may suggest the dominance of a particular ideology, the acceptance by the political establishment, and perhaps the bulk of the masses also, of a set of ideas which may become for a time the ruling political orthodoxy. Indeed, as some twentieth-century Marxists like Gramsci have argued, the dominance of such a single 'hegemonic' ideology may be more the norm than the exception. It may become so widely accepted and unchallenged that it is not even perceived as ideological, but simply common sense or 'the way things are', to which 'there is no alternative'. It is only when the assumptions behind such a dominant orthodoxy are eventually challenged that its ideological character is acknowledged.

Contemporary approaches towards the study of ideologies

As McLellan (1995, p. 1) has ironically observed, 'Ideology is someone *else's* thought, seldom our own,' underlining the pejorative interpretation of ideology both by Marxists and leading anti-Marxists, such as Oakeshott (1962) or Minogue (1985). An alternative approach assumes that all political thinking, including our own, is ideological (Freeden, 1996, 2003). The use of the term 'ideology' does not in itself imply any kind of judgement on the validity of the ideas discussed. Ideology is not necessarily to be identified with illusion or unreflecting dogma, nor should it be contrasted with 'truth' or 'science'. Moreover, while ideologies may be employed to legitimate existing systems or regimes, they can also be used to justify their overthrow. Ideologies may thus be conservative, reformist or revolutionary, moderate or extremist. They may be associated with conflicting interests in society, but also with a system of belief that appears to command general assent. This more inclusive approach to the study of ideology (Seliger, 1976, pp. 91–2), has now become sufficiently common to be described as mainstream, and implicitly or explicitly underpins a burgeoning literature surveying modern political ideologies (e.g. Vincent, 1995; Adams, 1993, 1998; Eatwell and Wright, 1999; Eccleshall *et al.*, 2003; Heywood, 2007).

While not neglecting the importance of social context, power and interests, some exponents of this modern approach to the study of ideology also draw more freely on the older study of political theory and philosophy, and treat political ideas as worth studying in their own right. Thus Freeden (1996, p. 7) seeks to 'reintegrate' the investigation of political ideologies 'into the mainstream of political theory.' He makes eclectic use of insights from Marxist analysis and modern social science in associating ideologies with 'social groups, not necessarily classes'. He argues that ideologies 'perform a range of services, such as legitimation, integration, socialization, ordering, simplification, and action orientation, without which societies could not function adequately, if at all.' He also sees ideologies as 'ubiquitous forms of political thinking' which are 'inevitably associated with power, though not invariably with the threatening or exploitative version of power.' But he also argues that 'ideologies are distinct thought-products that invite careful investigation in their own right' (1996, pp. 22–3), and goes on to treat them essentially as a specialist branch of political theory.

Studying ideology – the issue of bias

Vincent (1995, p. 20) observes 'We examine ideology as fellow sufferers, not as neutral observers.' The warning is apt. This is not a subject where one can expect objectivity. Those who write about ideologies in general have their own ideological convictions, which may be more or less apparent, however hard they seek to write dispassionately. Accounts of specific ideologies are even more likely to be partisan. Much of the literature on feminism or the Greens is written by committed supporters, and some is frankly propagandist. Modern accounts of racism and fascism are almost universally hostile. Accounts of the mainstream ideologies of conservatism, liberalism and socialism are more mixed. A few may be obviously and markedly critical (e.g. Honderich, 1990, on conservatism), but even where they are clearly sympathetic overall, they will frequently reflect a particular interpretation or tendency.

Such obvious bias by both proponents and antagonists is scarcely surprising. Ideologies are action-oriented – paraphrasing Marx, they seek to change the world, not just interpret it. Those who are ideologically committed seek converts to their cause. Even academics who affect greater detachment inevitably have their own views which consciously or unconsciously influence the way they treat their subject. Moreover, as we have seen, the study of ideology itself inevitably reflects ideological preconceptions. There are very different views on the definition and nature of ideology, and the relationship of ideology to power and interests on the one hand and science and truth on the other.

All this suggests some problems for students, both in terms of interpreting what others have written on specific ideologies and ideology in general, and in terms of formulating and presenting their own views. However, the contested nature of the subject matter does not mean that in the study of ideologies 'anything goes', allowing a free rein to the ventilation of personal prejudices. As in any subject for academic study there is an obligation to standards of accuracy over detail and rigour in analysis. Views attributed to particular thinkers, politicians, or parties require supporting evidence. The reasoning behind inferences and causal connections should be explained. Above all, awkward facts that do not fit a favoured interpretation should not be ignored. A particular standpoint or theory may ultimately be rejected, but in academic discourse there is a presumed obligation to present it fairly and accurately first.

Political ideologies are the very stuff of controversy, which is why many find them fascinating. But this means that no-one who comes to the study of political ideologies can be free of preconceptions. It may seem difficult to separate academic enquiry entirely from personal political allegiance, yet commitment to a particular political position should not preclude some reasonably dispassionate examination of its development, supporting interests, core principles and problematic areas. Equally, opposition to a particular ideology is not compromised by an attempt to understand its appeal to others. There are advantages to be derived from 'knowing your enemy'. Even ideologies such as fascism or racism that may inspire repugnance still require some reasonably detached analysis to explain their apparent appeal to many, both in the past and today.

A one-sided or inadequate view of an ideology may not reflect prior prejudice, but simply weaknesses or bias in the source material. The best safeguard against falling for a partial, narrow or eccentric interpretation of an ideology is to read widely, but always critically. Contrasting interpretations, including both hostile and sympathetic treatments, should be deliberately sought out. Such an approach will help to identify both points of agreement and controversy. In all reading a questioning, sceptical approach should be adopted. Nothing should be taken on trust (including what is written here!). It is often useful to attempt to discern the author's perspective. To know that a particular

writer is a Marxist, a conservative or a neo-liberal may assist in interpretation, and also suggest critical questions.

Elements of ideologies

Although political ideologies may differ radically in terms of assumptions and practical implications, it is possible to identify some key
elements that provide a basis for comparison. Three elements may be
broadly identified - an interpretation of existing economic, social and
political arrangements, a vision of the future, and a strategy for realis-
ing that future. While ideologies are essentially action-oriented and prescriptive, any prescription for political and social action must ultimately
rest on some assumptions, however crude, about existing society and
human behaviour. For those who are broadly happy with existing economic, social and political arrangements, the vision of the future may
closely resemble the present, and the strategy will be one of seeking to
maintain the *status quo*. Those profoundly dissatisfied with the present
will contemplate strategies for achieving radical change or revolution.

A view of existing circumstances will commonly include some
assumptions about human nature and individual motivation. Indeed,
such assumptions lie behind the ideas of most of the great political
thinkers of the past. Plato, Machiavelli, and Hobbes, for example, were
all fairly pessimistic about the capacity of human beings to live together
sociably and co-operatively, without a considerable element of coercion or brainwashing, while Aristotle, Rousseau, and, in the last analysis, Marx, had a more optimistic view of human potential for fruitful
co-operation. Among modern political ideologies, fascism makes some
fairly cynical assumptions about the pliability of men and women, while
socialism is essentially optimistic, and traditional conservatism rather
pessimistic about human nature. Free-market liberalism, drawing heavily
on classical economics, sees individuals as motivated by self-interest,
but suggests that the net consequence of all pursuing their self-interest
will be the greatest common good.

A linked consideration is the potential for changing human nature,
from which a further question naturally arises. Is human nature the
same everywhere, or is it substantially the product of the environment?
Does vicious behaviour reflect the immutable nature of humanity, or is
it the product of a particular environment, which might be changed?
Anarchists for example believe that power corrupts. A society without
hierarchies of authority, and without government in the sense of coercive

power, would lead to more co-operative and civilised human behaviour. Socialists may argue that highly self-interested competitive behaviour is the product of the capitalist economic system rather than a universal human characteristic. They also suggest that substantial inequalities in human capacities and attainments are not innate, but can be reduced through enlarging opportunities. Conservatives are usually rather more sceptical about the scope for improvements in human nature, although they may consider religious beliefs, cultural traditions or stable family background as possible ameliorative factors. Some feminists would draw a major distinction between male and female nature, suggesting that men are naturally aggressive and competitive, while women are naturally caring and co-operative, although other feminists would suggest that this behaviour is largely culturally determined. The capacity for changing human behaviour is clearly important where prescriptions for the future require people to behave in different ways.

This highlights the question of the relationship of the individual to society. To Aristotle a proper human existence was inconceivable outside society; man was naturally a social and political animal. At the opposite extreme, some liberal thinkers have viewed society as an artificial construct, requiring a conscious and deliberate effort to bring it into being, and having no meaning apart from its constituent individual elements. Mrs Thatcher lies comfortably within this strand of liberal political tradition in her assertion that there is no such thing as society, only individuals and their families. By contrast, both traditional conservatism (or Toryism) and socialism have tended to view the individual as inseparable from society, with individuals, groups and whole classes bound inextricably to each other through ties of mutual dependence, although of course conservatives and socialists have sharply contrasting views on existing social relations. Finally, in this connection, it may be observed that what have been described as totalitarian ideologies involve, in theory at least, the total subjugation of the individual to the state.

Ideologies will commonly involve all kinds of other assumptions about the way society currently operates - the extent of equality within society, the organisation of work and industrial relations, community relations, authority and power structures, and a host of further issues. Some of these assumptions may be substantially accurate, while others may be wildly inaccurate, but perceptions of how the world *is* inevitably colour perceptions of how it *should be*, so that description and prescription are closely interlinked.

Some people may be more fearful than desirous of change – for all sorts of reasons. They may be substantial beneficiaries of existing social arrangements. They may pessimistically fear that change is likely to be for the worse. They may be persuaded, perhaps against what others would regard as their objective interests, that change is impossible, dangerous, or undesirable. The essence of conservatism, as the term implies, is to avoid major change, and a radically different future is neither sought nor desired, although a degree of gradual reform may be countenanced. For conservatives the problem is rather how to maintain social stability, and avoid social unrest and revolution. The choice may often seem to lie between granting reforms to appease dissatisfied elements, or refusing any concessions for fear that these will only create more instability in the long run. In general, conservatives are much more sceptical of the scope for deliberate social engineering than liberals or socialists, and more wary of the possible dangers of change. Some reactionaries, in the proper sense of the term, may seek a future that resembles a past, real or imaginary, which they regret.

Others may strive for a future that is nothing like the present or immediate past. The construction of utopias has been a favourite preoccupation of political thinkers since classical times. The problem with utopias is how to achieve them. The proposed utopia may be far more appealing than existing society, but how does one progress from (a) to (b)? Ideologies thus generally involve some assumptions about social change, although this element can in practice be fairly weak. Marx was critical of some of his socialist predecessors for lacking any coherent theory of social change. They had a socialist vision of the future, but no realistic strategy for achieving it. A major debate among socialists since Marx's day has been over the prospects of the parliamentary road to socialism – whether socialism can be achieved solely or mainly through the ballot box and the election of governments with parliamentary majorities. Some socialists deny that this is possible. Parliamentary socialists tend to respond that the alternatives are even more problematic.

Classifying ideologies – left and right

One of the oldest ways of classifying ideologies involves locating them on the familiar left–right political spectrum. The terms derive from the seating positions in the National Assembly arising out of the 1789 French Revolution, where the most revolutionary groups sat on the left and the more conservative or reactionary sat on the right. Since then the terms 'left' and 'right' have gradually acquired a universal currency. In many legislatures, particularly where the chambers are semi-circular, seating arrangements still mirror those of the revolutionary National Assembly, but even in countries like the United Kingdom where they do not, politicians, parties, and political programmes are freely classified according to the terminology of left and right. A scale suggests that the terms are essentially relative, and that is how they are employed. Indeed, further sub-categories are often used, such as 'far (or hard) left', 'extreme right' or 'centre left', to describe the position occupied on the spectrum more precisely. Frequently, it is suggested that a certain politician, party or trade union is more left or more right than another, and the terms are also commonly used to describe intra-party factions. This can be confusing. Thus, a particular politician or group in the British Labour party might be described as 'right-wing', strictly within the context of his party, while more generally he would be regarded as 'on the left'. Similarly, factions within the Conservative party are often loosely termed left, right or centre to explain their ideological position relative to others within their party, while from an outsider perspective they all essentially belong to the right.

This emphasises the importance of context in interpretation. Yet if the classification is virtually universal, it is not unproblematic. What is the scale really about? A common interpretation is that the scale measures attitudes to change, with those seeking revolutionary change on the left, and those opposed to all change on the right, with cautious reformers somewhere in the middle (Figure 1.1). Thus, socialists and communists are on the left, conservatives on the right and progressive liberals in the centre.

Figure 1.1   Left–right: revolution and reaction

Yet if revolutionaries succeed and become the new establishment, should they then be placed on the right? In practice, Lenin's Bolsheviks continued to be regarded as 'left' after they seized power and established a new social and political system in Russia. Similarly, there is a problem with the 'radical right', almost a contradiction in terms if 'right' means opposition to change. Margaret Thatcher instituted radical change in Britain, although she and her allies were generally considered further to the right than the rather more cautious 'One Nation' Conservatives whom they had effectively displaced.

Another way of interpreting the left–right scale is in terms of attitudes to authority – with those championing individual liberty on the left, and those emphasising discipline and order on the right. This also does not always accord with general usage. Thus anarchists and communists, both generally considered on the left or far left, tend to display radically different attitudes to authority, and there are similar differences between the 'libertarian' and 'authoritarian' right. By contrast, the concept of 'totalitarianism' developed by some western theorists in the post-war period, implied that both communism and fascism, conventionally placed at opposite ends of the left–right scale, were essentially similar in subordinating individual liberty to state authority.

Perhaps rather more promising is a definition in terms of attitudes to state intervention in the economy, with 'left' associated with collectivism and 'right' with the free market (Figure 1.2). This definition is consistent with the description of communists and socialists as 'left' regardless of whether they constituted the establishment or the opposition, and also consistent with the common designation of free market Conservatives as more 'right wing' than the more interventionist 'One Nation' Conservatives. Yet fascism, commonly placed on the far right, favoured protection and substantial state direction rather than the free market.

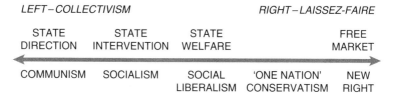

Figure 1.2   Left–right: collectivism and the free market

In view of the ambiguities associated with the left–right scale, some have sought to establish a more complex revised classification of political attitudes. Thus, Eysenck (1957) proposed a two-dimensional model, with attitudes measured on two scales, one labelled radical – conservative (roughly equivalent to that in Figure 1.1), the other tough and tender (close to the distinction between authoritarian and libertarian, above). Brittain (1968), by contrast, suggests the terminology of left and right is so misleading it should be dropped completely. Indeed, many more recent commentators have concluded that the terms are no longer useful or meaningful. However, it seems most unlikely that the long familiar language of left and right can ever be banished from political discourse.

Thus the conventional left–right scale is used here, despite the problems (Figure 1.3).

Figure 1.3   Left–right: conventional scale

Even so, this conventional left–right political spectrum is more readily applicable to some ideologies than others. There are particular problems in locating nationalism, feminism, and green thinking on a left–right continuum. They each cut across the familiar distinctions based on economic intervention or social class interests. Nationalism in different times and places has been associated with ideas across the political spectrum from the left to the far right. Feminism is generally linked with the left, but it is questionable whether it should be. Although most green activists are also more commonly associated with the left, the familiar green slogan 'neither left nor right but forward' suggests they see themselves on another dimension altogether. Thus, some argue that 'left' and 'right' describe the old obsolete politics, while the women's movement and the green movement and other currents of thought represent a new politics.

Levels of ideology

Ideologies can be interpreted and analysed at a number of different levels – from sophisticated intellectual constructs down to inferences from political behaviour. While the traditional study of political theory has tended to focus on the writings of great thinkers and the relatively tiny political elite familiar with their ideas, the study of political ideologies is concerned with mass as well as elite ideas and behaviour. Ideologies may be systematically articulated, through, for example, the writings of major thinkers, or expressed more selectively and persuasively through political pamphlets or speeches, or they may be essentially latent, and unsophisticated, expressed if at all in shorthand slogans, symbols and gestures. The clenched fist may seem a long way removed from Marx's *Das Kapital* but they are both aspects of one ideology.

Some 'great thinkers' studied within the political theory tradition have clearly made a significant contribution to particular political ideologies, for example, Marx to socialism, Burke to conservatism or Mill to liberalism. Yet it was often writers who were not themselves profound or original thinkers who did more to popularise particular doctrines. Harriet Martineau, who wrote little fables embodying the principles of classical economics, Edward Baines, the polemical editor of the *Leeds Mercury*, and Samuel Smiles, the purveyor of Victorian homilies on self help and other virtues were all more widely read and understood than the economists Ricardo or Nassau Senior. Indeed, these populist writers can be considered more typical of *laissez-faire* liberalism.

At another level, the pronouncements and achievements of active politicians, whose ideas are insufficiently original or systematic for consideration in histories of political theory, may play a critical role in the development of ideologies and their subsequent interpretation. There are very few 'great texts' which provide much of a guide to an understanding of conservatism. Many interpretations place particular emphasis on the contribution of past politicians, especially Prime Ministers, such as Peel, Disraeli, Salisbury, Macmillan, and Thatcher. Some of these politicians did articulate their ideas in articles, novels, speeches and manifestos, but the ideas of others must be substantially inferred from their decisions and policies. For while political ideologies, almost by definition, influence political behaviour, they can also sometimes appear as rationalisations of political behaviour. However, few politicians would put it quite as bluntly as Herbert Morrison (1888–1965), Labour's Deputy Prime Minister from 1945–51, who once declared that socialism was what the Labour government did.

Ideologies inform the beliefs and behaviour not just of politicians but of the masses. The popular version of an ideology may be less elaborate than that held by professional politicians and party activists, but it will shape the attitudes people have to the great questions of the day. Thus, ideological assumptions may influence how people vote, or indeed whether they vote, and their readiness to indulge in other political activity, such as demonstrations, law-breaking or even, on occasion, revolution. Although there may be a difference in sophistication between the elite and mass versions of particular ideologies, they normally reflect the same outlook on life, and inter-relate. Mrs Thatcher acknowledged the influence of the everyday maxims on, for example, the virtues of thrift and duty acquired during her upbringing in that celebrated grocer's shop in Grantham (Young, 1989, pp. 5–7). She also acknowledged a debt to Adam Smith and Hayek (Thatcher, 1977). It is difficult to assess which has made the more significant contribution to what came to be called 'Thatcherism'. It can be confidently asserted that it is the everyday maxims that have a greater resonance with the wider public. Newspaper headlines, slogans and graffiti, and non-verbal symbols, such as the British bulldog, or Britannia, or photographic images may reinforce or express particular ideological approaches. Some political ideologies are indeed almost entirely lacking in sophisticated intellectual expression. The Nuremberg rallies and the slogans painted in Mussolini's Italy, 'Believe, Obey, Fight', 'Live dangerously', 'Better one day as a lion than a thousand years as a sheep', perhaps tell us more about the nature of fascism, and almost certainly had more influence on political behaviour than fascist theory.

Power, influence and indoctrination

Consideration of the ideological perspectives of the masses raises some awkward questions on the transmission of ideas – over, for example, the potential for deliberate indoctrination. There are some celebrated fictional accounts of thought control, and plenty of real life illustrations of more or less successful attempts to mould opinion, by no means all of which are to be found in so-called totalitarian states. For example, the allied authorities in Germany after the Second World War embarked on a deliberate counter-indoctrination programme which employed many of the methods of their Nazi predecessors – censorship of newspapers, burning of books, screening teachers for ideological soundness and the like. Most attempts to influence people's minds on political issues are less extensive and systematic than this, but there is still a certain amount of quite conscious manipulation even in a supposedly liberal democracy like Britain.

If deliberate manipulation of people's minds by those in power was regularly employed and always successful, there would be no ideological conflict, just the universal acceptance of one ideology. Plato wanted to eliminate conflict in this way in his ideal state, and there have been celebrated recent fictional examples, such as Orwell's *1984* and Huxley's *Brave New World*. Real live governments have found it rather more difficult to stifle all dissent. However, at the very least it can be said that they have substantial means at their disposal to influence opinion.

The role of the media in shaping opinion is another controversial area. The narrow concentration of media ownership in the UK and the influence of a handful of media tycoons rather undermines the comfortable liberal pluralist assumption that people are exposed to a wide range of sources and views, enabling them to make up their own mind on political questions. Most national newspapers have long exhibited a marked political bias, while the assumption of television neutrality has been challenged from both left and right. Moreover, although the internet offers the prospect perhaps of more open and pluralist political debate, its full political potential has yet to be realised. Media concentration and bias may not matter that much if, as some academic research suggests, people use the media to reinforce their own ideas, and filter out messages which do not match preconceived attitudes. However, others argue that our thinking must be influenced, if sometimes subliminally, by the constant repetition of media images and associations. Thus, not only our perceptions of particular politicians and parties, but our images of women, our attitudes to minorities, and our views on a whole range issues from paedophiles to fuel protests, from fox hunting to the European Union, are inevitably influenced and perhaps even determined by the media. This is more likely to be the case on issues where we have no direct personal experience.

Too much emphasis can be placed on deliberate indoctrination by governments or on media propaganda. Far more significant, it might be argued, is the largely unconscious process by which beliefs are transmitted and sustained from the elite to the masses, and across generations. Existing institutions, work practices, patterns of social organisation, habits and beliefs may generally be taken for granted. In some cases it may require a considerable effort to even imagine alternatives. The weight of tradition is always likely to be a major constraint on political thinking, which will tend to justify the *status quo*, and serve the interests of those who benefit principally from the *status quo*. Thus, the ideas of established dominant groups may often be fairly generally accepted throughout society, without any deliberate action to ensure this. While the dominant ideology may not be all-pervasive, some of its core assumptions at least may gain wide acceptance among subordinate groups.

The battle of ideas, then, is inevitably fought with loaded dice. The failure of some political perspectives, such as radical feminism, or anarchism, or dark green environmentalism, to gain a wider following may reflect inherent weaknesses in the ideology. Alternatively, it may be an indication of the overwhelming difficulties any radical perspective faces in combating the mass of routinely accepted assumptions bound up with the existing economic, social and political order. Yet it may not just be radical left wing views which fail to secure a fair hearing. Both neo-liberals and neo-conservatives have claimed that the post-war progressive consensus effectively excluded their ideas from political debate until more recently.

Ideology and pragmatism in British politics

An explicit assumption of this book is that political ideas are important, and indeed that 'all politics is ideological' (Seliger, 1976, p. 146). However, not everyone would agree that ideas have generally been important in British politics, or even indeed should be. Much has been made of British empiricism, involving a rejection of abstract reasoning. Although Mrs Thatcher showed a positive enthusiasm for ideology this was markedly at variance with traditional British conservatism (as noted in Chapter 3). From Burke through Peel to Oakeshott (1962) and Minogue (1985) in the latter part of the twentieth century there has been a conservative distrust of abstract rational theory and doctrine and a positive aversion to 'ideology'. Yet an apparent British aversion to ideology is not just confined to conservatism, but can even be discerned in the British versions of liberalism and socialism. British liberalism, although more obviously influenced by theory than conservatism, has generally been flexible and pragmatic in execution. Even the British Labour Party was heavily constrained by the British empirical tradition and much less influenced by Marxist or any other theory than socialist or social democratic parties elsewhere.

Yet if 'ideology' clearly, for many, retains pejorative associations, 'pragmatism' is also, for some at least, a dirty word. Pragmatism 'all too easily slips into opportunism and is a synonym for short-term expediency' (Robertson, 1993, p. 394). Opportunism and short-term expediency were the charges critics often laid against former Labour Prime Minister, Harold Wilson, who coined the phrase 'a week is a long time in politics'. (The phrase was more recently updated by another Labour Prime Minister, Gordon Brown, in the midst of the 2008 financial crisis as 'an hour is a long time in politics'.) Indeed, pragmatism, the relative neglect of 'grand theory' and the absence of long-term vision is sometimes seen as a weakness of British politics.

Ultimately, however, the dichotomy between ideology and pragmatism is a false one (Seliger, 1976, pp. 123–47). Politics can hardly be conducted without reference to values and principles (or ideology), but also inevitably requires flexibility and compromise (or pragmatism) in pursuit of ideological goals. Moreover, 'pragmatism, with its dogmatic insistence on the impossibility of far-seeing deliberate reform, is itself a deliberate "ideological" standpoint on human nature' (Robertson, 1993, p. 394).

Thus, even those political thinkers such as Burke, Oakeshott and Minogue who apparently decry an ideological style of politics, themselves reflect ideological assumptions over, for example, human behaviour and motivation, the nature and distribution of property, and the scope and limitations of government. Indeed, for all their denunciation of 'reason', 'rationalism' and 'ideology', their writings were the product of a rational intellectual process, and were deliberately articulated as a persuasive interpretation of politics, with clear implications for political behaviour. Thus, traditional conservatism was as 'ideological' as the free market conservatism which succeeded it.

All politics reflects ideological assumptions. Thus, New Labour, for all its pragmatic emphasis on 'what works', is as ideological as old Labour. While ideologies may sometimes be inspired by utopian visions, they are all about influencing political attitudes and behaviour. They are not about pure ideas abstracted from reality but are 'action-oriented' and necessarily involve an interdependence between theory and practice, particularly when politicians obtain power and the chance to implement their ideas. Although policy is inevitably guided or constrained by ideological assumptions, its practice, over time, is bound to modify initial theoretical expectations, reinforcing some and leading to the modification or discarding of others. In this way ideologies evolve as they are tested against reality. While the New Right and, more recently, New Labour emerged out of a conscious intellectual debate over ideas and values, as they developed they both embodied some rationalisation of trial and error responses to specific problems and circumstances. They necessarily combine 'ideology' and 'pragmatism'.

Moderation and consensus in British politics

While British politics is inevitably ideological, it is generally associated with continuity, moderation, and compromise. Since the violent upheavals of the seventeenth century there have been no revolutions, regime changes or sharp breaks in the development of the political system. Periodic crises that threatened political stability have been peacefully resolved, and strong opposition to the government of the day has seldom been translated into significant opposition to the whole system of government. Revolutionary parties and ideologies have rarely attracted a mass following, and communism and fascism have never secured more than fringe support. The Labour party was never Marxist, and generally avoided the language of confrontation and class conflict. The Conservative party would not have survived and thrived had it remained tied to narrow reactionary interests. In terms of the left–right ideological spectrum, British voters have been offered a constrained choice between the centre-left and the centre-right. Extremism is of course a question of definition and perspective, but mainland British politics has rarely faced a significant internal challenge from those regarded as extremists (Ireland, of course, is another matter).

Indeed, it has often appeared that major British parties have been competing for the centre ground, and at times British politics has been more characterised by consensus (or agreement) than conflict. In war and periods of national emergency political leaders have been prepared to enter coalitions, or at least suspend normal party conflict. Yet at other times such as the 1950s and 1960s many have observed an absence of sharp ideological differences between the major parties. This 'post-war consensus' appeared to break down in the 1970s and early 1980s, as the Conservatives under Margaret Thatcher moved to the right and the Labour party increasingly appeared dominated by the left. Yet this period was followed by the more consensual style of John Major, and subsequently Tony Blair's attempts to bring Liberal Democrats and moderate Conservatives within his 'big tent'. More recently, commentators have drawn attention to the similarities between the political rhetoric of Gordon Brown, David Cameron and Nick Clegg (see Chapter 10).

The British political tradition

Yet if British politics has rarely been characterised by violent or extreme conflict, it has involved significant disagreements or tensions. The dominant theme in some older influential interpretations of British politics (see for example Spencer [1884] 1981, Dicey [1885] 1959 and [1905] 1914) has been the tensions between libertarianism and collectivism, or between the free market and the state, and this has been reaffirmed in more recent accounts. Thus Beer's *Modern British Politics* (1982) documented the victory of Conservative and Labour collectivism over traditional liberal individualism. Barker (1978, p. 5) 'used attitudes to the modern state' as the main organising principle behind his analysis of *Political Ideas in Modern Britain*. According to Greenleaf (1983, vol. 2, p. 5) 'the dialectic between the growing pressures of collectivism and the opposing libertarian tendency is the one supreme fact of our domestic political life as this has developed over the last century and a half'.

It is difficult to disagree that attitudes towards the state have been a massive theme in British politics, particularly for the mainstream ideologies of liberalism, conservatism and socialism. Nineteenth-century liberalism sought to uphold the liberty of the individual against the encroachment of the state, while the New Liberalism of the early twentieth century struggled to reconcile individual liberty with state-sponsored social reform (Chapter 2). Conservatives recurrently championed state protection of British agriculture and industry, and, subsequently, paternalist social reform (Chapter 3). The dominant British interpretation of socialism involved the growth of state intervention to provide public services (Chapter 4). Thus, much of the internal debate within these mainstream ideologies as well as between them has been over the powers of the government and the freedom of the individual, and the boundary between public and private spheres, or state and civil society.

Yet important though the state/market debate is in the 'battle of ideas', it is a mistake to regard it as the only debate that matters in British politics. Even the mainstream ideologies are concerned with many issues that are only tangentially, if at all, connected with the state/market dichotomy, while for other political perspectives the issue of state economic intervention is secondary. Nationalism, for example, generally assumes that nations should constitute states, but is essentially concerned with the politics of identity and allegiance rather than economic arguments about the functions of the state (Chapter 5). Similarly, the politics of race and ethnicity revolve more around issues of identity than economics, even if economic deprivation is among the factors that fuel racism (Chapter 6). Multiculturalism is a more recent political perspective stressing diversity that developed in response to exclusive nationalism and racism but with some contentious implications for mainstream ideologies also (Chapter 7). Feminism, particularly in its radical form, asserts the primacy of gender relations over economic class conflict; the feminist slogan 'the personal is political' has redrawn the boundaries of politics, and transcends the old liberal distinction between the state and civil society (Chapter 8). Finally, green ideas are about the relationship of humanity with its environment; the role of the state in this relationship is an important and controversial issue for Greens, but it is an essentially secondary question (Chapter 9).

Yet while the importance of these alternative perspectives should be emphasized, at the same time it remains fairly clear that mainstream British politics over the last few decades has (rightly or wrongly) centred substantially on the respective roles of the state and the market. Although other issues of foreign policy and security have sometimes taken centre stage in the wake of the attack on the World Trade Centre on 11 September 2001 and the wars in Afghanistan and Iraq, the financial crisis of 2007–8 and the ensuing economic recession has dramatically revived old ideological debates over the state and the free market. Keynesian intervention is back in fashion, and so, remarkably, is nationalisation. Bank nationalisation has secured, for a time, all-party support, a startling reversal of recent ideological assumptions, demonstrating how politics can be overwhelmed by unforeseen events. Prophecy, now more than ever, is hazardous. The book concludes with a brief survey of the implications for political ideologies in Britain (Chapter 10).

Further reading

Useful extended definitions of ideology and other concepts discussed in this chapter and throughout the book are provided in various specialist dictionaries such as those by Williams (1976), Bullock and Stallybrass (1977), Miller *et al.* (1987), Bottomore (1991), Robertson (1993), Maclean and McMillan (2003) and Scruton (2007). Particularly useful is Heywood's (2000) more extended analysis of *Key Concepts in Politics*. These are handy reference works from which to begin an exploration of the numerous highly contested concepts discussed throughout this book, but the reader should be warned that the treatment of ideas even in such reference books reflects the different perspectives of authors.

Students may wish to sample some of the alternative surveys of modern ideologies, including Adams, (1993), Vincent (1995), Eatwell and Wright (1999), Eccleshall *et al.* (2003) and Heywood (2007). Most of these include brief introductory discussions on the nature of ideology. This is usefully examined in a slim volume by McLellan (1995). Still the most useful and authoritative modern source is Seliger (1976). Freeden (1996) has contributed a thoughtful analysis of the relationship between ideology and political theory, which also includes his own analysis of the core components of mainstream ideologies, and a briefer discussion of feminism and green ideas. The same author's *Ideology: A Very Short Introduction* (2003) is much briefer, and stimulating, but despite the title, is not really an introductory text, and best read after other material.

British political ideas are summarised in Barker (1978, 1994) and Adams (1998). Beer (1982) provides one thought-provoking overall (but pre-Thatcherism) perspective, and Greenleaf (1983) another. The latter also explores the relationship between ideology and public pol-icy – as do George and Wilding (1980), Fraser (1984), and Pearson and Williams (1984). Gamble (2003) provides a stimulating broad survey of British politics in relation to Europe and America. Marquand (2008) offers a challenging alternative view of British ideological divisions. For books on specific ideologies see suggested further reading in subse-quent chapters.

2
Liberalism

Introduction

Liberalism remains the mainstream political philosophy of the modern western world, despite the decline of political parties describing themselves as 'liberal' both in Britain and elsewhere. Most other political ideologies are defined in relation to liberalism, and it is the necessary starting point for any analysis of political doctrines today.

Liberalism has evolved over a long period and has varied considerably over time and space, which presents some problems for analysis. Although the term 'liberalism' was not employed until the early nineteenth century (Manning, 1976, p. 9; Gray, 1986, p. ix) its roots can be traced back much earlier (Arblaster, 1984, p. 11). It drew its intellectual inspiration from the religious reformations of the sixteenth century, the seventeenth-century scientific revolution, and the eighteenth-century French or European enlightenment. It was, however, industrialisation from the eighteenth century onwards which transformed economic and social relations and created new class interests with a commitment to a capitalist economy and a liberal political programme of reform.

In the first half of the nineteenth century, liberalism appeared a revolutionary creed on the European continent where absolutist or reactionary regimes generally prevailed. The cause of individual liberty was there inextricably bound up with national self-determination. Movements for national freedom or national unity were closely associated with demands for civil and political rights and for constitutional limits on government. By contrast, Britain's national integrity and independence seemed then unproblematic, while absolutism had been defeated and parliamentary sovereignty established from the seventeenth century. British liberalism certainly involved support for these goals abroad, but as they were already substantially achieved at home the liberal domestic programme necessarily concentrated on other objectives such as parliamentary reform, religious toleration and free trade.

A distinction is commonly made between economic and political liberalism. Modern neo-liberals see the free market as the quintessential liberal value. However, nineteenth-century continental liberalism was primarily a political creed, while even in Britain the centrality of free markets to liberalism has been exaggerated. Victorian liberalism stood for political reform at home and support for national and constitutional movements abroad. Its inspiration was derived more from religion (and specifically radical nonconformism) than classical economics. Moreover, from the late nineteenth century onwards, British liberalism explicitly repudiated *laissez-faire* and accepted the need for state intervention, particularly in the area of social welfare. This New Liberalism has been variously regarded as a natural and inevitable development out of the old liberalism (Hobhouse, 1911; Freeden, 1978, 1996), as an aberration (Arblaster, 1984, ch. 16) or even as a betrayal (Gray, 1984, pp. 32–3).

In twentieth-century Britain, liberal ideas thrived while their former political vehicle, the Liberal Party, suffered decline. Until the 1970s the dominant political and economic orthodoxy was essentially derived from the New Liberalism which had flourished early in the century. Indeed, Keynes and Beveridge, the twin gurus of the post-Second World War political consensus, marked the culmination of New Liberal thinking. Moreover, when this consensus finally faced a challenge, that challenge came principally from an older free-market version of liberalism, or neo-liberalism. The battle of ideas in the postwar era was arguably not so much between conservatism and socialism, nor even between right and left, but between the old and the new liberalism.

Today the term 'liberal' has distinctly different connotations in different parts of the world. It is not even easy to place it on the 'left–right' political spectrum. The modern British Liberal Democrats and their Liberal predecessors have long been regarded as centre or even left of centre, while in continental Europe liberalism is more generally associated with the right. However, in the United States the term 'liberal' has become almost a term of abuse for radical-progressive and crypto-socialist ideas. Yet the 'liberal' or 'neo-liberal' label is also associated with advocates of the free market like Hayek and Friedman and their New Right disciples.

In some interpretations liberalism is the hegemonic ideology of the modern age. Almost all mainstream ideologies, even Marxism, may be regarded as variants of liberalism. One problem with this view of liberalism as an all-embracing hegemonic ideology is that any clear identity, coherence and consistency is in danger of being lost. But whatever view is taken of liberalism today, the historical importance of liberalism cannot be denied; liberal values and ideas have been central to the development of the western political tradition.

This chapter begins by exploring key liberal concepts and values. It proceeds to examine the development of British liberalism, including early influences, the Whig and Radical traditions, classical economics and utilitarianism, religious non-conformism and the New Liberalism (Table 2.1). The chapter concludes with a discussion of rival interpretations of liberalism today, and the ideas of the Liberal Democrats in Britain.

Liberalism: key concepts and values

While there are clearly major differences and tensions within the liberal tradition, as there are in other mainstream ideologies, it is possible to describe liberals or liberalism in terms that would command a wide measure of agreement. Stuart Hall (1986, p. 34) suggests that liberals are 'open-minded, tolerant, rational, freedom-loving people, sceptical of the claims of tradition and established authority, but strongly committed to the values of liberty, competition and individual freedom.' Nineteenth-century British liberalism, according to Hall 'stood for individualism in politics, civil and political rights, parliamentary government, moderate reform, limited state intervention, and a private enterprise economy'. This is a description (by a non-liberal) which most liberals would endorse. Thus there is widespread agreement over key liberal ideas and values, even if there is not always equal agreement over their subsequent development and interpretation.

Individualism

Individualism is the key liberal assumption. For the liberal, individual human beings, rather than nations, races or classes are the starting point for any theorising about society, politics or economics. Society is seen as an aggregate of individuals, and social behaviour is explained in terms of some fairly basic assumptions about individual human psychology (Macpherson, 1962; Arblaster, 1984, chs. 2, 3). Indeed, some thinkers within the liberal tradition saw society as an essentially artificial creation; they postulated a prior state of nature in which neither society nor government existed. Whether this state of nature was perceived as a hypothetical model or historical fact, the implication was that society and government were purposefully created by individual humans in pursuit of their own self-interest. Many liberals today still tend to see society as an aggregate of individuals; there

Table 2.1   The Whig–Liberal tradition in Britain

Period	Description	Politicians and thinkers
17th century	**Puritanism and Parliamentarism**	
Late 17th century and 18th century	**The Whig tradition**	
	'Glorious Revolution'	John Locke
	Constitutional monarchy	
	Government by consent	
	Division of powers	
	Oligarchy	
	Mercantilism	
	Religious toleration	Charles James Fox
Late 18th century and early 19th century	**Radicalism**	
	Revolution	Tom Paine
	Rationalism	
	Rights of Man	
	Classical liberalism	Adam Smith
	Individualism	Thomas Malthus
	Free markets	David Ricardo
	Utilitarianism	Jeremy Bentham
	Representative democracy	James Mill
Mid 19th century and later 19th century	**Victorian Liberalism**	John Stuart Mill
	Manchester liberalism	Richard Cobden
	Nonconformism	John Bright
	Free trade	William Gladstone
	Nationalism	
	Municipal gospel	Joseph Chamberlain
Late 19th century and early 20th century	**New Liberalism**	T.H. Green
	Social reform	Leonard Hobhouse
	State intervention	John Hobson
	National efficiency	Herbert Asquith
	Constitutional reform	David Lloyd George
1920s to 1960s	**Decline of Liberal Party**	J.M. Keynes
	(progressive liberal consensus?)	William Beveridge
Late 20th century and early 21st century	**Liberal revival?**	David Steel
	European Union	Paddy Ashdown
	Devolution	Charles Kennedy
	Civil liberties	Menzies Campbell
	International law	Nick Clegg

can be no social interests beyond the interests of the individuals that constitute society. The individual is logically and morally prior to society.

Rationalism

Rationalism is another core liberal assumption. Liberals assume that individuals pursue their own self-interest rationally. No one else, not rulers, nor priests nor civil servants can determine the individual's own interest for them. Yet liberals, such as the utilitarian thinker Jeremy Bentham, have optimistically assumed that the general pursuit of rational self-interest will produce not only individual satisfaction but also social progress and the happiness of the greatest number.

Universalism

Liberals tend to assume that human nature is universal and much the same everywhere, so that individual human beings all over the world are motivated by similar interests and impulses. Thus liberals theorise about 'humanity' (or more narrowly 'man') in the abstract, and today commonly assume there are universal human rights (see below). By contrast, conservatives generally reckon that behaviour is more culturally embedded in particular societies, while socialists, although advocating universal remedies for human woes, assume existing attitudes and behaviour are to a considerable extent socially determined.

Freedom

Freedom is, however, the quintessential liberal value; liberals require that individuals should be free from external constraints to enable them to pursue their own self-interest (Mill, 1859). An important application was the principle of toleration, particularly applied to freedom of religious belief and observance, and vigorously championed by Locke (1689, ed. Gough, 1966). The right to full freedom of thought and expression, and freedom of behaviour in so far as it did not involve harm to others, was to receive its most eloquent expression from John Stuart Mill (1859, ed. Warnock, 1962).

In the early history of liberalism this freedom from constraint entailed firm limits to the power of a potentially oppressive state to interfere with individual liberty. Classical liberals also assumed that freedom for the individual entailed free markets, where distribution and exchange were free from state interference. This conception of freedom was essentially negative, a freedom *from* coercion and control. Subsequently, some liberals (called New Liberals or 'social liberals') emphasised the freedom *to* enjoy certain benefits, a more positive conception of liberty which might entail extensive state intervention and interference with the free market to develop welfare services and enlarge individual freedom and potential (Green, 1881; Hobhouse, 1911; Berlin, 1975). The conflict between these two contrasting negative and positive views of freedom, and their widely divergent practical implications, has been a major theme in the development of liberalism for over a century.

Equality

If liberalism has always involved a commitment to liberty, however defined, it has also involved some egalitarian assumptions. Thus liberals have stressed equality before the law, and equal civil and political rights, although there has not always been agreement over what these should entail in practice. Egalitarian considerations have also led many liberals to justify state provision of education and other services to create greater equality of opportunity. But a commitment to an equality of worth and opportunity has generally been accompanied by a liberal acceptance of considerable inequality of income and wealth. Indeed, liberals have regarded private property as crucial to freedom. Thus, critics allege, liberals in practice sacrifice equality to liberty (Arblaster, 1984, pp. 84–91).

Justice

Liberals themselves have argued that freedom entails the freedom to be unequal, but they have also denied that individual liberty is inconsistent with social justice. Although liberalism is based on the assumption of self-seeking individualism, it has never involved the cynical equation of might and right. Rather, liberals have embraced the language of justice and attempted to make it consistent with the pursuit of rational self-interest (Rawls, 1971). There are implicit in such arguments some fairly optimistic assumptions about human nature and the scope for reconciling individual and collective goals. It is here that liberalism parts company with traditional conservatism on the one hand, and socialism on the other. Conservatives have shown less trust in the unguided capacity of individual humans to pursue their enlightened self-interest to the general benefit of society (see Chapter 3, below). Socialists, while sharing with liberals a more optimistic view of human nature, have not agreed that the pursuit of individual self-interest and social justice can be so easily reconciled (see Chapter 4, below).

Consent

Liberals have argued that government and law should rest on the consent of those over whom it is exercised. While some thought that this consent rested on an original contract between individuals to establish a society, government and law, others suggested that government and law rested on the implicit consent of those who remained within the borders of the state. However, as critics such as David Hume and others pointed out, it was often virtually impossible for individuals to exercise the freedom to leave a state for another. Even so, the notion that government should rest on the consent of the governed has important implications for the legitimacy of states and governments. It suggests that the allegiance of citizens is conditional rather than absolute, and can be forfeited if the power of government is exercised tyrannically. It implies limits to arbitrary state power, bound up in the notions of limited or constitutional government and the rule of law. Ultimately, the notion of government only with the consent of the governed implies democracy.

Rights

Most, but not all, liberals have argued that individual men (and later, women) have inviolable rights, which further imply constraints on government, but may also impose obligations on government. Sometimes it is suggested these rights come from God, or from nature, or are bound up with citizenship. Such rights have often been spelt out in documents, such as the *Declaration of the Rights of Man and Citizen,* published in France in 1789, or in state constitutions, such as the American constitution. Such rights may suggest their limitation to particular states and societies. However, today it is widely argued that everyone should enjoy what are described as universal human rights, as embodied in the UN Charter of Human Rights. Whereas some rights emphasise freedom *from* oppressive acts by governments, rights more recently proclaimed include rights *to* work, education and health care that impose obligations on government. It is also sometimes suggested that there is an inherent western bias in such documents, which effectively discriminate against other cultures, and deny what some minorities consider to be their rights (see later arguments about multiculturalism, Chapter 7).

Liberal democracy

While liberalism always involved limits to government, it did not originally entail democracy. Although liberals in the early nineteenth century favoured the principle that governments should be responsible to, and controlled by, elected assemblies, they did not necessarily believe that the whole adult population should have a right to vote, even it they generally favoured some extension of the franchise. Yet over time liberals came to support the principle of 'one man, one vote' and later 'one person, one vote.' Critics, however, have suggested that the liberal conception of democracy is limited. It does not involve 'government by the people' in the sense of full popular participation in government, but an occasional right to exercise a very constrained choice over those who are to govern. Morever, as Marxists in particular have argued, there can be no true political equality in the face of gross economic inequality. Those with economic power will effectively exercise political power, and thus under capitalism, where productive wealth remains concentrated in the hands of the few, democracy remains a sham. Liberals of course would respond that communist regimes have involved in practice much less personal freedom and no effective choice of government.

Internationalism

In the early nineteenth century, liberalism and nationalism appeared bound together, and there seemed no contradiction between the promotion of freedom of individuals, and the freedom, or self-determination of nations. However, while nineteenth-century liberals commonly supported nationalist movements, they did not believe there were profound differences in national characteristics, as they assumed human nature was much the same everywhere (see ***universalism***, above). Subsequently, perceiving some of the dangers of unrestrained competitive nationalism, liberals strongly favoured the development of international law, international institutions and collective security against acts of aggression by rogue states. Indeed, the theory of international relations associated with these ideas is commonly termed 'liberal'.

Early influences on liberalism in Britain

The sixteenth-century Protestant reformation was a significant factor in encouraging ideas later associated with liberalism. Protestantism had challenged the traditional authority of the church of Rome. Some forms of Protestantism, including Puritanism in England, and Presbyterianism in Scotland, went further in challenging the authority of bishops and the ecclesiastical hierarchy. Such Protestant dissent, or non-conformism (refusal to conform with the authority and doctrines of the Church of England) was to become a key strand of British liberalism and a major element in the support for the nineteenth century Liberal party.

Protestant dissent also had more immediate political implications. Much of the opposition to the crown and royal absolutism in the seventeenth century came from Puritans and dissenters. James the Sixth of Scotland and First of England declared, 'No bishop, no king', recognising the potential threat to royal authority from rejection of religious authority and the ecclesiastical hierarchy. It was Scottish Presbyterians, opposed to the attempt of Charles I to impose a new prayer book, who first rebelled against the king, obliging him to recall the English parliament to finance war with Scotland. It was English Puritans who were behind much of the parliamentary opposition to the crown that led to the English Civil War that culminated in the defeat of the royalists, the execution of the king in 1649, and a brief experiment with a republic. After the restoration of the monarchy in 1660, Protestants of various shades continued to provide parliamentary and popular opposition to the later Stuarts, leading to the 'Glorious Revolution' that substituted the Protestant William of Orange for the Roman Catholic James II. The cause of parliament was thus closely linked with Protestant dissent, and both fed into the Whig–Liberal tradition in British politics.

Some authorities (Weber, 1904, 1930; Tawney, 1926, 1938) have also suggested that a 'Protestant ethic' was a driving force behind the development of capitalism. The connection remains contentious, although it was in the Protestant countries of northern Europe and North America that the development of commerce and manufacturing became most marked from the seventeenth to the nineteenth centuries. Indeed, the rise of liberalism as a political ideology is closely associated with the rise of capitalism. If Calvinism and Puritanism helped promote capital accumulation, they also created an economic and social climate favourable to liberal ideas of individualism, self-reliance and enterprise.

The influence of Protestanism on liberalism, although particularly significant in Britain, should not be exaggerated however. The eighteenth-century enlightenment and the rise of science helped to stimulate a characteristically liberal trust in human reason and progress and also provided a challenge to traditional religious authority, both Catholic and Protestant. In Catholic countries, liberalism often became associated with anti-clericalism. Even in Britain some leading liberal political philosophers, including Paine, Bentham, and Mill, were not religious. Yet the continuing range and diversity of Christian communities in Britain encouraged a strong liberal commitment to religious toleration rather than anticlericalism and a rejection of religion.

The Whig tradition

Liberalism in Britain grew out of the Whig tradition, to the extent that it is not possible to mark precisely where the one ends and the other begins. Whigs originated in the seventeenth century as the party that opposed royal absolutism, and championed religious dissent. They supported the rights of parliament, and sought to place limits on royal power. John Locke (1632–1704) sought to ground this political programme in abstract principles. There were natural rights to life, liberty and property; government should rest on the consent of the governed, who were ultimately justified in rebellion if their rights were infringed. There should be constitutional limits on government, and a division between the executive and legislative powers (Locke, 1689, ed. Gough, 1966). These ideas came to be enshrined, albeit imperfectly, in the British constitution following the Glorious Revolution of 1688. They also later helped to inspire and justify the American and French Revolutions.

Yet there were always contradictory tendencies in Whiggism. Behind fine sentiments there were material interests to advance and defend. The great Whig aristocrats and their allies among the merchants and bankers sought to preserve their own power, property and privileges from a perceived threat from the crown. The massive inequalities in income and wealth in eighteenth-century Britain were for them unproblematic (Arblaster, 1984, ch. 8). Locke spoke for their interests in defending rights to life, liberty and property.

Moreover, the Whigs in general had no wish to spread power beyond the ranks of the propertied. Thus the constitution which they developed and defended was essentially oligarchic and conservative. Power was, furthermore, shamelessly exercised for the benefit of the wealthy, and prodigious fortunes were made out of war, the slave trade and India. Wealthy landowners enclosed land to enrich themselves at the expense of the rural poor in the name of agricultural progress. The game laws were ruthlessly enforced. Thus class interest apparently lay behind Whig political principles.

Yet Whig principles were capable of a radical as well as a conservative interpretation. 'No taxation without representation', the slogan of the parliamentary opposition to the Stuarts, became the cry of the American rebels against George III, and many Whigs found it difficult to deny the justice of their case. The Declaration of Independence (1776) was based on classic Whig principles. The French Revolution was more divisive, but was initially welcomed by most leading Whigs. Despite the reaction which the subsequent course of the revolution provoked, the Whig leader Charles James Fox continued to defend its principles, if not always its practice, and championed civil liberties in England until his death in 1806.

Their effective exclusion from power for most of the period from 1783 to 1830 permitted some reaffirmation and development of Whig principles. Free from the messy compromises of government, Fox's followers could proclaim their continued attachment to 'Peace, retrenchment and reform', with unsuccessful parliamentary reform bills introduced in 1797 and 1810 providing some precedent for the Great Reform Bill of 1832 (Watson, 1960, pp. 361–2, 450–1). The Foxite Whigs could also claim some credit for British abolition of the slave trade, while the traditional Whig demand for religious toleration was reaffirmed in their support for Catholic emancipation as well as Protestant dissent.

The defection of the 'Old Whigs' and the accommodation within the Foxite remnant of the party of a new generation of radicals with a strong commitment to reform, helped preserve or re-establish a politically progressive Whig tradition which ultimately merged into liberalism (Watson, 1960, pp. 436–7). The 1832 Reform Act can be seen as the culmination of that Whig tradition, but also underlines the cautious, essentially conservative nature of Whiggism (Wright, 1970, pp. 31–6). It was a strictly limited measure, involving a very modest extension of the franchise to incorporate elements of the respectable propertied middle classes, but even so it laid the foundation for Victorian liberalism by transforming the political geography of Britain. The new urban centres gained at the expense of the shires: manufacture and commerce at the expense of land. Whig aristocrats as well as Tory squires ultimately lost influence to the urban-based business and professional middle classes, who were to provide the effective muscle behind Victorian liberalism. Whiggism had developed in a pre-industrial, predominantly rural society in which land remained the overwhelming source of wealth. It was an approach to politics that was increasingly anachronistic in an industrial capitalist society, although Whigs remained an important but diminishing element within the Liberal coalition until the late nineteenth century.

Those who see liberalism almost exclusively in terms of free markets and industrial capitalism neglect the Whig foundations of British liberalism. Whiggism may have served economic interests but it was never essentially an economic doctrine. It was about parliamentary sovereignty, government by consent, freedom of conscience and religious observance, no taxation without representation, and a host of other slogans (often imperfectly applied). It was not about free trade or free markets. Whig foreign trade policy in the seventeenth and eighteenth centuries remained mercantilist. It aimed to secure, through colonisation, Navigation Acts, and war, as large a British share of world trade as possible.

Radicals

Radicals seek fundamental reform. Alongside the Whig tradition, at times interwoven with it, at times in opposition to it, there is a radical tradition that has had a marked effect on both British liberalism and, subsequently, socialism. The label 'radical' has been employed to cover a wide range of politicians, thinkers and ideas, and moreover has had different connotations for different periods. Yet although the label is imprecise, the influence of radicalism on the nineteenth-century British Liberal Party, and British liberalism generally, cannot be ignored. At the parliamentary level, the boundary line between Whigs and radicals was a shifting one. A succession of one-time dangerous radicals were subsequently absorbed into the Whig (and later Liberal) political establishment.

Tom Paine (1737–1809) was one major radical thinker who was never absorbed into that establishment. Although mainstream Whig politicians interpreted their proclaimed principles in ways that preserved their own power, property and privileges, Paine gave those same principles a far more radical interpretation. He argued that once ultimate sovereignty had been transferred from the monarchy to the people, once political equality had been accepted in theory, there was no logical case for restricting participation in the choice of a legislature. Paine himself championed full manhood suffrage (Paine, 1791–2, ed. Collinson, 1969). Although by turns reviled and neglected in Britain, his ideas were the logical outcome of Whig slogans. Indeed, it can be argued that the only coherent way to counter such a revolutionary democratic ideology was by assailing its egalitarian and rationalistic assumptions, as Burke realised.

Paine has been claimed for both liberalism and socialism. Some argue 'his political theory was vintage liberalism', citing his uncompromising individualism, his sympathies for manufacturers, and his hostility to government (Foot and Kramnick, 1987, pp. 22–9). Ayer (1988, ch. 7), by contrast, talks of 'Paine's blueprint ... for his Welfare State', and stresses his support for a highly redistributive graduated income tax. His writing enjoyed a wide circulation and later inspired the Chartists (Foot and Kramnick, 1987, p. 33) and other working-class movements. Yet Paine's ideas had more immediate impact in America and France than Britain, where his uncompromising republicanism, his total opposition to the hereditary principle, and his rejection of Christianity gave him a wild and dangerous reputation.

In the early nineteenth century some radicals like Cartwright and Hunt with a substantial popular following were distrusted or persecuted by the political establishment, while others such as Whitbread and Brougham constituted the progressive wing of the parliamentary Whig party. Also in touch with progressive Whig circles were the 'philosophical radicals' or utilitarians – Bentham and his followers (see below). More difficult to classify is William Cobbett, initially an arch-critic and later a champion of Paine. Yet Cobbett's radical populism harked back to a pre-industrial age, which was arguably true also of the so-called 'Tory radicals' such as Oastler and Shaftsbury. Very different was the radicalism of the Quaker manufacturer John Bright who belonged to the new generation of politicians who came to the fore after the 1832 Reform Act, and who in some ways personified the new age. However, Bright in turn lived long enough to be displaced by a new breed of radicals who took over the Liberal party in the latter part of the century, by which time the term 'radicalism' was beginning to be associated with socialism.

Thus, a variety of forms of radicalism influenced British politics in the nineteenth century. It was radical pressure which reinforced the Whig commitment to parliamentary reform in 1832 and subsequently. The association of radicalism with religious dissent in the second half of the nineteenth century imbued it with a strong moral character, and fuelled demands for non-denominational state education and disestablishment of the Church of England. Radicalism was also strongly associated with the 'municipal gospel' in local government. At the parliamentary level it was the fusion of Whigs and radicals with former Conservative Peelites that effectively created the British Liberal Party in

1859. While Whigs continued to predominate in Liberal Cabinets, radicals predominated at the increasingly important grassroots level, particularly following the formation of the National Liberal Federation. Yet it was a relatively restrained, religiously inspired, and peculiarly British strand of radicalism which eventually prevailed rather than the fiercely rationalist, republican radicalism of Thomas Paine.

Classical economics and utilitarianism

If the moral inspiration of Victorian liberalism was derived from radical nonconformism, it drew intellectual sustenance from the ideas of the classical economists and the utilitarians. It was Adam Smith (1732–90), Malthus (1766–1834) and Ricardo (1772–1823) who virtually founded the modern study of economics, and established the importance of the market in the allocation and distribution of resources. Similarly, Jeremy Bentham's (1748–1832) 'principle of utility' was applied to a wide range of institutions and practices. Tradition and long usage were no justification in the face of Bentham's fiercely rationalist analysis. 'What use is it?' was his brutal question, cutting through the mystique with which constitutional and legal issues were generally surrounded. The 'only right and proper end of government', he declared, was 'the greatest happiness of the greatest number'.

The classical economists and the utilitarians had much in common. Both stemmed from a similar intellectual climate – the eighteenth-century enlightenment. Both shared the individualist and rationalist assumptions underpinning liberalism, and there were also clear connections between them. Bentham and his associates broadly accepted the *laissez-faire* implications of the economic theories of Smith, Ricardo and Malthus, while Smith's friend and colleague, the philosopher and historian David Hume (1711–76), had earlier laid the philosophical foundations for utilitarianism. Some thinkers, like Nassau Senior (1790–1864) and John Stuart Mill, had a foot in both camps.

Yet modern neo-liberals have identified a fundamental distinction between Benthamism and the ideas of Adam Smith, arguing that it is Smith and Hume, the great thinkers of the eighteenth-century Scottish Enlightenment who represent the true spirit of liberalism. Bentham and his followers, by contrast, are blamed for ideas which 'provided a warrant for much later illiberal interventionist policy' (Gray, 1986, p. 24; Barry, 1986, pp. 19–21). It is not difficult to understand why neo-liberals opposed to state intervention should be critical of the utilitarians. Their 'greatest happiness principle' involved a potential breach with free-market economics. Bentham had been converted by his friend and associate James Mill to representative democracy, as only a government freely elected by the governed could be relied upon to promote the happiness of the greatest number (Dinwiddy, 1989). Yet democracy could involve electoral pressures for interference with free-market forces. Moreover, Bentham was an advocate of bureaucracy as well as democracy. He sought to redesign the whole system of British government from top to bottom on rationalist lines, involving the appointment of professionally qualified, salaried, public officials.

The contradictory implications of Benthamite thinking are evident in the utilitarian-influenced Poor Law Amendment Act of 1834. The Act's underlying assumptions were those of free-market economics. Incentives must be maintained. The able-bodied poor who sought relief must be prepared to enter a workhouse, where their condition would be 'less eligible' than that of the lowest independent labourer. Yet the New Poor Law also involved a comprehensive network of new administrative areas, a new hierarchy of administrative officials, and a novel form of central control and inspection that had rather different implications for the future. Bentham's formidable secretary, Edwin Chadwick (1800–90), a key figure in the development and the administration of the New Poor Law, was later converted from free-market orthodoxy to advocacy of state intervention, following his experiences in the public-health movement.

All this explains why modern neo-liberals have reservations about the utilitarians. Hayek (1975) is critical of Bentham's 'constructivist rationalism'. Gray (1986) similarly argues that because Bentham believed 'social institutions can be the object of successful rational redesign', his utilitarianism 'had an inherent tendency to spawn policies of interventionist social engineering'. For Norman Barry (1986), 'its central tenets stress artifice and design in the pursuit of collective ends'. All this is fair comment. However, the consequent refusal of neo-liberals to recognise Bentham as a liberal involves an artificial conception of liberalism which bears little relation to the British Whig/Liberal tradition, in which Bentham and his associates were directly and centrally involved, in terms of personal connections, ideas and practical influence on policy.

Although the major British classical economists – Smith, Malthus, Ricardo, Nassau Senior and, later, John Stuart Mill – contributed significantly to Victorian liberalism, their ideas were extensively vulgarised and oversimplified. While Adam Smith's 'invisible hand' provided a graphic and enduring vision of the beneficial operation of free-market forces, even Smith allowed for significant exceptions. It was popularisers such as Harriet Martineau, Edward Baines and Samuel Smiles who reduced the principles of classical economics to the simple injunctions of '*laissez-faire*' for governments and 'self-help' for individuals. Even so, *laissez-faire* was only one strand among many in Victorian liberalism, and public policy was never consistently informed by the principle. A series of interventionist Factory Acts, local and general Public Health Acts, and Acts to regulate the railways and banks were passed in the early Victorian period. Indeed, economic historians question whether there ever was an age of *laissez-faire*.

Victorian liberalism

A political ideology is not to be identified with the history of a political party, yet there is inevitably a strong connection between particular systems of ideas and their practical political expression. Thus any account of British liberalism must pay some attention to the composition, support, and record of the British Liberal Party, especially during its heyday in the second half of the nineteenth century.

Although the term 'liberal' was applied in British politics from the early nineteenth century, the British Liberal Party only emerged in the 1850s from a party realignment involving Whigs, radicals and Peelite Conservatives. Gladstone (1809–98), who had started his political career as a Conservative follower of Peel, became the embodiment of Victorian liberalism, and was four times Prime Minister. He so dominated the party that he was substantially able to shape it in his own image. He was an Anglican landowner with no past reputation as a radical in a party that was becoming increasingly associated with manufacturing, dissent, and radical reform. Yet Gladstone was a politician who became more radical and populist with age. Furthermore, and crucially, he was inspired by a Christian moral fervour which struck a receptive chord among his nonconformist followers. Gladstonian liberalism thus became something of a moral crusade (Vincent; 1966, Adelman, 1970, pp. 6–7).

This Gladstonian liberalism drew on several strands. Parliamentary reform was a theme derived from the Whig tradition, and the advocacy of Bright, and later Gladstone himself, turned it into a populist cause. Proposals for a fairly modest extension of the franchise soon developed into radical Liberal demands for full manhood suffrage. Nonconformism also loomed large. According to the religious census of 1851, almost half of the church-going population of the country was nonconformist, so that although the 1860s parliamentary party was 'still overwhelmingly Anglican', the Liberals were becoming 'the party of the Nonconformist conscience' (Vincent, 1966, pp. 61–2). Nonconformist pressures spawned the Liberation Society, to disestablish the Church of England, and later the National Education League to campaign for a national, free and secular system of education. The League in turn provided the model for the National Liberal Federation in 1877 that established a national organisation for the Liberal Party but tipped it decisively towards radical nonconformism. By the 1880s the parliamentary party as well as the party in the country was predominantly nonconformist (Adelman, 1970).

A similar attitude to foreign policy and Ireland helped unite Gladstone with the nonconformists. The importance of foreign affairs to British liberalism is often underestimated. It was support for liberal and nationalist movements on the continent, especially Italian unification, which helped create Palmerston's 1859 government and subsequently kept it together. It was Gladstone's campaign against the Bulgarian atrocities which brought him out of premature retirement and into close collaboration with the nonconformists. It was the religious fervour behind his mission to pacify Ireland which both split his party, but also strengthened the moral element in liberalism.

What has been called 'Manchester liberalism' was a significant but retrospectively exaggerated element of the Liberal Party after 1859. Free trade had certainly been clearly established as a liberal principle. Cobden and Bright, the leaders of that classic pressure group campaign, the Anti-Corn Law League, had seen their cause victorious in 1846. Repeal of the Corn Laws symbolically reflected the transfer of power from the landed to the manufacturing interest, which both Cobden and Bright represented. Gladstone as Chancellor of the Exchequer in Palmerston's government built on their work by abolishing a whole range of duties, while Cobden himself negotiated the Anglo–French trade treaty of 1860.

Yet free trade did not entail *laissez-faire* in domestic policy. Cobden's opposition to Factory Acts in particular and government intervention in general seemed increasingly out of tune with the times. As for Bright, his 'theory of history and of politics did not derive from any abstract attachment to *laissez-faire* or political economy, or from any construction of his business interests' (Vincent, 1966, p. 168). Rather, it was a moral and religious fervour that informed his views on economics and foreign affairs, and a detestation of 'privilege' that led him to champion parliamentary reform.

Liberal practice entailed increased state intervention. Major reforms in education, the army, the law and civil service were accomplished by Gladstone's 1868–74 administration. Subsequently, the Third Reform Act in 1884 involved the triumph of radical demands for reform over Whig caution. Chamberlain's 'Unauthorised Programme' of 1885, and the 'Newcastle Programme' of 1891 marked a decisive shift towards radicalism within the British Liberal Party.

Behind the evolution of Liberal political practice there was a considerable development in political thinking, and not all liberal thinkers were happy with the pace of change. Herbert Spencer (1820–1903) combined *laissez-faire* economics with evolutionary theories that emphasized the survival of the fittest. He opposed almost all forms of state intervention of the sort which Liberals of his day were increasingly advocating and introducing at both local and national level, and even argued for the privatization of the Royal Mint. Yet Spencer was out of step with his time. John Stuart Mill (1806–73), by contrast, was a key transitional figure in the evolution of liberalism. In most respects Mill was a thorough individualist:

> The sole end for which mankind are warranted, individually or collectively, in interfering with the liberty of action of any of their number is self-protection … Over himself, over his own body and mind, the individual is sovereign. (Mill, 1859)

Mill was eloquent in denouncing censorship and arguing for full liberty of thought and expression. It was his commitment to individuality that led him, despite his general advocacy of representative democracy (including the representation of women), to fear the 'tyranny of the majority'. He worried about the intolerance of public opinion and the 'despotism of custom' which he saw as a greater threat to individuality than deliberate actions by governments. Despite his individualism, Mill, unlike Spencer, increasingly allowed for considerable government intervention, despite his general espousal of the market in his *Principles of Political Economy* (1848). Indeed, Mill has been described as 'a watershed thinker' in the development of liberalism from individualism to collectivism (Gray, 1986, p. 30; Greenleaf, 1983, p. 103).

Liberalism, capitalism and democracy

Liberalism as a political ideology has been closely associated with the rise of industrial capitalism; it was pre-eminently the creed of the bourgeoisie, the owners of industrial and financial capital. Its political objectives involved the enfranchisement of the new middle classes and the effective transfer of political power to the major manufacturing urban centres of industrialised Britain. Its economic theory could be seen as the rationalisation of the interests of capital. Moreover, it was hardly coincidental that the British Liberal Party finally emerged in the 1850s when Britain's industrial and commercial dominance was unchallenged, the British bourgeoisie supremely self-confident, and the working classes still largely non-unionised and unenfranchised. The relative decline of British manufacturing and the rise of labour from the late nineteenth century onwards were part of the background to the subsequent decline of liberalism.

Even so, British liberalism cannot be simply derived from capitalism. The leading Whig parliamentarians, who retained a substantial presence in nineteenth-century Liberal governments despite their diminishing numbers, were large landowners. Many of the rank and file Liberal activists were not manufacturers but shopkeepers and tradesmen (Vincent, 1966). And even before their progressive enfranchisement, a substantial section of the working class had attached itself to the Liberal cause. Liberalism in practice involved a coalition of class interests. Some of the causes it embraced, such as temperance, religious disestablishment and Irish home rule were only tenuously, if at all, connected with the interests of capitalism. Leading British liberal thinkers such as John Stuart Mill, Ritchie, Hobhouse, Keynes and Beveridge gave only qualified support for capitalism.

The establishment of a capitalist economy was accompanied by the gradual establishment of a liberal democratic system in the United Kingdom, and this may not have been coincidental. Indeed, some Marxists have argued that representative democracy affords the best shell for capitalism. If that is so, then it was not surprising that the party of the bourgeoisie should have been in the forefront of the parliamentary reform movement in Britain. Moreover, support for parliamentary reform in the mid-nineteenth century commonly stopped short of support for full representative democracy, and some critics have denied any reciprocal tie of dependence between liberalism and democracy. Arblaster (1984, p. 264) talks of the 'fear of democracy' and argues that 'middle-class liberals were fearful, not only for wealth and property, but also for the position and values of their class'. From a neo-liberal perspective, unlimited democracy 'cannot be liberal government since it respects no domain of independence or liberty as being immune to invasion by governmental authority' (Gray, 1986, p. 74).

Such verdicts involve a rather strained interpretation of the evolution of liberalism over the last two centuries. Democracy in the eighteenth century was a remote theoretical model, interpreted by educated Britons, if at all, through Thucydides, Plato and Aristotle. Representative democracy in the early nineteenth century was a largely untried system. In these circumstances it is not surprising that liberals were apprehensive about its possible consequences. Yet, as we have seen, Paine was a consistent advocate of manhood suffrage, James Mill converted Bentham to adult male suffrage, while John Stuart Mill argued for the extension of full political rights to women. Commentators have been quick to seize on any shortcomings in the commitment of these writers to democracy – the exclusion of women from James Mill's franchise, and his son's flirtation with plural voting. Yet in so doing they ignore the substance of their support for what was then a radical minority cause.

While many Whigs and Liberals in the early and mid-nineteenth century were more cautious than these thinkers, once the logic of the movement for parliamentary reform was accepted and British liberals became finally committed to the theory and practice of representative democracy, their conversion was wholehearted. Indeed, the arrival of 'government by the people' was seen by many liberals as a justification for abandoning former limitations to government intervention. Thus Chamberlain argued in 1885:

> I quite understand the reason for timidity in dealing with this question [poverty] so long as the government was merely the expression of the will of a prejudiced and limited few ... But now we have a Government of the people by the people. (Schultz, 1972, p. 59)

Herbert Samuel in 1902 argued that a reformed state could be entrusted with social reform. 'Now democracy has been substituted for aristocracy as the root principle of the constitution ... the State today is held worthy to be the instrument of the community in many affairs for which the State of yesterday was clearly incompetent' (quoted in Schultz, 1972, p. 81). The acceptance of democracy marked a critical step towards the New Liberalism. There was an inexorable logic by which liberals progressed from parliamentary reform to representative democracy, to state intervention, and the apparent abandonment of some of the principles associated with earlier liberalism.

The New Liberalism

The New Liberalism flourished in the late nineteenth and early twentieth centuries and involved state economic and social reform that marked a repudiation of *laissez-faire* liberalism. It has been the subject of intense controversy. To its advocates, the New Liberalism developed naturally out of the old, extending and refining familiar liberal principles and concepts. Others, including some Liberals at the time and modern neo-liberals have perceived the New Liberalism as the culmination of 'anti-liberal elements' which 'began to enter the liberal tradition itself from the mid-1840s in the work of John Stuart Mill' (Gray, 1986, p. 33). However, radical and socialist critics have dismissed the New Liberalism as a forlorn attempt to revive and update an outmoded ideology (Arblaster, 1984, ch. 16).

The origins of the New Liberalism have been variously attributed. At the philosophical level it reflected the influence of Hegelian idealist philosophy (Pearson and Williams, 1984, p. 146). From a party political perspective it was partly stimulated by the need to head off the rising challenge from labour. It has also been linked to a perceived need to modernise the British economy and society and enable Britain to compete more effectively in the world economy (Hay, 1983). Yet it also involved a rationalisation of the substantial growth in government intervention that had been taking place throughout the Victorian period, much of it actively promoted by Liberals.

While Mill played an important transitional role in the evolution of liberal thought, the key New Liberal thinkers were Green, Hobson and Hobhouse. T. H. Green (1836–82) was an influential Oxford philosopher who derived his 'political obligations' from Kant and Hegel, and served as a local councillor. Leonard Hobhouse (1864–1929) was a philosopher and sociologist who wrote a seminal text on *Liberalism* (1911, reprinted 1964). John Hobson was an economist who believed that under-consumption was the cause of unemployment. They were essentially engaged in an extensive project to redefine old liberal concepts and values in line with new political practice. Thus, freedom, the key liberal value, meant for Green 'a positive power or capacity of doing or enjoying something worth doing or enjoying.' 'The ideal of true freedom is the maximum of power for all members of human society alike to make the best of themselves.' While individual liberty remained the touchstone of liberalism, the New Liberalism, according to Hobson involved 'a fuller realisation of individual liberty contained in the provision of equal opportunities for self-development' (quoted in Eccleshall, 1986, p. 204). Thus, state intervention might be necessary to remove obstacles to self-development. However,

> Liberals must ever insist that each enlargement of the authority and functions of the State must justify itself as an enlargement of personal liberty, interfering with individuals only in order to set free new and larger opportunities. (Eccleshall, 1986, p. 206)

Some New Liberals advocated extensive programmes of state action. Hobhouse justified interference with the market to secure 'the right to work' and 'the right to a living wage'. There was, he argued, 'a defect in the social system, a hitch in the economic machine'. Individual workers could do nothing. 'The individual workman cannot put the machine straight ... He does not direct and regulate industry. He is not responsible for its ups and downs, but he has to pay for them' (Hobhouse, 1911, 1964 edition, pp. 83–4).

Liberal politicians were not always prepared to go as far as these New Liberal ideologues, although Liberals at both local and national level were increasingly interventionist. In local government, enthusiasm for civic improvements amounted to a 'municipal gospel'. Radical Liberals saw city government as a test-bed for policies that could be applied nationally. A key figure here was Joseph Chamberlain (1836–1914) who made his name as a radical Liberal mayor of Birmingham before making a successful transition to national politics. His campaign for the 'Unauthorised Programme' in 1885 drew extensively on his own local government experience, which involved the public provision of hospitals, schools, libraries, art galleries, baths and parks. Chamberlain explicitly rejected the principles of *laissez-faire*. The problem of poverty was, he said, one which 'some men would put aside by reference to the eternal laws of supply and demand, to the necessity of freedom and contract, and to the sanctity of every private right of property'. But, he observed, 'these phrases are the convenient cant of selfish wealth'. He went on to brush aside allegations that what he was advocating involved socialism:

Of course it is Socialism. The Poor Law is Socialism. The Education Act is Socialism. The greater part of municipal work is Socialism, and every kindly act of legislation by which the community has sought to discharge its responsibilities and its obligations to the poor is Socialism, but is none the worse for that. (Schultz, 1972, pp. 58–9)

Chamberlain has rarely been claimed for New Liberalism because of his later split with Gladstone and alliance with the Conservatives. Yet, as a radical reformer with roots in local government, Chamberlain was only the most prominent of a whole new breed of Liberals who were coming to prominence in the party in the late nineteenth century. The radical, reforming approach of the 1885 Unauthorised Programme was echoed in the Liberal Party's 1891 Newcastle programme, although at national level there was little opportunity to implement the New Liberalism before the Liberal landslide victory of 1906.

Key figures in the 1906–14 Liberal Government were Asquith (1852–1928) and Lloyd George (1863–1945), although Winston Churchill (1874–1965), a recent convert from the Conservatives, also made a significant contribution. Welfare reforms included the provision of school meals and old-age pensions, and Lloyd George's introduction of national health and unemployment insurance in 1911. Lloyd George's controversial 1909 budget also involved some modest redistribution of income and wealth through his land tax and progressive income tax, while Churchill's labour exchanges indicated a readiness to intervene in the operations of the labour market (Fraser, 1984, ch. 7).

How far was the New Liberalism stimulated by the 'rising challenge of labour', about which Liberals were undoubtedly concerned? Some hoped that social reforms would win votes; others feared they could be an electoral liability. They were not necessarily popular with working-class voters, and might frighten the middle classes. Rosebery, briefly Liberal Prime Minister after Gladstone, was convinced that the radical Newcastle programme had cost the party support (Bernstein, 1986, ch. 2). By contrast, Rosebery's Liberal imperialism could appeal to a chauvinistic working class. Rosebery's own more modest economic and social reform programme sought to promote 'National Efficiency' that progressive businessmen believed was necessary to enable the British empire to compete successfully with the rising political economies of Germany, the USA and Japan.

The decline of the Liberal party – and the triumph of liberalism?

The New Liberalism ultimately failed to prevent the decline of the Liberal Party. It is debatable how far this decline was inevitable (Dangerfield, 1966; Clarke, 1971, ch. 15). However, the 1914–18 war undermined Liberal internationalism, while the pressures towards collectivism and coercion associated with modern warfare created huge strains for Liberal individualism, particularly on the symbolically significant issue of conscription. After the war, some of the causes with which British liberalism had been identified, such as religious nonconformism, temperance and, above all, free trade, seemed less relevant.

Yet, conversely, it has been argued that 'the disintegration of the Liberal Party signifies the triumph of liberalism ... If liberalism is now partly invisible, this is because so many of its assumptions and ideals have infiltrated political practice and current awareness' (Eccleshall, 1986, p. 56). Indeed, the culmination of New Liberal thought can be

seen in the social welfare proposals of Beveridge and the economic
theory of Keynes that provided the basis of the post-Second World
War ideological consensus. Keynes and Beveridge were both large 'L'
as well as small 'l' liberals. The 1942 Beveridge Report was based on
the insurance principle, and, although far more comprehensive, was in
keeping with the spirit of the Lloyd George insurance scheme of 1911.
Keynes' economic theory involved government intervention at the
macro-level but allowed markets to operate freely at the micro-level.
Neither Beveridge nor Keynes saw any need for an end to the private
ownership of the means of production. It was precisely this kind of state
intervention to promote employment and welfare provision that was
favoured by earlier New Liberals like Green and Hobhouse (George and
Wilding, 1980).

Other liberal ideas have long been put into practice and absorbed
into British political culture. Thus a number of legislative changes in
the 1960s, including divorce, homosexual and abortion law reform, and
some relaxation of censorship, were compatible with the principles of
individual liberty proclaimed by Mill in 1859. Subsequent legislation
on equal pay, equal opportunities, and race and sex discrimination in
the 1970s is also thoroughly consistent with liberal ideology. Thus a
progressive 'liberal' orthodoxy was established, supported by leading
Labour and Conservative politicians as well as the much diminished
Liberal Party. (Although the continuing widespread prevalence of sexist, racist and homophobic views suggests also significant continuing
resistance to this orthodoxy.)

Yet this apparent triumph of the economic and social ideas of the
New Liberalism has been considerably complicated by the revival, from
the 1970s onwards, of an older form of liberalism, the free-market liberalism associated with classical economics. As a consequence, the
term 'liberal' today can only be invested with more precision by quali-
fying it with some modifying adjective or prefix. There are progressive
or social liberals who are enthusiastic about penal reform, civil liberties, the protection of the rights of minorities, freedom of expression
and open government, and who are generally unashamed intervention-
ists in the economic sphere. There are also neo-liberals, market liberals
or economic liberals, such as Hayek and Friedman, who favour free-
market ideas and are generally regarded as on the right of the political spectrum. These thinkers influenced the New Right and the brand of
Conservatism associated with Mrs Thatcher (and are discussed further
in Chapter 3).

The ideas of modern Liberals and Liberal Democrats

A modest revival in Liberal Party fortunes began in the 1960s, accelerated in the mid-1970s and was given renewed impetus by the alliance with the Social Democratic Party (SDP), launched by Labour defectors in 1981. The two parties eventually merged to form the Liberal Democrats, who by the twenty-first century were briefly involved in coalition in the devolved governments of Scotland and Wales, and had a substantial role in English local government. The Liberal Democrats also doubled their number of MPs at Westminster to 46 in 1997, and improved their representation further in 2001 and 2005, when they had 62 MPs, more than in any election since 1923. This revival in party political fortunes has been accompanied by some renewal of interest in associated political ideas.

The policies of the Liberals and Liberal Democrats have substantially involved a continuation of the New Liberal tradition – welfare capitalism with a strong emphasis on individual rights. Distinctive Liberal policies included early advocacy of UK entry into what was then the EEC, devolution, incomes policies, partnership in industry, electoral reform, and a focus on community politics (Tivey and Wright, 1989, pp. 83–6). This last element has been closely linked with Liberal successes in local government.

Whether the post-war British Liberal Party really did much to extend or develop liberalism may be doubted, however. The party was fertile in policy proposals, without producing any startling new ideas or major thinkers. Neither its electoral successes nor its failures seem to have owed much to liberal ideology. The crucial decisions with which its leadership was faced were tactical rather than ideological – whether to accept Heath's offer of a coalition in 1974, whether to support the Labour government after 1977, how to handle the SDP breakaway from Labour after 1981. All these decisions had ideological implications, but they were not ideologically driven.

In fact, there was rather more intellectual ferment among the modern Liberal Party's uneasy allies, the SDP, and their post-merger remnants (Owen, 1981; Williams, 1981; Marquand, 1988). It could be argued that the dividing line between New Liberalism and Fabian socialism or social democracy was always thin. Hobhouse talked of 'liberal socialism' in 1911, while Hobson made the transition to Labour following the First World War. It has perhaps grown thinner still as a consequence of revisionist tendencies on the right of the Labour Party in the 1950s, and the SDP breakaway in the 1980s. In this context, the Liberal/SDP Alliance and subsequent merger can be seen as the practical expression of an ideological convergence which was already well underway (Behrens, 1989). Thus social democrats like David Marquand could be claimed for liberalism (although Marquand eventually rejoined Labour in 1995). Yet, ultimately, the Liberals effectively swallowed the SDP rather than the other way around, and the modern Liberal Democrats are the clear lineal descendants of the old Liberal Party.

Paradoxically, as the fortunes of the party have risen, Liberal Democrat ideas have become less distinctive. This is hardly their fault. For most of the post-Second World War period Liberals adopted an intermediate position between the two major parties. Briefly, in the early 1980s, the Liberals and their allies could offer a clear middle way between right-wing Thatcherism and left-wing socialism. Since then, Labour in particular has re-occupied the centre ground it had previously vacated, leaving the Liberal Democrats with little ideological space and few distinctive ideas and policies. On economic management, constitutional reform, Europe, defence and foreign policy, the differences between the two parties increasingly appeared more of degree than kind. Under the leadership of Ashdown, coalition with Labour appeared logical, and for a time likely. Blair seemed keen to heal the divisions on the centre-left that had left the Conservative party dominant for most of the twentieth century. Labour–Liberal Democrat coalitions in local government and, later, devolved government in Scotland and (briefly) Wales, provided some continuing impetus, but the sheer scale of Labour's victory in 1997 and resistance within both parties weakened the Blair–Ashdown project.

Under Ashdown's successor, Charles Kennedy, the Liberal Democrats pursued a more independent and critical line, without returning to the old stance of equi-distance between the major parties. Indeed, on some policy issues the Liberal Democrats appeared to the left of Labour, favouring higher taxation for the better-off and a penny on the standard rate of income tax to fund increased education expenditure. The invasion of Iraq drove the Liberal Democrats further apart from both Labour and the Conservative opposition that backed the invasion. Kennedy and foreign affairs spokesperson Menzies Campbell led a united party in opposition to war, and gave them a distinctive principled stand that attracted considerable popular support that paid electoral dividends in 2005. Whereas the Liberal Democrats had won seats from the Conservatives in 1997, in part on Labour's coat-tails, aided by some tactical voting by Labour supporters, in 2005 they made gains at Labour's expense.

Yet some Liberal Democrats thought the party should have done better in the circumstances and blamed their leader, whose drink problem had become public knowledge. Kennedy's resignation in January 2006 and the ensuing leadership election involved further unwelcome publicity, although Liberal Democrat MPs hoped that Kennedy's successor, the widely respected but elderly Menzies Campbell, would improve the party's prospects.

There were some suggestions that the new leader might encourage rapprochement with Labour, as Campbell was personally friendly with Gordon Brown, Blair's heir apparent and soon to be his successor. In the event, Campbell failed to make much impression with the public. Brown's decision not to call an early election in 2007 provided an opportunity for disaffected Liberal Democrats to push for Campbell's resignation.

The Liberal Democrats today

The outcome of the 2007 leadership election was a narrow victory for Nick Clegg over Chris Huhne in a close-fought contest. Nick Clegg has been compared with David Cameron, the Conservative Leader (indeed, hostile critics have suggested he is 'Cameron-lite'). He is young (just three months younger than Cameron), and educated at a leading public school (Westminster) and Cambridge. He was a Member of the European Parliament from 1999 to 2004, and only entered the Commons in 2005. Thus, like Cameron, he carried little political baggage from the past.

Previous Liberal and Liberal Democrat leaders from David Steel onwards had moved away from the traditional Liberal equi-distance between the two major parties. Steel (1976–88) had negotiated a Lib–Lab pact to keep Callaghan's Labour government in office in 1977–8 and presided over the electoral alliance and subsequent merger with the SDP from 1980–88. Paddy Ashdown, the first leader of the merged party, the Liberal Democrats (1988–99), worked closely with Labour on devolution and constitutional reform and planned an electoral coalition with Blair (see above). Charles Kennedy (1999–2006) had originally been elected for the SDP in 1983, and appeared to be positioning his party to the left of Labour. Menzies Campbell (2006–7) had been closely involved at the centre of party decision-making for many years before he became leader. Clegg had been one of 25 Liberal Democrat MPs who declined to serve under Kennedy, but as a recent arrival at

Westminster he had not been associated with previous internal parliamentary party debates. Indeed, he had little direct experience of domestic UK politics, which had some advantages (like Cameron he appeared a fresh face), but was also a potential weakness.

Clegg has emphasised his own liberalism, and appears to be distancing his party from its twenty-five year embrace of social democracy and its past links with Labour, implying a return of the Liberal Democrats to the former traditional Liberal equi-distance between the major parties. Indeed, there are some indications that the party under Clegg is repositioning itself to the right. If they are to be involved in coalition government in the future it seems more likely that this would be with the Conservatives rather than Labour. This partly reflects electoral calculations. The Liberal Democrats are defending seats won mainly from the Conservatives, and need to appeal to former Conservative voters if they are to retain them against a revival of Conservative fortunes, and they also hope to capitalise on criticism of Labour's record. So distancing the party from Labour makes political sense. Yet there are also clear signs that Clegg and the parliamentary party are repositioning themselves ideologically. While Clegg has stressed his own radical liberal credentials in his defence of civil liberties and has also maintained his party's left wing stance on foreign policy, he has appeared to shift to the right on economic policy.

Within both the old Liberal party and its Liberal Democrat successors there has long been a tension between social liberalism (inherited partly from the New Liberals, but also from the SDP Alliance) and economic liberalism. Although economic liberals have generally been in a small minority, there are signs of their increasing influence. Already under Kennedy a party pressure group had challenged the leader's commitment to 'tax and spend' policies, and published a volume of essays, *The Orange Book: Reclaiming Liberalism* (Marshall and Laws, eds., 2004) calling for a return to economic liberalism, including a flat rate tax system. Since then, the party has ditched its former commitment to increase taxes. Under Clegg's leadership the Orange Book Liberal Democrats, including Vince Cable, David Laws and Ed Davey, have become more prominent. Significantly Clegg soon reversed his party's past line by advocating tax and spending cuts, a policy previously associated with the Conservative right.

Any marked move towards economic liberalism is likely to arouse opposition from party activists in the country, many of whom continue to see themselves as radicals, and to the left of Labour. However, the development of the economic crisis in 2008 has had further implications for the Liberal Democrats, as it has had for the other parties. Vincent Cable, the party's economic spokesperson, showed more prescience than most politicians (and indeed other observers) both in warning of the economic dangers and proposing action. (Thus he advocated nationalising the failed bank Northern Rock in 2007 while the Labour government long sought to avoid this eventuality.) The Liberal Democrats have also been less critical than the Conservatives of Gordon Brown's measures to boost the economy in the latter half of 2008, and indeed partly anticipated them, advocating increased taxes on higher incomes, and cuts in taxes for those on lower incomes.

So where do the Liberal Democrats stand today?. It remains difficult to articulate a distinctive Liberal Democrat philosophy in the context of modern British politics (Wallace, 1997; Russell, 1999; Ballard, 2000; Marshall and Laws, 2004). Many key concepts and values are apparently shared with Brown's Labour and Cameron's Conservatives. There is no longer much distinctive ideological ground for the Liberal Democrats to occupy, although that underlines the widespread acceptance of liberal ideas across mainstream British parties.

There has long been a considerable diversity of views within the ranks of the party, which still contains 'free market Liberals, social liberals, conservatives with a social conscience and dissatisfied ex-Labour voters, greens, anarchists...' This may demonstrate tolerance and inclusiveness as Ballard (2000) claimed, but hardly ideological coherence. If the Liberal Democrats are ever to become a party of government again (most plausibly in coalition with either of the major parties) they will have to make some awkward choices.

Further reading

Eccleshall (1986) provides a good reader on liberalism, with a useful introduction – see also his own account of liberalism in Eccleshall *et al.* (2003). An earlier reader by Shultz (1972) is particularly useful on the New Liberalism. 'Variants of Liberalism' are briefly but cogently discussed from a Marxist perspective by Stuart Hall in Donald and Hall (eds, 1986). Gray (1986) provides a provocative neo-liberal interpretation of liberalism, while Arblaster (1984) offers a critical socialist perspective. Greenleaf (1983) and Freeden (1996) advance contrasting views of the British liberal tradition. The New Liberalism is explored from different angles by Freeden (1978), Clarke (1971) and Hay (1983).

Among liberal texts, John Stuart Mill's *On Liberty* (1859) provides the classic defence of free speech and toleration, and much of his other writing is at least worth dipping into (many modern editions). Hobhouse's *Liberalism* (1911, 1964) was written at the height of the New Liberalism. Wallace (1997), Russell (1999) and Ballard (2000) have explored modern Liberal Democrat ideas, while Marshall and Laws (2004) edited an influential collection of essays by Liberal Democrats favouring a return to economic liberalism.

3
Conservatism

Introduction

It is as difficult to give an authoritative account of conservatism as for other mainstream ideologies. As with liberalism and socialism, interpretations of conservatism vary over space and time. Thus O'Sullivan (1976) devotes separate chapters to the French, German and British conservative traditions, and also discusses modern American interpretations of conservatism (and more recently 'neo-conservatism'). Here the concern is primarily with conservatism in Britain, although this necessarily includes some comparison with conservatism elsewhere, as well as external influences on the development of British conservative thought and practice. However, there are noted tensions and ambiguities in British conservatism, which has changed markedly over a considerable period of time and has been very variously explained.

This is hardly surprising. In British politics the term 'conservatism' dates back to the 1830s, but the roots of the philosophy much further – through the 'Toryism' established from the late seventeenth century, and arguably further back. It would be surprising had Toryism/conservatism not evolved and changed considerably in response to altered circumstances. Moreover, terms commonly associated with conservatism are 'pragmatism' and 'flexibility'. The British Conservative Party has sometimes been characterised as a pragmatic rather than an ideological party, responding to immediate practical problems instead of pre-conceived theory. Moreover, conservatives have frequently denied that their political convictions constitute an ideology.

Indeed, conservative theory is rather thin. There are few key texts or authoritative statements of conservative philosophy. Often ideological inspiration has come from outsiders – from the Whig, Edmund Burke, from the radical Liberal Unionist Joseph Chamberlain, from Keynes, and more recently from classical liberalism and neo-liberalism. Thus conservative ideas sometimes have to be inferred from the practice of the Conservative Party and individual Conservative politicians. The party has been notably flexible in adapting policies to altered circumstances, which explains much of its enduring success in holding on to power, and its capacity to bounce back from occasional electoral disaster (e.g. 1832, 1906, 1945 and 1997).

This chapter begins with an examination of key conservative values and concepts that draw on wider conservative thought and practice, but with more particular reference to British conservatism. It goes on to examine the evolution of British conservative ideas and practice over time, culminating in a review of the contemporary British Conservative Party's ideas, policies and prospects.

What is conservatism really about? Key values and concepts

The introductory discussion (above) suggests that it may be difficult to provide a definitive list of key conservative values and concepts. Indeed, there are fierce debates among conservatives, both practitioners and academics, over core conservative concepts and their interpretation. The account provided below is inevitably contentious, and should be compared with the analysis of others, including conservative insiders, relative outsiders and hostile critics.

Conservation, reaction and change

Conservatism at its simplest suggests 'conserving', keeping things as they are, with a sceptical attitude to change, summed up in the well-known aphorism, 'If it ain't broke, don't fix it.' According to Michael Oakeshott, an influential twentieth-century British conservative thinker, 'To be conservative is to prefer the known to the unknown, to prefer the tried to the untried, fact to mystery, the actual to the possible, the limited to the unbounded.' Thus the conservative regards innovation with caution and suspicion. 'Innovation entails certain loss and possible gain, therefore, the onus of proof ... rests with the would-be innovator ... The man of conservative temperament believes that a known good is not lightly to be surrendered for an unknown better' (Oakeshott, 1962, pp. 168ff).

Hostility to change is a common human sentiment. Many people appear more comfortable with what is old and familiar and are wary of anything new and different. Such feelings have been expressed throughout recorded history, and the origins of conservatism have been traced back as far as Plato, whose theory of history suggested that change involved not progress but degeneration (*Republic*, 4th century BC, tr. Cornford, 1945, Part IV). However, the emergence of a coherent conservative ideology is commonly identified with reaction against the major upheavals in the western world from the late eighteenth century onwards. Here there is a clear contrast with liberalism, which was a product of the Enlightenment, the American and French revolutions, and most of all industrial capitalism. Conservatism involved a reaction against all these. It was suspicious of the claims made for rationalism and science by writers of the Enlightenment, and with the threat these presented to traditional religious and secular authority. It was hostile to the language of liberty and equal rights expressed by the American and French revolutionaries, and particularly horrified by the course of the French revolution. It was fearful of many of the changes associated with industrialisation. Traditional interests felt threatened by the new wealth and its growing political weight.

However, conservatives, although temperamentally averse to change, have responded to it in various ways in different contexts. In France, conservatives like de Maistre sought to put the clock back, restore the *ancien régime* and the authority of both the monarchy and the Catholic church. In Germany after the revolutionary and Napoleonic wars, the restoration of the pre-revolutionary political system was neither feasible, nor even desirable for most conservatives, inspired instead by a romantic nationalist interpretation of a (largely mythical) distant German past. In Britain, fear of revolution was balanced by a cautious acceptance of limited reform, which conservatives from Edmund Burke (1729–97), through Peel to Disraeli, considered necessary to preserve traditional values and institutions. Thus, as Burke argued, 'A state without the means of some change is without the means of its conservation' (1790, ed. Hill 1975, p. 285). However, Burke parted from his former Whig colleagues over the 1789 French Revolution, which they initially welcomed and he utterly condemned. 'The very idea of the fabrication of a new government is enough to fill us with disgust and horror.' Reform should grow organically out of the past and should be based on 'precedent, authority and example' rather than abstract reason (Burke, 1790, ed. Hill, 1975, p. 296).

Tradition

As compared with most liberals and socialists, conservatives have generally stressed the limitations of human reason and rationalism, preferring to rely on tradition and the perceived wisdom inherent in traditional values, institutions and processes. Thus, Edmund Burke argued, 'We are afraid to put men to live and trade each on his private stock of reason, because we suspect that the stock in each man is small, and that the individuals would do better to avail themselves of the general bank and capital of nations and of ages' (Hill, 1975, p. 354). 'Rationalism in politics' was later the main focus of the attack of conservative thinker Michael Oakeshott (1962, pp. 1–36). 'To the Rationalist nothing is of value merely because it exists ... familiarity has no worth.' This rationalist assumption was wholly at variance with Oakeshott's own view of the conservative temperament.

Human imperfection

Conservatism has been called a 'philosophy of imperfection' (O'Sullivan 1976, Quinton 1978). Compared with liberalism or socialism, less reliance is placed on the reason or the inherent goodness of humans, and there is accordingly less optimism about the prospects for improving society. Quintin Hogg has commented that 'man is an imperfect creature with a streak of evil as well as good in his inmost nature' (Hogg, 1947, p. 11). T. E. Utley (1949) has trenchantly observed, 'Human nature is violent and predatory and can be held in check only by three forces, the Grace of God, the fear of the gallows, and the pressure of social tradition, subtly and unconsciously operating as a brake on human instinct' (Utley, 1949). Norman St John Stevas (1982) has noted that belief in the perfectability of man is a liberal or socialist error – conservatives have on the contrary a consciousness of original sin, (although Stevas acknowledges that not everyone would illustrate the point in religious language). Many conservatives (although by no means all) have emphasised the importance of established religion in keeping erring humans on the straight and narrow.

Organic society

While liberal theorising started with the individual, and sometimes assumed society was no more than a mere aggregate of the individuals composing it, conservatives have commonly perceived society as more than the sum of its individual parts. Individual human beings do not exist in isolation but are born into and embedded within specific societies that give them identity and security. Society exists naturally. It is not some artificial construction deliberately and consciously manufactured by rational self-interested individuals, but a complex living organism, necessarily involving ties of mutual dependence between the individuals, families, groups and classes that form it. An organic conception of society and the state can be traced back to Plato, but it has often been articulated by conservatives (e.g. Hogg, 1947, pp. 24–30). One implication is that humans should be extremely cautious in meddling with any part of the whole, for fear this will damage the delicate balance that enables the organism to survive and thrive. A more positive implication is that all the individuals and groups within a society are dependent on each other, and this entails social duties and responsibilities and not just the pursuit of individual rights and self interest.

Authority and leadership

Partly because of human intellectual and moral weakness, conservatives commonly emphasise the need for authority, leadership (both secular and religious) and a strong state and government to maintain law and order and the fabric of society. Conservatives also generally assume that those called to undertake leadership roles will perceive these as a public duty and govern in the wider public interest, rather than their own interest. An emphasis on leadership and authority has not always appeared compatible with democracy. In the early nineteenth century conservatives feared democracy. Thus Lord Salisbury opposed further extension of the vote in 1860, arguing 'Wherever democracy has prevailed, the power of the State has been used in some form or other to plunder the well-to-do classes for the benefit of the poor' (in Buck, 1975, p. 104). Conservatives only moved to a qualified acceptance of democracy when it became clear that it was compatible with maintenance of the existing social order and the defence of property. Yet the conservative conception of democracy is one in which all the initiative comes, through strong leadership, from an authoritative government (Beer, 1982, pp. 94–8). Conservative parties generally vest considerable power and discretion in their leaders, as compared with socialist parties that, theoretically at least, constrain the power of the leadership with internal democratic controls within the party.

Defence of property

Conservatives have generally been unequivocal in their defence of property (Nisbet, 1986, p. 55 ff). This contrasts strongly not only with early socialists who sought substantial redistribution, and sometimes the abolition of private property, but also with liberals who, starting from libertarian and egalitarian assumptions, have felt a need to produce elaborate justifications for property, based for example on natural rights, labour, or utility. Conservatives have generally devoted less time and space to the justification of private property, as the issue for them is unproblematic. Existing property rights are part of traditional social arrangements endorsed by conservatives. Inequality in property reflects profound inequalities in abilities and energies. While the existing distribution of property may not reflect desert or meet need, conservatives deny that ideal social justice is obtainable. Interference with existing property rights in pursuit of social justice threatens the whole institution of private property. The most the conservative is generally prepared to concede is that the possession of property entails obligations and responsibilities to the less fortunate.

Thus, conservatives have wholeheartedly defended private property, and justified its extremely unequal distribution. Burke argued that 'the characteristic essence of property, formed out of the combined principles of its acquisition and conservation, is to be unequal.' Great concentrations of property 'form a natural rampart about the lesser properties in all their gradations.' Inherited property is also strongly defended. (Hill, 1975, pp. 316–17). Modern conservatives have been as committed to the defence of property. Oakeshott associates the possession of private property with freedom, and goes on to suggest that private ownership of the means of production, essentially capitalism, is also necessary for liberty. Scruton (1980, p. 99) talks of 'man's absolute and ineradicable need of private property,' which, he says, 'represents the common intuition of every labouring person.' The problem with property for conservatives has been more one of strategy rather than of principle – how to persuade the majority with little or no property to accept its existing distribution. In practice, conservatives have attempted to widen and extend property ownership, particularly through encouraging home ownership and shareholding, and thus establish a 'property-owning democracy' and 'popular capitalism'.

Hierarchy and inequality

It follows from their strong defence of property rights and the existing distribution of property that conservatives see inequality and hierarchy in human society as natural and inevitable. There will always be huge differences in income, wealth, and social status between individuals, groups and classes in any society. Some are bound to have more power and influence than others. Poverty may be alleviated, but can never be eliminated.

To preach equality and social justice is to stir up envy, hatred and unhappiness, for the passions aroused can never be satisfied. The most conservatives are prepared to urge is a need for more equality of opportunity, to enable the talented and industrious to better themselves, and encourage a degree of social mobility, through 'levelling up' rather than 'levelling down'.

Paternalism, social reform and collectivism

The conservative defence of private property and hierarchy has not generally implied an unqualified defence also of the free market. Indeed, from a conservative perspective, many people were incapable of perceiving and pursuing their own rational self-interest. Those more fortunately placed in terms of natural endowments or wealth had an obligation to provide help, guidance and control. For many conservatives charity and voluntary activity was much the more preferable means of alleviating social distress. It was part of the conception of an organic society with mutually dependent classes. It links with the notion that property carried with it obligations and duties as well as rights. Yet where voluntary activity proved inadequate, some conservatives were increasingly prepared to use the state to help those unable or incapable of helping themselves. Indeed conservatives often had fewer inhibitions about using the power of the state than old-fashioned *laissez-faire* liberals. Conservative leader Benjamin Disraeli in 1872 described the 'elevation of the condition of the people' as the third great object of his party. By the middle of the twentieth century leading Conservative politicians embraced social reform. As the Conservative statesman R.A. Butler declared in 1947, 'We are not frightened at the use of the State. A good Tory has never in history been afraid of the use of the State.' This was a verdict endorsed by his colleague (and future Conservative Prime Minister) Anthony Eden. 'We are not the political children of the *laissez-faire* school. We opposed them decade after decade' (both quotations from Beer, 1982, p. 271). Indeed, S.H. Beer (1982) saw the interventionist postwar Conservative governments as the culmination of a Tory collectivist tradition (although this involved a rather selective interpretation of conservative history.)

Libertarianism

As with liberal critics of the New Liberalism, there are some conservatives who would regard the whole notion of Tory collectivism as a monstrous aberration, a departure from true conservatism. Other conservatives through history have championed the freedom of individuals against a meddling and potentially oppressive 'nanny state'. This tendency was strengthened by the revival of free market economics in the hands of neo-liberals such as Hayek, Friedman, Buchanan, Tullock and Niskanen, particularly when conservatives were railing against the perceived excesses of socialist collectivism in the 1960s and 1970s. Economic libertarianism was later exemplified to some degree in the Conservative governments of Margaret Thatcher (see below). More recently, another strand of libertarianism has been articulated by some conservative critics against aspects of post-1997 New Labour policies on security and law and order, especially powers to hold suspects longer without charge, increased monitoring and surveillance of citizens (e.g. through CCTV) and proposals for identity cards. (Thus the former Conservative leadership candidate and shadow Home Secretary, David Davis, resigned his Commons seat to fight and win a by-election on a civil liberties platform in 2008.)

It may be observed, however, that conservative libertarianism has been most powerfully expressed at times when the Conservative Party was in opposition, against a state temporarily in the hands of a New Liberal or Labour government. When the Conservatives have been in government they have more generally emphasised the need to maintain and strengthen the authority of the state against perceived internal and external threats. This may appear inconsistent, although it is not necessarily hypocritical. Governing parties of all complexions routinely claim, and no doubt sincerely believe, that they are using the power and authority of the state to protect and enhance the liberty and security of citizens.

One influential interpretation of British conservatism (Greenleaf, 1973, 1983) perceives a lasting tension between libertarian and collectivist strands in conservative thought. This suggests that what came to be described as Thatcherism was simply a re-emphasis of the libertarian tradition after a period when the collectivist strand had been more dominant. However, Freeden (1996, ch. 9) has described this 'dual conservative tradition' as a chimera. The contradictions, he argues, were more apparent than real, and partly reflected a rhetorical conservative response to the contrasting challenges of liberalism and socialism in different periods.

Nationalism

Accounts of political ideologies frequently ignore or underestimate the importance of conceptions of the nation and the national interest at home and abroad. This is particularly unwise with reference to conservatism. International relations and foreign policy are key aspects of modern American neo-conservatism. Similar considerations have been central to British conservatism from the latter nineteenth century onwards. For half a century or more imperialism, unionism, national defence and economic protection were key elements of the party creed, as compared with liberal and socialist support for 'Home Rule' within Britain and free trade and internationalism abroad. More recently, conservatives have been concerned to maintain the union of the United Kingdom against devolution and the threat of separatism, and British national sovereignty against perceived threats from international institutions and the European Union. To many conservatives these are fundamental rather than marginal concerns.

The Tory tradition

Just as British liberalism emerged out of the Whig tradition, British conservatism grew out of Toryism (Table 3.1). This creates some additional complications in the case of conservatism, for while the term 'Whig' is no long used, in Britain 'Tory' is still a familiar synonym for 'conservative'. Here we are essentially concerned with the Tory foundations of modern British conservatism. Historically, Toryism, like Whiggism, dates from the seventeenth century, whereas conservatism derives from Sir Robert Peel's modernisation of his party, and more specifically from the 1834 Tamworth manifesto. Strictly, the label 'Conservative' should not be used before then. However, just as the term 'liberalism' is often extended backwards in time to include earlier thinkers who would not have used or even known the word, so the conservative tradition is frequently and not unreasonably taken to encompass thinkers and ideas which influenced conservative thought. In this context, the rather unhistorical use of the term 'conservative' rather than 'Tory' is useful in claiming for conservatism individuals like Edmund Burke, who was actually a Whig politician in his lifetime, and could not be described as a Tory. Thus, conservatism can be projected backwards before 1834

Table 3.1 The evolution of British conservatism

Period	Description	Politicians and thinkers
Late 17th and 18th Century	TORYISM Monarchy, Church of England, landed interest	Bolingbroke David Hume (Edmund Burke)
Early 19th century	REACTIONARY TORYISM Fear of revolution, repression, agricultural protection	Liverpool Castlereagh
1820s	LIBERAL TORYISM 'Liberal' foreign policy, reform, Catholic Emancipation	Canning Robinson Huskisson
1830s, 1840s	PEELITE CONSERVATISM Pragmatism, gradualism, acceptance of parliamentary reform, repeal of Corn Laws	Peel
1860s, 1870s	DISRAELI CONSERVATISM 'One nation', paternalism, patriotism and imperialism, 'Tory democracy'	Disraeli R. Churchill
Mid-1880s to 1930s	UNIONISM Preservation of Union with Ireland, imperial preference, protection, social reform	Salisbury J. Chamberlain Balfour Baldwin
1940s to 1960s	POST-WAR ONE-NATION CONSERVATISM Keynesianism, mixed economy, welfare state, conciliation of trade unions, end of empire, planning	W. Churchill Macmillan Butler Macleod
1970s, 1980s	'THATCHERISM' Free market, competition, privatisation and traditional conservative values – strong state, national sovereignty	Thatcher Joseph (Hayek) (Friedman)
1990–2005	CONSERVATISM AFTER THATCHER	Major, Hague, Duncan Smith, Howard
2005–	CONTEMPORARY CONSERVATISM	Cameron, Osborne

in a sense which distinguishes it from Toryism. Some writers would also project the term 'Tory' forwards after 1834, to denote the older, traditional ideas and interests within the conservative tradition, but this has never involved a clear-cut distinction with conservatism, rather a difference in emphasis. In common parlance a 'Tory' is simply a conservative.

The labels 'Whig' and 'Tory' were admittedly lacking in precision and variable over time, but some reasonably valid generalisations can be made. While the Whigs wished to limit royal authority, the Tories supported the monarchy. While the Whigs upheld the right to religious dissent, the Tories were the party of the Church of England. Most important of all perhaps, the Whigs, although led by aristocratic landowners, were associated with developing commercial and manufacturing interests, while the Tories were the party of the landed gentry. Behind these interests the Tories stood for traditional authority and hierarchy in society, although such ideas were less systematically articulated than by their Whig counterparts. These Tory values and interests were largely carried forward into conservatism.

Reaction and reform

Both Toryism and early conservatism involved a reaction against the major upheavals in the western world from the late eighteenth century onwards, including the eighteenth-century Enlightenment, the French revolution, and industrialisation. Fearing revolution during and after the wars with France, predominantly reactionary Tory governments pursued repression. However, in the 1820s more progressive Tories (sometimes described as liberal Tories) allowed or initiated some reform, including the legalisation of trade unions and Catholic emancipation. Although, after their defeat in 1830, the Tories strongly resisted electoral reform, a new party leader, Sir Robert Peel, finally accepted the 1832 Reform Act and articulated his own cautious and gradualist approach to reform in the 1834 Tamworth manifesto. This is usually taken to mark his party's transition from Toryism to conservatism. Yet although he rehabilitated his party and eventually brought it back to power, he caused bitter divisions within it particularly when, as Prime Minister, he once more accepted the need for a major reversal of past policy (the protection of agriculture) introducing corn law repeal in 1846.

It was another younger Conservative, Benjamin Disraeli, who helped lead the opposition against Peel. However, it was Disraeli who subsequently was responsible for an even more remarkable political 'U-turn', when he persuaded his party to support a second electoral reform Act in 1867, and thus 'caught the Whigs bathing and stole their clothes.' Disraeli in one of his novels had written of 'two nations' in Britain, the rich and the poor, implying the need to forge one nation. In a speech in 1872 he described 'the elevation of the condition of the people' as the third 'great object' of his party (in Eccleshall, 1990, p. 137), and went on to lead a reforming administration from 1874–80. Conservative electoral and social reform won wider electoral support, even among the working classes, and made more credible the novel concept of 'Tory democracy' (later associated with Lord Randolph Churchill, Winston Churchill's father).

Some historians, however, have suggested that the Conservative commitment to both democracy and welfare reform has been exaggerated. It was less in evidence in the period of Conservative dominance from 1886–1906, which the American academic S.H. Beer (1982, pp. 271–6) has described as a period of 'Conservative inertia'.

Imperialism, unionism and protection

Beer (1982, p. 272) suggests that this inertia (at least with regard to social reform) was because 'in imperialism ... the Conservative party had found a cause with a mighty appeal to the voter'. Indeed, he goes on to conclude that social reform 'was a theme Conservatives could be induced forcefully to support only when defeat left it no other way of winning power'. It was Disraeli's strong assertion of Britain's national interest in international relations, and particularly his promotion of imperialism that perhaps secured more popular support than his rather limited social reforms. This support for imperialism was if anything more pronounced under Lord Salisbury (Prime Minister 1886–1892 and 1895–1902). Moreover, by this time imperialism was linked with another popular cause, unionism, in reaction to the Liberal leader Gladstone's conversion to Irish Home Rule, a policy that divided his own party, provoking an alliance between Conservatives and Liberal Unionists.

The association of conservatism with imperialism and unionism was to be joined by a third cause, protection. Those only familiar with the modern Conservative Party may wrongly assume that conservatives have always supported free markets and free trade. In the first half of the nineteenth century Tories and conservatives strongly maintained protection for British agriculture. Later in the nineteenth century, as cheaper foreign imports threatened British manufacturing, some conservatives demanded 'fair trade' rather than 'free trade'. The growing empire that was a source of raw materials and a potential market for British goods led to demands for 'imperial preference' or 'empire free trade', linking the cause of protection with that of imperialism. Yet the politician who committed the party to protection was the former radical Liberal, now Liberal Unionist, Joseph Chamberlain, who had subordinated his old passion for social reform to the cause of empire, particularly after he served as Colonial Secretary in Salisbury's second administration.

Robert Blake, the leading historian of the Conservative Party, notes 'The success of tariff reform within the party is something of a puzzle, given its total failure outside', and he confesses to being baffled by 'the persistence of the party in a cause that was politically so calamitous.' Indeed, it led to desertions from the party (including the young MP Winston Churchill), contributed to the Liberal electoral landslide of 1906, and kept the party out of power until 1915, and from a Conservative-led government until 1922. Joseph Chamberlain thus succeeded in dividing and weakening both major parties, although he founded a political dynasty that remained committed to his programme. It was his son Neville Chamberlain who, as Conservative Chancellor of the Exchequer in a Conservative-dominated National Government, introduced import duties in 1932.

It was only after the Second World War that the British Conservative Party dropped its enthusiasm for protection. Nationalism (or patriotism) and imperialism remained key conservative themes through the early post-war period, although colonialism became increasingly difficult to support in both theory and practice, and empire over time disappeared from conservative rhetoric. Unionism persisted longer. The party remained the Conservative and Unionist Party, even though the Ulster Unionists parted company from the party in mainland Britain from 1974. As the party of the union, the Conservative party continued to oppose devolution to Scotland and Wales under the leadership of Thatcher and Major. While it has since accepted devolved institutions in Scotland and Wales, it maintains support for the union, (although this may no longer be in its electoral interests). Indeed, in 2008 the much-depleted Ulster Unionists re-united with David Cameron's Conservatives, re-emphasising the party's traditional unionism.

'One-Nation' conservatism

'One-Nation' Conservatism is associated with some leading Conservative politicians who became prominent from the Second World War onwards, especially Harold Macmillan and R.A. Butler. Those who come across the term 'One Nation' for the first time may, understandably but mistakenly, relate it to the more consistent conservative themes of nationalism and unionism. However, it relates back to a phrase of Benjamin Disraeli, implying the need to overcome the divisions between the two 'nations' of rich and poor. One Nation Conservatism involved the enthusiastic embrace of welfare reform, Keynesian policies to maintain full employment, and other forms of state intervention.

Thus, Harold Macmillan, a Conservative rebel in the 1930s, had preached an interventionist 'Middle Way' between *laissez-faire* capitalism and socialist state planning. The wartime Tory Reform Group urged the acceptance of social reform and more specifically the state welfare recommendations of the Beveridge Report which was declared the 'very essence of Toryism' (Beer 1982, p. 307). R. A. Butler, the architect of the 1944 Education Act in Churchill's coalition war time government, helped firm up the commitment to social reform in opposition from 1945–51, and as Churchill's Chancellor of the Exchequer from 1951 continued to pursue the Keynesian full employment economic policies of his Labour predecessor.

Indeed, Conservative governments from 1951 to 1964 did not seek to reverse much that the 1945–51 Labour government had established. The Welfare State was maintained and even, in certain respects, enhanced. Thus the former rebel Macmillan, as Housing Minister, fulfilled his promise to build three hundred thousand houses a year, many of them council houses. A policy of compromise and accommodation was applied to the trade unions and industrial relations. Most remarkably perhaps, after the initial denationalisation of steel and road haulage, other state-owned industries were maintained. Overall, the role of government continued to expand, and public expenditure continued to rise. As Prime Minister Harold Macmillan accepted the resignation of his entire Treasury team in 1958 rather than the cuts in spending which they demanded. Confronted with persistent problems such as low growth, balance of payments deficits and weak sterling, Macmillan's government moved towards more intervention rather than free market solutions. The National Economic Development Council signalled a new interest in long term economic planning, and the National Incomes

Commission institutionalised the new Conservative concern with incomes policy. This was perhaps the high-water mark of post-war Tory collectivism.

Macmillan had once provocatively declared that Toryism had always been a kind of paternal socialism. As with liberal critics of the New Liberalism, there were some conservatives who regarded 'One-Nation' conservatism as a monstrous aberration, a departure from true conservatism. Indeed, some who participated in these governments, most notably, Lord Joseph (1976), later recanted, and declared they only discovered true conservatism subsequently. Others such as Sir Ian Gilmour (1978) have continued to claim that Butler and Macmillan represent the mainstream Tory tradition, and that it is the free market neo-liberal ideas of the New Right which are heretical.

The New Right and Thatcherism

In 1975 Margaret Thatcher became leader of the Conservative Party. Her victory was unexpected, and arose because the bulk of the parliamentary party wished to be rid of Ted Heath, not primarily for reasons of policy or philosophy but because of personality factors and electoral failure (he had lost three elections out of four). Most of her new Shadow Cabinet had been members of Heath's Cabinet, of which Mrs Thatcher had been a loyal and fairly junior member. Thus no sharp change of party direction was anticipated. Some assumed the new leader would not last long. In the event, Mrs Thatcher was to remain party leader for 15 years and was to serve as Prime Minister for 11, longer than any predecessor since Lord Liverpool. Moreover, she presided over a marked change in the direction of British conservatism.

What marked Prime Minister Margaret Thatcher off from most of her predecessors and the mainstream conservative tradition was her overtly ideological approach to politics, her populism, and her radicalism, in contrast with past pragmatism, elitism and cautious gradualism. She was first and foremost a conviction politician, determined to put ideas and principles into practice and consequently averse to traditional conservative compromise and consensus. She was a populist in the sense that she sometimes appeared the champion of ordinary people against established interests (although she was not always particularly popular, and aroused some strong antipathy). Finally, many of the changes she began were not of the 'small and limited' nature associated with conservative gradualism, but very radical. Nigel Lawson (1988) observed that she had 'transformed the politics of Britain – indeed Britain itself – to an extent that no other Government has achieved since the Attlee Government of 1945–51'.

Yet 'Thatcherism' is hardly an ideal term to describe the ideology associated with Mrs Thatcher. While she took ideas seriously, she was never herself an original thinker. She had absorbed her convictions from many sources, some long dead, others still active and influential. Academics and think-tanks played a larger role in the dissemination of ideas. Even the policies pursued by her governments owed much to energetic colleagues such as Geoffrey Howe, Nigel Lawson, Nicholas Ridley and Norman Tebbit, who all contributed significantly to aspects of 'Thatcherism'. Thus, some commentators from the start preferred the less personalised description 'New Right', which can also be employed to cover similar ideas advanced in other countries.

Indeed, many of the political developments described under the heading of 'Thatcherism' in Britain show similarities to changes over much of the western world in the last quarter of the twentieth century. Thus 'Thatcherism' might be seen as a UK manifestation of a wider transition to a post-modern, post-industrial, global economy. Even so, Mrs Thatcher herself made such an impression not only on British politics but on the western world that the term 'Thatcherism' has survived her personal fall, and is not entirely inappropriate.

The ideas associated with 'Thatcherism' or the 'New Right' involved an interesting mix. There were two principal strands. Firstly there were the free market ideas derived ultimately from classical liberalism, but more recently expressed by thinkers such as Hayek and Friedman who were dubbed 'neo-liberals'. Secondly, there was a neo-conservative strand which emphasized more traditional Tory and Conservative themes such as authority, sovereignty, law and order and the national interest. Clearly neither strand was really new, although both seemed relatively novel in the context of the formerly dominant 'One Nation' strand of post-Second World War conservatism. Mrs Thatcher herself did not even pioneer the blend of neo-liberal and neo-conservative ideas: Enoch Powell had articulated a mixture of free-market liberalism and ultra-traditional Toryism a decade or so earlier. Mrs Thatcher's version was less provocative than Powell's, although it still contained tensions and contradictions which have posed problems for the Conservative party under Mrs Thatcher herself and her successors.

Classical liberalism, neo-liberalism and the free market

Capitalism and Freedom was the title of an influential book written by the American economist Milton Friedman in 1962, which propounded the virtues of the free market. Neither the free market nor the term capitalism were then fashionable in Britain. Even Conservative governments had embraced the welfare state, Keynesian demand management and the mixed economy. Indeed, in the same year, 1962, as Friedman's book appeared, Harold Macmillan had established the National Economic Development Council, and embraced a form of planning. Macmillan's government did contain at least one heretic, Enoch Powell, who was to become a prominent exponent of free-market capitalism, and a future heretic, Keith Joseph, who was then however as keen on state housing and public spending as his chief. Well outside the Cabinet there was a recently appointed young, very junior minister, Margaret Thatcher, whose ideological leanings were as yet unrevealed to the wider political world.

Friedman's advocacy of the free market derived from the classical liberal economic theory of Adam Smith ([1776], 1976). Smith had argued that wealth was created through the pursuit by individuals of their own self-interest in the free market that guided production like an 'invisible hand'. Those governments did best which governed least. This became the economic orthodoxy of classical liberalism. A passionate belief in free markets and free trade had become the key characteristic of the 'Manchester liberalism' of Cobden and Bright, and subsequently Gladstonian liberalism. This was at a time when conservatism remained committed to protection and 'fair trade' rather than free trade and was beginning to be associated with paternalist social reform (see above). As we have seen (Chapter 2), classical free-market liberalism gave place to the more interventionist New Liberalism in the British Liberal party, and these reforming ideas also took root in the twentieth-century Conservative and Labour parties. Two world wars, the depression and the rise of new state-centred ideologies marginalised the old free-market orthodoxies.

Friedrich von Hayek was one important thinker who unfashionably attempted to turn back the collectivist tide. All state planning, he argued, involved a *Road to Serfdom* (1944, 1976), whether undertaken by fascist, communist, moderate social democratic, or even conservative governments. Another key influence on Thatcherism was the public (or rational) choice theory of a school of American writers including Downs, Tullock, Buchanan and Niskanen who applied classical liberal economic analysis to government and the public sector. Thus Niskanen

(1971) argued that public sector bureaucrats would pursue their own interests rather than that of the public they were supposed to serve. Instead of profit maximisation they would seek 'bureau maximisation' – the growth of programmes, employment and spending associated with their own department or bureau – as this would enhance their status, pay and prospects. This would always tend to produce a higher level of provision and public spending ('bureaucratic oversupply') than would be demanded and supplied in the free market. Thus public bureaucracies were inherently inefficient and wasteful. These ideas were to influence the Thatcher government's reforms of the civil service, local government and National Health Service.

More immediately influential were the increasingly vocal critics of Keynesian orthodoxy, including Friedman himself and the economists Alfred Sherman and Alan Walters. They argued that Keynesian budgeting was inflationary, and that control of inflation required tight control of the money supply. 'Monetarism' was thus the term initially associated with Mrs Thatcher's brand of conservatism but it was never a satisfactory label. It was actually the Labour Prime Minister Callaghan and his Chancellor Healey rather than Mrs Thatcher who first adopted monetary targets, while her political philosophy was always about much more than controlling the money supply (which received less emphasis subsequently).

All these free-market ideas belonged more to the liberal than the conservative tradition, although Greenleaf (1973, 1983) has associated them with a 'libertarian' strand of Conservative thought. Significantly, Hayek considered himself a liberal rather than a conservative although he carefully distinguished his own liberalism from what he described as the 'constructivist rationalism' of Voltaire, Rousseau and the English Utilitarians. Milton Friedman similarly described himself as a 'Liberal of the nineteenth-century variety', which was how he also described Mrs Thatcher herself:

> Mrs Thatcher is not in terms of belief a Tory. She is a nineteenth century Liberal. But her party consists largely of Tories. They don't really believe in free markets. They don't believe in free trade. They never have, as a party. They believe in an elite governing, which is a very different conception to hers. (Friedman, *Observer*, 26 September 1982)

Yet before she became leader these ideological convictions were less evident. Although she claimed to have read Hayek's *Road to Serfdom* as a student at Oxford, she showed few signs that she was a disciple in her early political career. Her biographer Hugo Young (1989, p. 56) observes, 'What is striking about this period is how small and tentative were her contributions to the debate which raged about the future of Conservatism.' As a loyal member of Heath's Cabinet she was 'responsible for the abolition of more grammar schools than any Secretary of State before or since' (Young, 1989, p. 68), and fiercely defended education spending. Nor did she indicate any criticism of the general direction of government policy under Heath, although scorn for Heath's 'U-turn' in 1972 subsequently became Thatcherite orthodoxy. Following Heath's election defeats in 1974, it was Sir Keith Joseph who took the lead in advocating free-market rather than Keynesian policies, with Margaret Thatcher giving quiet support.

It was only after Mrs Thatcher emerged as the unlikely winner from the leadership contest in 1975 that her own free-market convictions became manifest. In speeches she extolled Victorian virtues of self-reliance, attacked collectivism, and dismissively referred to 'bourgeois guilt', a phrase widely interpreted as a criticism of Tory paternalism as much as socialism. She also acknowledged the influence of two celebrated neo-liberals, Friedman and Hayek, and, behind them, the virtual founder of classical economics, Adam Smith (Thatcher, 1977).

Detailed analyses of the policies of the Thatcher governments can be found elsewhere (Young, 1989; Kavanagh, 1990; Gilmour, 1992). Here it is sufficient to indicate how far free-market ideas informed the broad direction of policy. Control of the money supply, early seen as the very essence of the new approach, was found to be difficult in terms of definition and execution and was accorded less priority. There was a more determined attempt to 'rein back the state' although public spending was effectively restructured rather than reduced. The sale of council houses and the privatisation of most of the former nationalised industries marked, however, a significant transformation of the hitherto mixed economy. A shrunken public sector was systematically overhauled through the injection of competition and free-market principles. A managerial revolution challenged the old administrative culture of the civil service, which saw most of its tasks and personnel transferred to semi-autonomous Executive Agencies. Compulsory competitive tendering was imposed on a range of services, transport was deregulated and internal markets introduced into reorganised health and education services.

All this amounts to a formidable redirection of policy inspired by what might be described as neo-liberal free-market ideas. Even so, the Thatcher government did not go as far or as fast as some of the free-market enthusiasts would have liked. While the administration of health and education was reorganised, the principle of state provision of those services was substantially unaffected. The fashionable New Right notion of vouchers for education and health was considered but not implemented. The state was still substantially funding 'social housing' but through voluntary housing associations rather than local councils. Even privatisation disappointed some critics because many of the newly-privatised services initially involved little effective competition, while the state retained an extensive regulatory role.

Moreover, despite the free-market rhetoric that emphasised decentralisation to consumers, customers and patients, the reality often seemed to involve increased centralisation. Thatcherite reforms appeared to strengthen rather than weaken the authority of the state, which did not match liberal or neo-liberal assumptions although it did sit comfortably within the mainstream Tory or conservative tradition and the neo-conservative strand of Thatcherism.

Neo-conservatism

Early accounts of Thatcherism and the New Right played down its traditional conservative or neo-conservative elements, emphasising its roots in liberal and neo-liberal free-market ideology (Bosanquet, 1983; Green, 1987). Even while Mrs Thatcher was still in opposition, her liberal rhetoric disturbed both critics and some admirers within the Conservative Party. Sir Ian Gilmour, later sacked from Mrs Thatcher's Cabinet, carefully distinguished between conservatism and liberalism in his book *Inside Right* (1978). William Waldegrave (1978), a future member of both the Thatcher and Major governments, attacked neo-liberalism and reasserted a conservative tradition involving the acceptance of state power. Several contributors to a generally sympathetic volume of *Conservative Essays* (ed. Cowling, 1978) were expressly critical of liberal ideas:

> The urgent need today is for the State to regain control over 'the people', to re-exert its authority, and it is useless to imagine that this will be helped by some libertarian mishmash drawn from the writings of Adam Smith, John Stuart Mill, and the warmed up milk of nineteenth century liberalism. (Worsthorne, in Cowling, 1978, p. 149)

Yet Peregrine Worsthorne need not have worried about Mrs Thatcher's rhetorical commitment to 'set the people free'. She shared his belief in firm government and restoring the authority of the state. Her 'nineteenth-century liberalism' was distinctly partial; she never exhibited much sympathy for the libertarian implications of Mill's thought in the field of tastes and morality, nor John Bright's pacifist internationalism. The Falklands War, Mrs Thatcher's approach to Europe, firm controls on immigration, tough penal policies and the National Curriculum in education were hardly inspired by free-market ideas. An influential radical Marxist critique of Thatcherism coined the term 'authoritarian populism' to describe its combination of free-market economics with some traditional conservative elements with popular appeal – patriotism, law and order, authority and strong government (Hall and Jacques, 1983; Edgar, 1984; Gamble, 1989). These moral, authoritarian and patriotic elements of New Right thinking were clearly evident in other countries, particularly among Mrs Thatcher's right-wing Republican allies in the United States.

It is a confusing consequence of the elastic and ambiguous definition of key concepts in the study of ideology that Thatcherism can be interpreted as both a product of one form of liberalism and a reaction against another. Just as neo-liberalism involved a reaction against Keynesianism and the welfare state, so neo-conservativism involved a reaction against another dominant orthodoxy of the recent past – in this case the progressive 'liberal' permissiveness of the 1960s. The 1960s saw the abolition of capital punishment, the relaxation of censorship, divorce law reform and the legalisation of abortion and homosexuality, advanced and supported by 'liberal' progressive politicians from all parties. These measures both reflected changes in public opinion and contributed to further changes in attitude and behaviour. Some critics, largely on the right, blamed the breakdown of marriage, family life and moral standards more generally on the 'permissive society'.

The 'family-values' reaction by the 'moral majority' against 'liberal permissiveness' was never as vocal or prominent an element in Thatcherism as it was in the Republicanism of Ronald Reagan. Although the moral campaigners believed she was sympathetic, Mrs Thatcher herself generally avoided explicit commitments on issues of personal morality, and indeed showed a resigned tolerance towards the publicised sexual misdeeds of her male colleagues. Norman Tebbit was much less restrained, however, and blamed the 1960s for the breakdown of family life and traditional morality. His language found a strong answering chord in the rank-and-file membership of the Conservative party, and this, to an extent, influenced the political agenda of Mrs Thatcher's successors, John Major and William Hague.

Tensions within Thatcherism

There are tensions and ambiguities in all ideologies and the contrasting neo-liberal and neo-conservative strands of Thatcherism have always provided a potential source of conflict (see Figure 3.1). To a degree, however, the two strands were compatible; both implied hostility to trade unionism, bureaucracy and corporatist tendencies in government. From a neo-liberal perspective trade-union practices, corporatist policies (such as incomes policy) and bureaucracy all involved unjustified interference with free-market forces. From a neo-conservative perspective, strikes and other union activities, concessions to powerful producer groups under corporatism and the entrenched influence of the higher civil service all posed a threat to the authority of the state and its elected government. Moreover, the free economy advocated by neo-liberals required a strong state to enforce competition, uphold contracts and resist the pressures and claims upon it from powerful sectional interests.

Yet there were also some obvious tensions. For example, on the environment neo-conservatives tended to be right-wing conservationists, while neo-liberals sought to remove controls on planning and development which interfered with market forces. There were also differences on a host of moral issues such as abortion, censorship and addiction issues (including alcohol, tobacco and drugs). Sunday trading involved a symbolically important clash of values. Neo-liberals wanted restrictions on Sunday trading abolished in the interests of free-market forces. Neo-conservatives wished to 'keep Sunday special' in accordance with traditional values and also protect the vulnerable interests of small shopkeepers and shopworkers. It was on this issue that the Thatcher government suffered a rare and embarrassing defeat.

However, the most important divisions were over foreign policy and particularly Europe. Thus some Conservatives saw the European Community (as it then was) in terms of their own free-market convictions, while others perceived a threat to national sovereignty and national interests. The European Community seemed to embody the free-market capitalist values dear to Mrs Thatcher, which is why she supported British entry and enthusiastically signed the Single European Act. Yet it was also associated with bureaucratic and corporatist tendencies which she opposed in Britain. More seriously, intensifying pressures towards closer political union apparently threatened Britain's national sovereignty and independence, a core conservative value. Mrs Thatcher's personal schizophrenia over Europe reflected the tensions between the neo-liberal and neo-conservative elements in her own political philosophy. This schizophrenia has been bequeathed to her party, with damaging consequences.

Arguably, however, the tensions within Thatcherism reflect older tensions within the Conservative tradition. The neo-conservative authoritarian streak in Thatcherism involved a change in emphasis from the liberal progressive attitudes of Macmillan, Butler, Macleod, Boyle and Heath, but reflected the attitudes and demands which regularly surfaced from the rank and file at Conservative party conferences throughout the post-war period. Also, the libertarian strand in conservatism was not altogether new (Greenleaf, 1973). Even in the supposed heyday of Tory collectivism there were strong pressures for competition. The Conservatives were re-elected to the slogan 'Set the People Free' in 1951, and proceeded to dismantle rationing and controls, denationalise steel and road haulage, establish commercial television, and later commercial radio, relax rent controls, and abolish resale price maintenance. The sale of council houses, sometimes regarded as quintessential

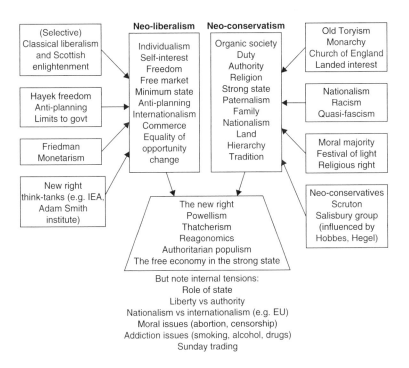

Figure 3.1 Tensions within Thatcherism and the New Right

Thatcherism, was Conservative policy in the 1950s. Here Mrs Thatcher differed from her predecessors in her more ruthless application of policy.

Ideology and pragmatism

Even the ideological drive behind Thatcherism can be exaggerated. The forced sale of council houses at substantial discounts, and the privatisation of the former nationalised industries perhaps had as much to do with pragmatic political objectives as free-market ideas. The extension of home ownership and share ownership gave more voters a stake in property and popular capitalism, while reducing Labour's traditional constituency of council tenants, public-sector employees and trade unionists. It can be seen in terms of the politics of statecraft, the construction of new coalitions of interests (Bulpitt, 1987). Mrs Thatcher, like Disraeli over a century before, was making a bid for the skilled working-class vote.

At another level it can be argued that Thatcherism was a response to altered circumstances. In the earlier post-war period it seemed that commitment to the welfare state and full employment was necessary to win elections, but by the 1970s both the economic assumptions behind those commitments and their political rationale were seen as questionable. Faith in Keynesian demand management was undermined by mounting economic problems, while a growing proportion of the electorate seemed disillusioned with both the benefits of the welfare state and its mounting cost, with adverse consequences for taxation and take-home pay. Thatcherism thus involved a response to the new mood; it was as much the politics of electoral calculation as the politics of conviction.

There is clearly something in such analysis. Mrs Thatcher was more pragmatic than some of her enthusiastic acolytes and advisers would have wished. Thus she declared that the National Health Service was safe in her hands, and rejected rail and Post Office privatisation. However some of the policies of Mrs Thatcher's third term, most notably the poll tax, seemed to have a clearer ideological than electoral rationale (although it certainly appealed to many Conservative Party activists).

A problem for any radical administration, of the right or the left, is whether to maintain the momentum of reform or seek to consolidate after initial objectives are achieved. Both Mrs Thatcher's government and Attlee's government after the Second World War had completed the more popular aspects of their programmes well before their end.

The Attlee government chose consolidation, appeared politically and ideologically exhausted, and lost office. The Thatcher government preferred permanent revolution and moved on to the more controversial privatisation of water and the decidedly unpopular poll tax, and broke up. Perhaps consolidation was never an option for Mrs Thatcher, because she was in the last analysis an ideological rather than a pragmatic politician. Ideas were clearly important to her, and she had argued that the Conservatives needed an ideology to counter socialism. She spurned the traditional civil service sources of policy advice, consulting ideologically sympathetic New Right think-tanks such as the Institute of Economic Affairs and the Adam Smith Institute, and, with Keith Joseph, founding the Centre for Policy Studies. Hers were the politics of conviction rather than pragmatism.

The legacy of Thatcherism

Ideologies are action-oriented and if they are scored in terms of their measurable impact, Thatcherism scores highly. The Thatcher governments did substantially transform Britain, more than any previous administration since Attlee's. Moreover, many of the changes, like those of the Attlee government, seem irreversible for the foreseeable future. Even a Labour government with a huge majority has not contemplated renationalising privatised industries (although Brown's government later felt obliged to nationalise banks in 2007–8), and has modified rather than reversed Thatcher reforms in local government and the NHS. Mrs Thatcher's governments have altered the terms of political trade in ways that have affected her Labour as well as her Conservative successors.

Even so, 'Thatcherism' never really conquered the country (Crewe, in Skidelsky, 1988). It was the electoral system combined with the divisions within the opposition that delivered a series of impressive victories at the polls. Mrs Thatcher in three elections failed to achieve anything approaching the proportion of the popular vote won by Eden in 1955 or Macmillan in 1959. She won her biggest parliamentary majority in 1983 with a smaller proportion of the vote than that secured by the defeated Sir Alec Douglas Home in 1964. Moreover, between the peaks of the General Election years, there were deep troughs in which the party lost heavily in local elections and parliamentary by-elections. Neither Mrs Thatcher herself, nor her party, nor its policies and underpinning ideas were ever as popular as some commentators have suggested.

Yet if Thatcherism was never that popular it caught the mood for change. The old assumptions that had governed policy-making since the end of the Second World War until the early 1970s appeared untenable. Keynesian remedies no longer seemed to work; the welfare state had failed to eradicate poverty; the public sector appeared insensitive and inefficient; and compromise in industrial relations had failed to deliver industrial peace. While Mrs Thatcher's abrasive style and particular remedies did not always inspire approval, her governments were tackling what were widely perceived as problems – high public spending and taxation, inflation, bureaucracy and waste, union power. Moreover, the acronym TINA ('There Is No Alternative') which was proclaimed by enthusiasts was also reluctantly conceded by many more. There did not seem to be a credible alternative in terms of ideas or policies. Thatcherism involved some nasty medicine but appeared necessary to many to purge the British state, society and economy of manifold weaknesses.

The legacy for the Conservative Party is mixed. If Mrs Thatcher can be credited with restoring the fortunes of her party to the extent of winning three successive General Elections and a long, almost unprecedented, period of unbroken Conservative rule, she also left a legacy of internal party division. Differences over policies and ideas were intensified by personal and factional rivalries, to the extent that dissecting the faultlines in post-Thatcher conservatism was to become something of an academic industry. In part, these differences only mirror old tensions between, for example, the libertarian and collectivist strands in conservatism (Greenleaf, 1973, 1983). Yet they were exacerbated by Mrs Thatcher's own abrasive and uncompromising style. Divisions were not accommodated; dissenting colleagues (Gilmour, Prior, Pym, Heseltine) and even former allies (Tebbit, Lawson, Howe) were removed or provoked to resign. Thus, a party for which unity was long said to be its secret weapon (Blake, 1997, 405) became deeply divided, while the embrace of ideology obstructed the party's former pragmatic flexibility in pursuit of power.

From Thatcher to Major

Mrs Thatcher's fall sparked off some speculation over the future direction of British conservatism. Yet too many leading Conservatives were implicated in Thatcherism to make total repudiation a credible option. Moreover, the victory of John Major, Mrs Thatcher's preferred successor, first in the leadership election of 1990 and then in the General Election of 1992, apparently confirmed that the Thatcher legacy was safe.

However, the particular circumstances of Mrs Thatcher's fall left a legacy of bitterness and internal recriminations within the Conservative party. In retrospect it might have been better for the party had Mrs Thatcher been eventually rejected by the electorate rather than by her own Cabinet and parliamentary colleagues; then the need for a change in leadership and direction might perhaps have been acknowledged. As it was, her numerous admirers both within the parliamentary party and the wider party in the country considered she had been betrayed, and they never forgave those deemed directly or indirectly responsible. John Major's government never acquired full legitimacy for those of the true Thatcherite faith, and only briefly from the wider public. The authority derived from the unexpected election victory in 1992 was swiftly followed by 'Black Wednesday', disastrous poll ratings and party splits. He was not helped by the slighting observations of his predecessor, 'the queen over the water', who soon became disillusioned with her anointed heir.

Although the Major government involved a marked change in political style, there were few significant differences in policy and ideas (Kavanagh and Seldon, 1994). The poll tax, incautiously described as the flagship of Thatcherism, was an early casualty, but this had become a political necessity. Otherwise, the Major government energetically pursued the changes in education and health begun under Mrs Thatcher, and extended competition in public services. There was no slackening in the privatisation programme. The politically contentious break-up of British Rail was forced through, while the government was only diverted from its intention to privatise the Royal Mail (which Mrs Thatcher had avoided) by the lack of a sufficient parliamentary majority. Major's only significant innovation was the Citizen's Charter, hailed by some as a new deal for the public services, but viewed by critics (not entirely fairly) as essentially cosmetic. Thus Major's government appeared more of an extended coda to his predecessor's than a new and distinctive administration (Kavanagh and Seldon, 1994).

In retrospect, John Major had a difficult, perhaps impossible, role. He had to appease the Thatcherite zealots of the 'No Turning Back' group and yet at the same time satisfy the demands for change in the party and the country. His own personality and style was consensual, in marked contrast to Thatcher's, and circumstances required that he should strive to contain widening party divisions. Yet the tensions between the neo-liberal and neo-conservative elements of the New Right, evident within the party when Mrs Thatcher was still Prime Minister, became rather more apparent after she left office.

The divisions were most obvious over Europe. Initially, John Major indicated that he was more sympathetic towards the European ideal than Mrs Thatcher, while still standing for British interests within Europe. Thus his conduct of the negotiations leading to the Maastricht Treaty (in which he secured exemptions for Britain from the Social Chapter and from monetary union) was presented as a diplomatic triumph. Even so, a small hardcore of rebels opposed Maastricht from the start, exploiting a growing general hostility to Europe following the disastrous 'Black Wednesday' when Britain was ignominiously forced out of the Exchange Rate Mechanism, and, even more, the escalating BSE crisis affecting British beef. Major faced a challenge to his leadership from John Redwood in 1995 and a threat to his party's electoral prospects from the newly-established Referendum Party (demanding a referendum on the EU) and UK Independence Party. Yet he could not appease the Euro-sceptics without risking losing the support of the most powerful ministers within his own Cabinet (Major, 1999, pp. 342–85, 578–607).

Thus Conservatism appeared increasingly on the defensive during John Major's period as Prime Minister. Under Mrs Thatcher, the party offered a radical challenge to the Butskellite consensus of the post-war era. The very success of that challenge had now transformed Conservatives into defenders of a new *status quo*, increasingly subject to criticism, particularly on the management of the reformed Health Service and the privatised utilities. Moreover, Conservatives were obliged to defend a chequered economic record. Two recessions, culminating in the effective forced devaluation of Black Wednesday, had undermined their claims to economic competence. Tax rises after 1992, coupled with the collapse of the housing market, helped to alienate a substantial section of the middle classes on whom Conservatives relied for their core electoral support. It was also unfortunate that Major launched a 'back to basics' initiative, which was misinterpreted and subsequently undermined when his government became mired in sleaze, following a series of financial and sexual scandals involving ministers and backbenchers (Major, 1999, pp. 554–77).

Of course, it is also true that some of the problems with which Conservative governments had been grappling reflected changes both in British society and the wider world. These included demographic change, the breakdown of traditional families and communities, technological change and unemployment, resource depletion and pollution, and the changing relationships between the developed and the developing worlds. In such circumstances, it is unsurprising that New Right prescriptions had failed to produce magic solutions. The free market was the 'big idea' which the New Right had claimed would transform the British economy and society, but following two decades of free-market orthodoxy some of the familiar problems of market failure were being rediscovered both in Britain and the wider world.

Conservatism in opposition – from Hague to Howard

The reversal of Conservative political fortunes from the last years of the twentieth century and into the new millennium was rapid and massive. After a fourth successive election victory in 1992 the party seemed unassailable and its opponents unelectable. In the space of a few years the roles had been reversed.

Defeat was always going to be traumatic for the Conservatives; the 'natural party of government' had become accustomed to the fruits of office. The sheer scale of the 1997 defeat, even though predicted by the polls, was a worse shock – the heaviest defeat since 1906, or, some suggested, since 1832. A direct consequence was the removal from Parliament of some former Cabinet Ministers. This electoral cull of some of the party's leading lights was swiftly followed by the retirement to the back benches of the former Prime Minister, John Major, and Deputy Prime Minister, Michael Heseltine, and then, as a consequence of the ensuing leadership election, the departure from the shadow cabinet of Clarke, and soon afterwards Howard, Lilley, Dorrell and Redwood. Thus the 1997 election produced an almost unprecedented turnover of the party's collective leadership.

Like Thatcher and Major before him, William Hague won the subsequent leadership election for negative reasons. Relatively unknown, he was less tarnished by the perceived failures of the Major government and carried less baggage than his rivals. Fresh faces at the top of the party apparently offered the prospect of a clean break with the past, and there were early indications that Hague favoured a more inclusive, tolerant party. Indeed, he quickly moved to reform the party's internal organisation and decision-making, with the expectation of creating a more modern democratic party with a wider popular appeal.

Yet giving more power and influence to the party's dwindling ageing membership (Whiteley *et al.*, 1994, p. 50) was hardly compatible with broadening its electoral appeal. While some leading Conservatives were aware of the need for change, it proved difficult to persuade constituency activists to accept the practical implications of gender equality, multiculturalism, toleration of different patterns of sexual behaviour and non-conventional families. A speech by Peter Lilley that sought to distance the party from Thatcherism, backfired disastrously. Thus, prospects for a softer, more inclusive conservatism receded. Subsequently, the party's uncompromising ideas on crime, asylum seekers, sex and drugs (articulated by Shadow Home Secretary Anne Widdecombe) were largely at one with those of (generally elderly) Conservative members.

So, apart from some pragmatic post-election concessions to realism including the acceptance of devolution and the minimum wage, against which the party had campaigned fiercely, there was no real attempt to redefine or update the party philosophy, such as took place after the Conservative defeats of 1945, 1966 and 1974. Instead, Hague concentrated on attacking the government, capitalising on events and issues raised by others (such as the Countryside Alliance, or the fuel protest lobby) rather than seeking to win the battle of ideas by articulating an alternative vision of the future.

Indeed, the ideological visions most widely canvassed related to the past rather than the future. Some advocated a return to One Nation conservatism of the post-war era, but this had depended on a symbiotic relationship between a paternalist leadership and a deferential loyal party which enabled Conservative governments to pursue progressive welfare policies out of tune with the interests and values of many Conservative supporters. More recently, the party in parliament and the constituencies have become less deferential, and less inclined to acquiesce in policies which run counter to their own gut instincts. Moreover, the old 'One Nation' project has been transformed by changing class interests and loyalties, and the increasing political salience of ethnic, gender and other divisions. Thus, the Conservative Party had lost a large slice of its previous core middle-class vote, without being able to reach out successfully to the new multi-ethnic, multi-faith nation containing a diversity of lifestyles and family groupings.

The favoured alternative for many Conservatives was a return to the moral certainties and electoral successes associated with Mrs Thatcher, who continued to cast a long shadow over her party. Significantly, she campaigned hard for Hague in the 2001 election, having taken a back seat in 1992 and 1997. While she enthused party activists, many commentators thought her rhetoric alienated voters, for whom she belonged to the past rather than the future. Indeed, for the party, Mrs Thatcher's brand of conviction politics had become an ideological straitjacket, preventing any significant rethinking.

One imperative for the new Conservative opposition was to rethink its economic policies and particularly its approach to taxing and spending. This was never going to be easy. It was no longer true that state spending mainly benefited the working class and was paid for by taxes raised from the middle classes. While the middle classes gained substantially and disproportionately from some state spending (for example spending on higher education, subsidised rail transport, and the arts), taxation had become more regressive. Indeed, an increasing proportion of the middle classes (particularly those employed in the NHS and other public services) favoured 'tax and spend' policies, while the old working class might be tempted by tax cuts. Attempting to respond to these diverse pressures, the Conservative opposition unconvincingly promised both improved public services and tax cuts. Their task was rendered much more difficult by Labour's apparently successful management of the economy between 1997 and 2007. The previous Conservative trumpcard, proven economic competence, was now held by their Labour opponents. It was now Conservative sums which 'did not add up'.

Constitutional reform, particularly devolution, presented another threat to traditional conservative values. The party which had been the party of the Union for well over a century had little choice but to accept devolution once it was achieved, and help to make it work, and preserve what Hague described as 'four nations in one'. Yet the Conservatives had lost their links with the Ulster Unionists in the early 1970s and their Westminster representation from Scotland and Wales was almost wiped out (although ironically the proportional electoral system that they opposed has preserved a significant Conservative presence in the devolved assemblies). Thus, increasingly, they appear an English party and as such might benefit in electoral terms from the break-up of the Union that they have long sought to maintain. Elsewhere, they have sought to exploit Labour's problems over Lords reform, but they have yet to develop a more comprehensive Conservative approach to constitutional reform.

Divisions over Europe have continued to damage the former reputation of the Conservatives for unity and moderation. Hague chose to adopt a harder Eurosceptic position which isolated the dwindling number of Conservative Europhiles, and drove a few out of the party. It was assumed a clear line would banish the ambiguities of the Major years, and appeal to a Eurosceptic electorate. Thus Hague fought the 2001 election as a single-issue campaign to 'save the pound'. It is now almost universally recognised that this was a mistake. Although the majority of voters shared Conservative opposition to the euro, it was well down their list of priorities. Hague's obsession with Europe meant that Labour's general record and Conservative alternatives never received detailed scrutiny. His tough line with dissent meant that the party was perceived as 'dogmatic', and 'extreme' rather than united, particularly among those voters who recalled that all the main developments in the UK's relationship with Europe had been undertaken by previous Conservative Governments. The party was effectively denying its own past.

The 2001 election was in some respects more disastrous than that of 1997 for the Conservatives, as they had failed to make any significant recovery despite the problems and weakening popularity of the Blair government. The prompt resignation of Hague offered another opportunity for a fresh start. However, the new mechanism for electing a leader, introduced under Hague, left the final choice of his successor to the party's ageing activist members rather than MPs. They chose the Eurosceptic and former Maastricht rebel, Iain Duncan Smith, over the experienced and popular pro-European former Chancellor, Kenneth Clarke. The leadership of Duncan Smith proved more moderate and sensitive to the need for change than might have been expected, but he failed to establish his reputation with the wider public or his own parliamentary party, who passed a vote of no confidence in his leadership in 2003.

After Duncan Smith's prompt resignation, the parliamentary party preferred not to risk another leadership choice by party members, and only one candidate was nominated, the experienced former minister, Michael Howard. While the party united behind Howard, he proved no more successful in appealing to the public than his predecessor. Although the Blair government had lost popularity, particularly over the Iraq war, the official opposition under Duncan Smith and Howard continued to back the war. In other respects, Howard played on some traditional party themes, such as law and order and immigration, but failed to inspire the public. Although the Conservatives won more seats in the 2005 election than in 2001, they lost their third election in succession, and Howard resigned.

For fifteen years from the fall of Thatcher the party had failed to move on. Her successors, Major, Hague, Duncan Smith and Howard, were all her candidates. Her influence helped to ensure the defeat of rival contenders from the leadership, who might conceivably have changed the party's direction and fortune, such as Heseltine and Clarke.

The party of government that had dominated British politics for much of the twentieth century had become the party of largely ineffective opposition. After the 2005 defeat it was widely recognised within the parliamentary party, and even among the wider party membership that change was necessary.

Conservatism today

It was an outsider, David Cameron, who was to succeed Howard as party leader. It was a victory for youth (he was only 39 when first elected) over experience. Kenneth Clarke stood for the third time, having been runner-up in 1997 and 2001, but was this time eliminated in the early rounds. A notably successful speech at the Conservative Party conference gave Cameron an impetus that he never lost, eventually defeating the early front runner David Davis in the final poll of party members by a margin of two to one in December 2005.

Cameron carried little political baggage. Unlike his predecessors, he had neither been a minister nor even an MP under Thatcher or Major. He had only been elected to Westminster in 2001, and was not linked with past divisions, nor closely associated with any wing or group within the party. He was a new face who could provide a credible fresh start, and, as some commentators put it, decontanimate the Conservative brand. He was compared with Tony Blair, another young man with little political baggage who had successfully transformed his party. Cameron's team was similarly largely new, and lacking in ministerial experience (apart from the former leader William Hague who had been Welsh Secretary under John Major), yet this meant they too were not associated with the Thatcher and Major years. Next to Cameron himself the most prominent figure was his Shadow Chancellor, George Osborne. Both men belong to the wealthy elite, educated at elite public schools and Oxbridge, once associated with the leadership of the Conservative Party. In that respect they differ from some of their more recent predecessors. However much they differed in other ways, Heath, Thatcher, Major, Hague and Duncan Smith were all initially outsiders, not drawn from this traditional Conservative governing circle.

Since his election as leader, Cameron has done much to transform the image of his party. He has gained some credit by establishing his party's green credentials, with a new oak tree logo (replacing the old freedom torch), and the election slogan 'Think Green, Vote Blue', although environmental conservatism is not as new as sometimes imagined. It was

Margaret Thatcher who declared at the Conservative conference back in 1988, 'We Conservatives are not merely friends of the Earth – we are its guardians and trustees. The core of Tory philosophy and the case for protecting the environment are the same.' Indeed, as the party that has long had the support of landowners, the Conservatives have a vested interest in the conservation of the countryside. Conservatives featured prominently in the pressure group the Countryside Alliance that from 1998 until 2005 mounted some well-organised demonstrations, largely in favour of fox-hunting, but capitalising on other rural issues. Cameron has sought to broaden his party's green credentials by his personal life style, cycling, running an environmentally friendly car, and installing a wind turbine on his house. How far such essentially gesture politics will be followed up by hard choices on controlling carbon emissions and conserving energy remains to be seen.

Rather more significantly, Cameron and Osborne have, with some success, colonised what was once Labour's ideological ground. Thus they initially accepted the need to spend more on public services such as health and education. Here they praise Labour's aspirations to improve public services, but criticise their centralised control and fail-ure to secure sufficient benefits from the substantial additional money poured into the National Health Service in particular.

Perhaps more surprisingly, the Conservatives have appeared keener on preserving civil liberties than a Labour government that was pre-pared to introduce detention without trial for up to forty-two days, in the interests of national security and the 'war against terror' (Labour has more recently quietly dropped these proposals). Conservative oppos-ition to imprisonment without trial, identity cards and increased sur-veillance over citizens largely reflected the libertarian convictions of Cameron's defeated rival for the party leadership, David Davis. Davis subsequently resigned his parliamentary seat and his post as shadow Home Secretary to fight an eventually successful by-election on a civil liberties platform in 2008. No longer on the front bench, Davis remains popular among Conservatives, although how far the party's enthusiasm for civil liberties survives the possible exchange of opposition for office remains to be seen.

However, the most audacious Conservative incursion into what might be regarded as Labour's ideological ground is over social justice, fair-ness and tackling poverty. While it is true that the former Conservative leader William Hague had borrowed the notion of 'compassionate conservatism' from the American republicans, and Iain Duncan Smith established a social justice commission, it is Cameron and Osborne who have really taken the argument over inequality and social justice to their opponents. Thus Osborne, in a speech to the left-leaning think tank Demos in August 2008, praised New Labour's aim in pursuing social justice, but castigated their performance in markedly failing to secure it. Osborne even cited the American liberal philosopher John Rawls on justice as fairness, a source more usually quoted by progressive liberals and social democrats. Whether the Conservatives might achieve more success in promoting social justice through voluntary agencies rather than state redistribution is unclear. However, Labour no longer has a monopoly of the fairness agenda.

On the issue of relations with Europe, Cameron's Conservatives remain strongly Euro-sceptic and as far apart from Labour as under previous leaders. Indeed, the small group of pro-Europe Conservatives has become more isolated under David Cameron, who remains pledged to take the UK Conservative Members of the European Parliament (MEPs) out of the moderate right European Peoples Party in the European Parliament. Cameron is also still demanding a referendum on the European Lisbon Treaty, which Conservatives insist is essentially similar to the proposed European Constitution that was rejected by French and Dutch voters in 2005, allowing former Prime Minister Blair to avoid the referendum on the constitution that he had promised. On relations with Europe generally, the Conservatives are, however, closer to the views of British voters than Labour or the Liberal Democrats. Thus there seems no immediate prospect of the United Kingdom exchanging the pound for the Euro, even though this has been suggested by some commentators in the wake of the credit crunch and the pound's slide on currency markets in late 2008.

Perhaps, surprisingly, it is the credit crunch and economic recession that has apparently stalled the Conservative revival under Cameron. After a brief initial 'Brown bounce' following the change in Prime Ministers in 2007, the Conservatives gained an increasing poll lead, until by the early summer of 2008 there was widespread speculation that Gordon Brown would be forced out by Labour MPs fearing an electoral massacre. It might have been expected that subsequent economic problems would ensure the end of his premiership. Earlier, Brown's apparently successful management of the economy as Chancellor had stolen what had once been the Conservative's strongest trump card, that only they could be trusted with the economy. The credit crunch, inflation in food and energy prices and the housing crisis, all experienced under Brown's premiership, apparently presented the Conservatives with a golden opportunity to regain the initiative on the crucial issue of economic competence.

It did not initially work out that way. The credit crunch and global economic recession instead contributed to a partial recovery by a re-energised Brown and his party. By contrast, Cameron and particularly his shadow Chancellor George Osborne attracted some Conservative criticism for their handling of the crisis. Part of the problem is that oppositions can only talk, while governments can act, which is inevitably frustrating. The initial reaction of the opposition was to offer the government broad support in measures to deal with the crisis, while criticising Brown's past management of the economy that they argued had contributed to the scale of the crisis. This was perhaps tactically sensible, but Conservative supporters became increasingly restless as Brown earned credit for his high profile activity. Thus, Cameron and Osborne became far more critical of the government's measures, arguing that increased spending and tax cuts would place a huge burden on taxpayers in the future, and that the large rise in government debt would produce a run on the pound. Labour responded by castigating them as the 'do-nothing' party, while attacking specific Conservative proposals as impractical or ineffective.

However, part of the Conservative problem with the economic crisis had more to do with basic ideology and core beliefs. Cameron had appeared to distance his party from some aspects of Thatcherism, particularly what was perceived as its uncaring and uncompassionate side. Thus, he could commit his party to improved public services and social justice, suggesting that the Conservatives could out-perform Labour on these issues. Yet he and Osborne could hardly repudiate Thatcherite economics. Although both Labour and Conservative government politicians had first embraced and subsequently abandoned Keynesianism in the post-war decades, Labour had done so reluctantly and never wholeheartedly, while the Conservatives became keen converts to free-market economics along with strict government control of the money supply. Thus Labour could enthusiastically rediscover Keynes, whose ideas remained compatible with moderate social democracy, while the Conservative leadership, still fundamentally committed to the principles of the free market and sound money, could not accept the deficit finance involved with tax cuts combined with increased government spending. Yet even so, and perhaps inevitably, some of their own proposals to deal with the crisis were criticised by the government as 'unfunded', and insufficiently covered by tax revenues or savings elsewhere in government spending. Thus, economic policy remains a problematic area for the Conservatives-one reason for the recall of former chancellor Ken Clarke to the conservative front bench in January 2009.

Perhaps none of this will matter in the longer run. Voters tend to punish governing parties for bad times, whether the responsibility is largely theirs or not. The crisis occurred under Labour's watch, when they had been in power already for a decade. Thus, the Conservatives may ultimately benefit a growing demand for change, whatever happens to the British economy. Indeed, if the outlook for the economy improves, the risks of entrusting government to an untried team are reduced (which was arguably the situation when Labour secured its landslide majority in 1997). We may only find out what Cameron's Conservatism really involves if and when opposition is exchanged for office.

Further reading

A useful and reliable introduction to British conservative thinking is the anthology, with introduction and notes, by Eccleshall (1990). Other anthologies include those edited by Buck (1975) and Kirk (1982). O'Sullivan (1976) and Nisbet (1986) both offer interesting interpretations of conservatism in an international context. Scruton (1980) provides a provocative and idiosyncratic account from his own neo-conservative perspective and Honderich (1991) a sledgehammer demolition. Contrasting analyses of Tory/conservative thought are contained in Beer (1982), Greenleaf (1973, 1983) and Freeden (1996). Blake's one volume history of the Conservative Party (1997) also gives a valuable insight into conservative thought at different periods. On specific periods, Quinton (1978) is useful on the seventeenth- and eighteenth-century foundations of conservative thinking, while Barnes in Seldon and Ball (1994) discusses twentieth-century conservative ideas.

Classic conservative texts include Burke's *Reflections on the Revolution in France* (various editions, for example Hill 1975) and Oakeshott's elegant collection of essays *Rationalism in Politics*. An insight into Disraeli's ideas can be gathered from his novels *Sybil* and *Coningsby*, although a more balanced account of the contribution of the mature Disraeli to conservativism might be derived from his biography by Blake (1966).

On Thatcherism and the New Right the literature is extensive and daunting. For the neo-liberal ideas which influenced Thatcherism see especially Hayek's classic neo-liberal text *Road to Serfdom* and Friedman (1962). There is a useful discussion of Powellism in Gamble (1974), and Powell's ideas are also explored in biographies (for example Cosgrave, 1989) and his own writings (1991). Joseph's ideas can be sampled in *Stranded in the Middle Ground* (1976). A neo-conservative perspective is to found in the collection of essays edited by Cowling (1978) and in Scruton (1980). On Thatcherism, Bosanquet (1983), Keegan (1984), Green (1987) and King (1987) concentrate largely on monetarism and the free-market aspects of the New Right, while Hall and Jaques (1983), Levitas (1986), Gamble (1988) and Skidelsky (1988) also acknowledge the importance of traditional conservative and neo-conservative themes.

Young's (1989) illuminating biography of Mrs Thatcher can be contrasted with her own account (1993) and that of other leading protagonists such as Gilmour (1992) and Lawson (1992). Ranelagh (1992) is useful on influences, while Kavanagh (1990) and Adonis and Hames (1994) provide a useful overall perspective.

Conservatism after Thatcher has been less exhaustively explored. Kavanagh and Seldon (1994) and Ludlam and Smith (1996) have both edited useful collections of essays on Major whose own autobiography (1999) is illuminating. Whiteley *et al.* (1994) is useful on Conservative Party members, while Patten (1995) has reviewed Conservative ideas. Post-1997 premature obituaries for Conservatism include Gilmour and Garnett (1997) and Gray and Willetts (1997). There is not yet an extensive academic literature on Cameron's conservatism. Until there is, recent developments are best explored on the party website, www.conservatives.com, and through newspapers and periodicals.

4

Socialism

Introduction

Socialism, like liberalism, was a product of the modern world – of the rise of science, industrialisation and associated political upheavals. Socialism thus shared with liberalism a post-Enlightenment rationalism, and optimism over progress. It adopted much of the liberal political programme, most notably for a reform and extension of the franchise, and the establishment of civil rights, and embodied many liberal values.

Yet socialism also involved a reaction against, and a radical alternative to, liberal capitalism. In terms of class interests, socialism can be seen as the political ideology of the new urban working class, effectively created by industrialization, just as conservatism was, initially, the ideology of the landed interest and liberalism the ideology of the bourgeoisie. While conservatism involved a defence of traditional social arrangements, and liberalism provided a justification and support for an ongoing industrial transformation, socialism developed as a radical or revolutionary ideology requiring a fundamental transformation of existing society and its underlying assumptions and values.

Thus socialists sought a radical overhaul of existing property relations and a massive redistribution of income and wealth in favour of the working classes. This was linked with a rejection of the free-market values and competition lauded by liberals in favour of planning and co-operation. Most socialists instinctively felt that it should be possible to improve on the unplanned outcome of market forces under capitalism, its periodic booms and slumps, and associated unemployment and misery.

Further generalization is difficult as socialism has many variants, which this chapter proceeds to examine. Key concepts and values associated with socialism are then explored. There follows an analysis of the British experience of socialism, which has been distinctive. While in many other countries variants of socialism are represented in contending political parties – communists, anarchists, socialists, social

democrats – in Britain there has never been a significant left-wing or
socialist rival to the Labour party. Yet Labour's socialist credentials are
contested. Some critics deny that Labour has ever been a socialist party
and use the term 'labourist' to describe it (Miliband, 1972; Saville,
1988). The more recent development of the party's ideology towards
what is now described as 'New Labour' is then examined.

Evolutionary and revolutionary socialism

A fundamental distinction can be drawn between those favouring an
evolutionary, gradualist route to socialism, relying on rational or moral
persuasion, and those who, enthusiastically or reluctantly, endorse revolution. Evolutionary socialism has always been the dominant strain in
Britain and western Europe, although ideas and analysis have sometimes been borrowed and adapted from the alternative revolutionary
tradition.

Revolutionary socialism was inspired by the French revolution (1789
onwards), which provided a precedent for further attempts to secure
the transformation of society through insurrection. But many socialists
rejected the revolutionary route to socialism. The French Revolution
had disappointed many early enthusiasts for it had 'destroyed its own
children', and culminated in dictatorship. Thus, it was not an example
to be followed but a failure and a warning.

By contrast, some early socialists hoped to build socialism peacefully, from the bottom up. This sometimes involved attempts to
establish small-scale model socialist communities, but more usually
practical experiments in mutual aid and self-help for working people,
such as consumer and producer co-operatives, friendly societies and
trade unions. Yet attempts to build socialism from the bottom up substantially ignored the problem of power. Such initiatives could not,
in isolation, produce that fundamental transformation of society and
redistribution of income and wealth which socialists sought. Marx and
Engels thus attacked this form of socialism as 'utopian', as there was no
realistic strategy for its achievement.

The alternative revolutionary socialism or communism proclaimed
by Marx and Engels anticipated that economic forces would inexorably lead to revolution. They saw class conflict as the motor of historical
change. In the modern industrial capitalist societies that were emerging in the west in the nineteenth century, increasingly the only two
classes that mattered were the capitalists or bourgeoisie who owned and

controlled the means of industrial production and the industrial workers (or proletariat) who owned only their own labour. But capitalism would ultimately be destroyed by its own internal contradictions. Competition between capitalists would lead to falling rates of profit, driving some out of business. Those who survived would be compelled to increase the exploitation of their workers, until poverty and hardship drove them to revolution.

Marx's followers believed that his economic analysis provided a scientific foundation for socialism, and superseded earlier interpretations of socialism. Marx's revolutionary socialism provided the inspiration for the 1917 Russian revolution, and numerous other revolutions since, although neither the background circumstances nor the actual course of these revolutions have closely reflected Marx's analysis. Lenin, in particular, provided his own gloss on Marx, extending the notion of a temporary dictatorship of the proletariat, and developing the concept of democratic centralism to establish an authoritarian, highly centralised state socialism, which was imitated in eastern Europe and China after the Second World War.

Meanwhile, an alternative evolutionary, parliamentary route to socialism seemed increasingly plausible with the extension of the franchise to the workingclass in Britain and other liberal capitalist countries from the second half of the nineteenth century onwards. The parliamentary route involved the formation of socialist parties that competed for votes and parliamentary seats, and ultimately the capture of the apparatus of the state through a parliamentary majority. Thus power could be won, and socialism established, through peaceful and democratic struggle. Indeed, for many, socialism seemed the natural corollary of democracy. Political equality would lead inexorably to social equality.

But although socialist parties were to enjoy considerable electoral success in western Europe, progress towards socialism has been, for many, disappointing. Sometimes this has been ascribed to betrayal by the parliamentary leadership – a familiar complaint on the left. Indeed, there are, arguably, endemic pressures towards accommodation and compromise within the parliamentary system (Michels, 1962). Compromises with socialist objectives were necessary to win votes and were thus an inescapable consequence of the electoral strategy. It was too readily assumed, both by early socialists and some of their opponents, that political democracy would lead rapidly to a major redistribution of income and wealth in favour of the masses. The extent to which the values of liberal capitalism were embedded in society as a whole

---

Box 4.1 Marxism, Marxism–Leninism, communism, socialism and social democracy

These terms are all highly contested and, moreover, have been used in different senses over particular periods, particularly following the Russian revolution of 1917, in the decades after the Second World War, and after the implosion of communist regimes in Russia and eastern Europe from 1989 onwards.

Marxism is the label given to the thought of Marx and his followers, and is also an appropriate term to describe the forms of socialism they endorsed. The specific interpretation of socialism in Russia after the second 1917 revolution is commonly described as *Marxism–Leninism*; Marxism as interpreted in theory and developed in practice by Lenin and his successors. There were, however, other interpretations and developments of Marxism both before and after the 1917 revolution. Some Marxists who sought to update or modify Marxism were condemned as revisionists.

Communism suggests the common or collective ownership of wealth and the abolition of private enterprise (and in the purist sense, all private property). Communism was a term employed by Marx to describe the ultimate outcome of a successful worker's revolution, although he freely used both 'socialism' and 'communism' to describe his political programme. Later, the term communism was widely used to describe the political systems established in Russia, eastern Europe and China, where economic activity was planned and controlled by the state rather than the free market. These regimes continued to describe themselves also as socialist, although in the western world many increasingly distinguished socialism from communism, partly because the latter appeared in practice to involve a one party dictatorship and a rejection of western democracy. Those

$\longrightarrow$

---

was insufficiently appreciated, and the task of converting the working class to fundamentally different values in a hostile climate was correspondingly underestimated (Coates, 1980). Some would further argue that parliamentary socialism inevitably involves a 'top-down', elitist or paternalist approach, producing a centralised state socialism that is the antithesis of the participative, co-operative socialist ideal.

⟶

in the west who were more sympathetic to Soviet communism continued to defend it as 'actually existing socialism', not perfect, but the only working alternative to capitalism. Communist parties also attracted strong support for a time in parts of western Europe, although the Italian communist party in particular later worked within and accepted the principle of parliamentary democracy, a compromise sometimes describes as 'Euro-communism'. Communism fell abruptly from favour both in the former eastern bloc and in the west following the 1989 revolutions. Many former communist parties (including the Italian) renamed themselves.

Socialism in the west after 1917 still implied an alternative to capitalism. While socialism did not entail the abolition of all private property, it was widely assumed that it involved the collective (or public) ownership of the means of production, and socialist parties sought to nationalise key industries. However after the Second World War, and in the face of rising prosperity (not least for industrial workers) socialist parties increasingly sought to manage rather than abolish capitalism, and downplayed or dropped policies of public ownership. Some politicians and thinkers attempted to redefine socialism as the promotion of greater equality and social justice. Some adopted the label 'social democracy' to describe this modified form of socialism.

Social democracy was a term adopted by many socialist parties in the nineteenth century to imply that they were both socialist and democratic. Some social democratic parties were explicitly Marxist. (Marx and Engels accepted the term.) Yet after 1917 the term 'social democracy' was used in a sense that marked it off both from Soviet communism and Marxism. After 1945 it has come to mean a reformed, moderate version of socialism (or 'managed capitalism') as opposed to the older more fundamentalist socialism involving public ownership of industry.

State socialism, anarchism and syndicalism

Attitudes to the state have varied markedly among socialists. While anarchists would totally reject the authority of the centralised state, others such as the British Fabian socialist, Sidney Webb, have identified the expansion of the state with socialism. Marxists argue that the existing state apparatus in a capitalist society inevitably reflects a narrow class interest and involves coercion, and thus must be replaced by new institutions. But while Marx suggested that the state would 'wither away' after the revolution, this was not the experience in communist political systems. The state established by Lenin in the Soviet Union was highly visible and centralised. Western parliamentary socialists, while abhorring the Leninist state, have still tended to see socialism in terms of centralised state economic planning and state welfare provision. More local decentralised, participative forms of socialism have had strong advocates, particularly by those influenced by anarchism, but there has been little by way of successful practice.

Anarchism, a term derived from ancient Greek, meaning 'no rule', is an ideology that suggests that states, governments, and all forms of coercive authority are neither necessary, nor desirable. The nihilistic violence of a few anarchists has contributed to a negative popular stereotype, but anarchism is a serious and in many respects attractive political philosophy. Anarchist thinkers, such as William Godwin (1756–1836), Pierre-Joseph Proudhon (1809–1865), Michael Bakunin (1814–1876), and Peter Kropotkin (1842–1921), argue that states are inevitably oppressive and limit freedom. Humans are not naturally aggressive and competitive, but social and co-operative, and would realise their true nature and full potential through voluntary association and mutual aid in stateless societies. Critics argue that anarchism is utopian, impractical and incapable of realisation, and indeed it is difficult to identify any modern society where its principles have been applied, with any degree of success.

Even so, anarchist ideas have had some influence on mainstream ideologies across the political spectrum. Thus a libertarian distrust of the state is found among variants of liberalism and conservatism. Indeed, some who have described themselves as anarchists have defended private property as critical to the defence of individual liberty against state interference. Such libertarian anarchism influenced the American political philosopher Robert Nozick (1938–2002), while the American political scientist Murray Rothbard (1926–95) has developed a theory of anarcho-capitalism.

However, such right wing anarchism is historically rare, and anarchism is much more frequently associated with socialism and the left or far left. Among leading anarchist thinkers, Proudhon figures in histories of socialism. Bakunin competed with Marx for control of the First International, while Kropotkin's ideas have been described under the heading communist anarchism. The French thinker Georges Sorel

(1847–1922) is associated with anarcho-syndicalism, combining anarchist ideas with radical trade unionism, seeking revolution through mass industrial action, or a general strike. All this suggests that most forms of anarchism are not only anti-state, but also strongly anti-capitalist, involving the collective ownership of property, or at least the collective management of the means of production. It is only this left-wing anarchism that has ever attracted a significant mass following, for example in France, Italy, Russia, and, particularly, Spain.

Socialists have also disagreed over the relative merits of parliamentary and extra-parliamentary (particularly industrial) action as a means to achieve social and political change. While trade unionism was predominantly legalistic, respectable and limited to immediate practical objectives concerned with pay and conditions, industrial muscle could also be employed to achieve wider economic and political ends. Anarcho-syndicalism (articulated by the French thinker Georges Sorel) had a brief passing influence on trade unionism either side of the 1914–18 Great War. Anarcho-syndicalism rejected parliamentarism in favour of such industrial action. Workers should use their power to seize control of industry. In theory this could be non-violent. Disciplined strikes would immobilise the country and lead to a peaceful revolution. In practice, such industrial action was often associated with violence. Syndicalism involved a clear class-conflict view of politics, and thus belongs more properly in the revolutionary rather than the evolutionary strand of socialism.

Socialism: key concepts and values

Despite the considerable differences within socialism, similar values have been proclaimed (if not always practised) by virtually all those who called themselves socialist. It is these values that still mark off the socialist tradition from the other mainstream ideologies, liberalism and conservatism. Thus, against conservatives, socialists generally advocate radical change. They continue to uphold the French Revolutionary principles, 'liberty, equality, fraternity', although in contrast with liberals many socialists emphasise equality and fraternity over liberty. In keeping with these values they attach importance to the notion of social justice, which implies in practice some redistribution of income and wealth incompatible with conservative assumptions of the inviolability of property rights. Socialists also have a more optimistic view of human nature than either liberals or conservatives, and assume that human beings can work together for the common good. Thus they stress the values of co-operation, planning and collectivism, rather than the competition, free markets and individualism assumed by liberals.

Equality

Equality is the defining socialist value, contrasting with the conservative emphasis on hierarchy, leadership and natural inequality, and the more limited liberal commitment to formal legal and political equality rather than economic and social equality. Socialism involved from the beginning a critique of existing inequality under capitalism and a programme for redistribution of income, wealth and power. Yet socialists have not always agreed over the meaning of equality. For a few it means the total abolition of personal private property: for others it is only the private ownership of the means of production that needs to be replaced by common or public ownership. Revisionist socialists, often described as social democrats (see Box 4.1), claim the promotion of greater equality no longer requires wholesale public ownership; they argue that progressive taxation coupled with state welfare benefits will lead to a more egalitarian society.

Liberty

While both advocates and critics acknowledge that socialism is about equality, the importance attached to liberty is rather more contestable (Freeden, 1996, ch. 12). Conservatives and liberals have often accused socialists of sacrificing liberty to equality. Socialists have generally maintained that equality is a condition of liberty. Equality does not mean uniformity, but rather frees individuals to develop their full and different potentials. Socialists, like some New Liberals, tend to see freedom in a positive rather than a negative sense – freedom *to* enjoy something that is valued, rather than freedom *from* restraint and coercion. 'Liberty implies the ability to act, not merely to resist' (Tawney, 1964, p. 165). The socialist commitment to liberty has also been strongly re-emphasised by recent British Labour Party politicians (Hattersley, 1987). Critics argue that socialism inevitably involves loss of liberty. Neo-liberals like Hayek identify freedom with the market order. Any state intervention or planning, even of the milder kind associated with moderate parliamentary socialism, restricts freedom. By contrast, socialists have generally argued that the freedom celebrated by classical liberals and neo-liberals is fairly meaningless in the context of severe economic and social deprivation. Thus, freedom in a capitalist society is largely illusory for the majority.

Fraternity

Behind the notion of fraternity or the 'brotherhood of man' lies an affirmation of the inherent worth of all humanity, regardless of class, nation, colour, creed or gender (despite the sexist terminology which leads some socialists to prefer allied concepts such as 'solidarity', 'community' or 'fellowship'). All these values focus on the interrelations between human beings and on the value and importance of social interaction. There is an implicit assumption that human beings have the capacity to live peacefully and co-operatively with each other. This conception of humans as essentially social and potentially selfless contrasts markedly with both conservative notions of a fatal flaw or evil streak in human nature and the competitive, self-seeking individualism which underpins liberalism. It is upon these optimistic assumptions that the feasibility of socialism essentially depends. Many conservatives regard the socialist view of human nature as naive and unrealistic, invalidated by the abundant evidence of 'man's inhumanity to man'. Liberals assume a need for individual rewards and incentives. Socialists argue that violent, competitive and acquisitive behaviour is socially determined – it is learned rather than natural. A socialist society would foster different values and behaviour.

Social justice

Social justice is sometimes called 'distributional justice' to distinguish it from the retributive justice administered in civil and criminal courts of law. Social justice implies that income and wealth should be more fairly (in practice more equally) distributed. Yet there is inevitably considerable debate over the extent of redistribution that social justice should entail. While modern socialists favour greater equality rather than absolute equality, this provides no clear measure for socialist policy-makers in pursuit of social justice, as well as inevitably involving interference with individual liberty, as hostile critics such as Hayek (1944, pp. 80–84) have pointed out. The American liberal political philosopher, John Rawls' *A Theory of Justice* (1971), has provided one approach that has appealed to some modern social democrats as well as progressive liberals.

Co-operation

While liberals have emphasised competitive individualism, socialists have stressed the importance of human co-operation as the means of improving the well-being of individuals, communities and society as a whole. Early socialists, like Robert Owen, supported voluntary organisations founded on the co-operative principle, such as consumer and producer co-operatives, jointly operated and owned by their members, who shared the proceeds of the enterprise. In some countries this led to the establishment of flourishing producer co-operatives, in agriculture (particularly among wine growers), industry and services. In Britain, the most enduring has been the Co-operative Society, which continues to run retail outlets, banking, insurance and burial services, although attempts to establish worker co-operatives in manufacturing industries in the 1970s were less successful. A Co-operative political party was established in 1917, although this soon affiliated with the Labour party. Today, a number of British MPs are still elected under the label, 'Labour and Co-operative Party'.

Planning

While classical liberals and modern neo-liberals value the free market as the most efficient means of determining the production and distribution of goods and services, socialists have generally criticised unregulated markets as both inefficient (leading to periodic booms and slumps) and unfair (producing massive inequalities). Instead, they have advocated economic and land-use planning. However, socialists have disagreed over the form of economic planning. While Soviet communism involved detailed planning of output, involving state ownership and control of economic activities, western socialists have relied more on indicative planning and Keynesian macro-economic planning. Critics, such as Hayek, have argued that such state planning is more inefficient than market outcomes, and leads to massive interference with the freedom of the individual. Such critics argue that socialist planning involves a 'nanny state' and a massive state bureaucracy telling people what is good for them.

Collectivism

Collectivism at one level simply emphasises the importance of collective rather than individual interests. At another it implies the need for state intervention in the interests of society as a whole, including the state provision of services and state regulation of economic activity. Thus, conservatives have sometimes been associated with policies that might be described as collectivist in this sense, such as protectionist trade policies, the subsidisation of agriculture and industry and, later, state welfare services. However, collectivism is sometimes more narrowly and specifically identified with the collectivisation of agriculture and the public ownership or nationalisation of industry. While the latter involved the state ownership of virtually all industrial activity in the Soviet Union, western social democrats took industries into public ownership more selectively (and have since largely abandoned nationalisation, at least until the banking crisis of 2007–8).

Internationalism

Socialism has long been international in theory (although not always in practice) favouring co-operation between peoples and states across national borders. Marx argued that the working man had no country; nationalism was just another way in which the ruling classes tried concealed from the workers their common class interest transcending national boundaries. Marx and Engels were instrumental in the establishment of the International Working Men's Association (the First International) in 1864 (dissolved in 1876). The Second International was founded in 1889, as a loose federation of socialist and social democratic parties, and trade unions. Although it had strongly opposed war, in 1914 socialists mostly supported their own national governments in backing war. After the war the Second International was re-established, to become the organisation of western socialism, while a rival Third International was set up by Lenin in Moscow as the organisation of international communism (the Comintern) in 1919. The British Labour party is still affiliated to the Socialist International and is also affiliated to the socialist group in the European Union. It supports international institutions, such as the United Nations. Such international concerns have sometimes influenced Labour foreign and defence polices. However, as with socialist and social democratic parties in other countries, Labour has often pursued narrower national interests.

Socialism in nineteenth-century Britain

If socialism reflects the interests of the industrial working class, Britain should have afforded a suitable environment for its rapid development. As the first major industrialising nation, Britain was the first country in which something like a modern industrial working class emerged. Industrialisation involved a new concentration of workers, both in workplaces and in fast-growing urban settlements. This facilitated organisation and the communication of ideas, and made the working class a factor in politics that could no longer be ignored.

There was certainly plenty of evidence of discontent among the labouring classes in Britain in the early nineteenth century, as shown by riots, demonstrations and revolutionary plots (Thompson, 1980). Subsequently, Chartism emerged in the 1830s as a broad-based working-class movement with radical political objectives, including the vote for all adult males, but involving a variety of ideas and strategies. Whether any of this working-class political activity posed a real danger to the existing social order is debatable, although the political establishment feared intensifying class conflict and revolution.

Increased political activism by British workers did not necessarily involve socialism, but socialist ideas were advanced in Britain in the first half of the nineteenth century. Thus, William Thompson (1775–1833) and Thomas Hodgskin (1783–1869) derived socialist conclusions from Ricardo's labour theory of value. The most influential early British socialist was, however, Robert Owen (1771–1858). Owen had demonstrated at his model factory and worker's houses at New Lanark, Scotland, that it was possible to make money by enlightened capitalism, and at his more ambitious American model community, New Harmony, that it was equally possible to lose a fortune. But even in his early years he was more than just an enlightened philanthropist. His work at New Lanark reflected a conviction (characteristic of socialism) that people are moulded, for good or ill, by their environment. Such a view contradicted the conventional religious notion of personal moral responsibility, and indeed Owen's irreligion soon lost him the respectful attention he had briefly enjoyed in parliamentary circles. But as his influence with the political establishment declined, his reputation among the radical working class grew, and Owen was strongly associated with an ambitious spread of trade unions in the 1830s and the establishment of the co-operative movement in the 1840s (Owen, ed. Claeys, 1991).

Owen's legacy was considerable and controversial. Marx and Engels attacked him in the *Communist Manifesto* as a utopian socialist, along with the French theorists, Saint-Simon (1760–1825) and Fourier (1772–1837). The charge reflects Owens' involvement in model socialist utopias and his failure to develop a plausible strategy to achieve socialism. Owen eschewed revolution, while his support for trade unionism and the co-operative movement could be comfortably accommodated within Victorian working-class self-help. Yet Owen thoroughly immersed himself in working-class politics and causes, and Engels later delivered another more generous verdict: 'Every social movement, every real advance in England on behalf of the workers links itself to the name of Robert Owen' (Marx and Engels, 1962, vol. 2, p. 127).

From the 1850s socialism made little headway. British working-class leaders were largely prepared to work within the existing political system. Political and social reforms seemingly confirmed the existing system's capacity for change. Religious and other divisions that cut across class divisions helped blunt social conflict. The benefits of early industrialisation and imperialism improved living standards among elements of the working class, particularly from the mid-nineteenth century onwards, when skilled craftsmen organised themselves into effective unions, creating an 'aristocracy of labour' (Gray, 1981). Many leaders of organised labour saw no reason to go beyond radical liberalism in their political demands (Pelling, 1965, p. 6).

Thus there was virtually no organised socialist activity before the 1880s (Pelling, 1965, pp. 13–15). By this time socialist parties with a mass following were already established in several other European countries. Yet even after distinct socialist organisations emerged in Britain from the 1880s onwards, radical liberal thinkers such as Bentham, Mill, Hobhouse, Hobson, and later Keynes and Beveridge, strongly influenced the character and development of British socialism.

Marxism and the British labour movement

The failure of British workers to develop a revolutionary socialist programme was sadly noted by two celebrated foreign observers of British politics. Marx and Engels spent the bulk of their working lives in England, studied conditions in England extensively and involved themselves in British working-class politics. Moreover, Britain, as the most advanced capitalist country in their day, might appear the prime candidate for a Marxist-style socialist revolution. Despite all this, Marxist ideas have had less influence in Britain than in Germany, France, Italy, Russia, China and many other countries where the ground for their reception might seem less fertile.

Indeed, although the British authorities kept a watchful eye on the socialist agitator in their midst, they concluded he was not particularly dangerous. Grant Duff, a Liberal MP who arranged a meeting with Marx at the suggestion of Queen Victoria's eldest daughter, enjoyed three hours civilised conversation with him and concluded, 'It will not be Marx who, whether he wishes it or not, will turn the world upside down' (McLellan, 1976, p. 445). Yet this erroneous prediction might have proved more accurate had the world followed Britain. The relatively weak influence of Marxist ideas in Britain can be largely attributed to factors already explored above. These include political stability and a tradition of gradualism, a blurred and fluid class system, the existence in Owenism of a distinct native strand of socialism, the relative prosperity of sections of the working class, the extension of the franchise and the reforms apparently secured through parliament. It was further aided by the growing acceptance of trade unionism by the political establishment. Marx's theories were familiar in British socialist circles, although not always fully understood or appreciated. In general, early British socialism was eclectic, and Marx was only one influence among many.

Hyndman's Social Democratic Federation (SDF) was the leading British Marxist organisation in the late nineteenth and early twentieth centuries. Hyndman (1842–1921) was particularly scathing about the theory and practice of trade unionism. While the SDF helped form the Labour Representation Committee (LRC) in 1900, it left within a year. It was subsequently transformed into the British Socialist Party, which in turn combined with others to form the Communist Party of Great Britain in 1920 following the Bolshevik revolution of 1917 which renewed interest in Marxist ideas both inside and outside the Labour Party (Callaghan, 1990, ch. 7).

The subsequent refusal of the Labour Party to allow Communist Party affiliation emphasised the split between revolutionary and evolutionary socialism, in Britain as elsewhere. The hardening division between western parliamentary socialism (represented by the Second International) and Soviet-style communism (represented by the Third International) rendered Marxism suspect in Labour circles. Meanwhile, the electoral progress of the Labour Party in the 1920s apparently confirmed the faith of the leadership in parliamentarism and constitutionalism.

Later, the economic crisis and collapse of the Labour government in 1931 rendered the alternative Soviet model of socialism more attractive (ironically at the height of the Stalinist terror), even to the arch gradualists, Sidney and Beatrice Webb (see below). Marxism and Russian-style communism remained intellectually fashionable throughout the 1930s, but its influence on the leadership of the Labour Party and the bulk of the working class remained marginal (Pimlott, 1977). After 1945, the Cold War and growing economic prosperity in the west again rendered Marxist analysis suspect or seemingly irrelevant, although it remained fashionable in left-wing academic circles. In the 1980s, sophisticated Marxist analysis had some impact on thinking within the Labour Party (especially through the journal *Marxism Today*), and at another level there were some highly publicised attempts at infiltration of constituency parties and trade unions by the Militant Tendency, and its more fundamentalist Marxism. Even so, the real influence of Marxist ideas on the Labour Party remained relatively weak (Coates 1980, p. 163).

Trade unionism and labourism

The failure of revolutionary socialism to have much impact in Britain might be ascribed in part to the strength and character of British trade unionism. Trade unionism and socialism share a concern to advance the interests of the working class; they place a similar emphasis on collective values, but otherwise do not necessarily coincide on ultimate objectives or strategy. Trade unions exist to promote the interests of their members, largely in terms of pay and conditions, through collective bargaining, backed by sanctions, including ultimately the withdrawal of labour. They do not necessarily seek, as socialists do, a fundamental transformation of the economic and social system. Indeed, free collective bargaining implies some accommodation within a capitalist system. Moreover, immediate interests in the workplace are not identical with the collective interests of the working class as a whole, including those outside the paid labour force – children, the old, the sick, disabled, unemployed, and unwaged women. Most British trade unions were moderate in their methods and objectives, and many were initially indifferent or hostile to socialism; indeed many retained strong links with radical liberalism. Until the late nineteenth and early twentieth centuries many trade unionists preferred to concentrate on the immediate issues of wages and conditions, avoiding wider political activity.

Yet, ultimately, the British Labour Party 'emerged from the bowels of the trade union movement' (Ernest Bevin). Several factors caused a change in outlook, including the reluctance of the established parties to endorse working-class candidates, some bitter industrial disputes in the early 1890s and, most significantly, growing anxieties about the legal position of trade unions. The latter followed a series of disquieting court cases culminating in a judgement in 1901 that trade unions were liable for damages caused by industrial action (Pelling, 1965, 200–13). Thus some unions joined with three socialist societies to establish the Labour Representation Committee in 1900, and affiliations tripled following the 1901 'Taff Vale' judgement. Subsequently, the commitment of the trade union movement to what was soon renamed the Labour Party was never in serious doubt.

However that commitment remained initially (and arguably always essentially) to labour representation rather than socialism, although there were already some reciprocal ties between trade unionism and socialism. Socialists had given encouragement and support to the New Unionism from the 1880s, while some trade union activists were themselves socialists. Moreover, those unions who joined the Labour Representation Committee were plainly prepared to enter an alliance with established socialist organisations. But there were considerable mutual suspicions. Hyndman's general hostility to the limitations of trade unions soon led to the SDF's withdrawal from the LRC (see above), while the Fabian socialists were patronising and disparaging about both the unions and the working classes (Adelman, 1986, p. 10). It is scarcely surprising that some trade unionists were in turn critical of middle-class intellectual socialists whose commitment to trade unionism and the labour movement seemed at best doubtful. Yet the 'contentious alliance' (Minkin, 1992) between the trade unions and the Labour Party survived and thrived. While there was always potential for ideological conflict between the two wings of the labour movement, this was minimised by the general compatibility between British trade unionism and the mainstream British interpretation of socialism. Both were essentially moderate, reformist and gradualist. Both were content to work legally within the existing state apparatus.

Indeed, one perhaps surprising consequence of the major role of trade unions in the British Labour Party was to establish the primacy of parliamentary rather than industrial action as the strategy for the achievement of socialism. Once the Trades Union Congress (TUC) decided to back parliamentary representation, it committed the trade union movement wholeheartedly to parliamentarism. While some trade unionists were briefly attracted to anarcho-syndicalist ideas and industrial action to achieve political objectives, these were a minority within the trade union and labour movement. The General Strike of 1926 illustrated the moderate, non-revolutionary character of both wings of the labour movement. The unions showed an impressive collective solidarity in obedience to the strike call, but neither the TUC General Council nor the Labour parliamentary leadership was remotely interested in the strike as a political weapon. Indeed, the outcome confirmed to both the Labour parliamentary and trade unionist leadership the futility of industrial action for political purposes, and reinforced parliamentarism (Miliband, 1972, p. 151). Trade unions long continued to supply the bulk of the party's money, and control the majority of places on its National Executive Committee and the overwhelming majority of votes at the annual conference. Yet this power was seldom used to embarrass the parliamentary leadership, despite Conservative claims that the party was effectively controlled by the unions (McKenzie, 1963).

However, trade union attitudes and values strongly coloured the Labour Party's ideology, which arguably remained essentially 'labourist' rather than socialist (Miliband, 1972, 61; Saville, 1988). The term 'labourism' implies an ideology that articulates the felt interests of labour, or the (then largely male) paid work force. These interests included the protection of free collective bargaining, improvements in living standards and welfare benefits, such as cheap public housing and free health care, but accommodation with, rather than a fundamental challenge to, the dominant economic, social and political order.

Ethical socialism

If Labour began essentially as a trade union party, it always contained socialists, and from 1918 at least was apparently committed to socialist objectives. Yet the extent and nature of the Labour Party's socialism has been contentious since its origins. In marked contrast with some continental socialist parties that began as revolutionary and became reformist over time, Labour began as a trade unionist reformist party that moved tentatively towards socialism. However, it was not a form of socialism that owed much to Marx; instead it involved a blend of the ethical socialism particularly associated with the Independent Labour Party (ILP) and the gradualist and social scientific outlook of the Fabians.

Ethical socialism was sometimes inspired by religion (in marked contrast to many socialist movements abroad that were indifferent or hostile to established religion). There has been a significant strand of Christian socialism within Britain, from Kingsley (1819–75) and Maurice (1805–72) in the nineteenth century, through Tawney (1880–1962) and Cripps (1889–1952) in the early and mid-twentieth century, to John Smith and Tony Blair. Some of these Christian socialists were Anglicans and others Roman Catholics, but there were particularly strong links between nonconformist Christian groups, especially Methodism, and the British labour movement.

For others, socialism was almost a religion itself. Religious language and imagery pervaded much turn-of-the-century socialist propaganda, particularly the Independent Labour Party founded by Keir Hardie in 1893, and one of the three socialist organisations which in 1900 joined with the trade unions to form the Labour Representation

Committee. Hardie (1856–1915), Labour's first leader, contrasted the 'glorious Gospel of Socialism' with 'the gospel of selfishness'. John Glasier referred to the 'Religion of Socialism' and the 'sacrament of socialism' (Foote, 1985, p. 34). Such language came easily to working people brought up in an atmosphere of Christian evangelism in non-conformist chapels, and served the same function of conversion to the faith, whether Christian or socialist (Greenleaf, 1983, Vol. II, p. 414; Callaghan, 1990, p. 67).

A strong moral element has been evident in the ideology of the Labour party down to the present day (notably including party leaders Smith, Blair and Brown). Socialists were consciously articulating a new morality involving unselfish, cooperative behaviour, which challenged the self-interested individualist assumptions behind classical economics and *laissez-faire* liberalism. This ethical approach emphasised the 'brotherhood of man'. Hardie, and after him most British socialists, explicitly rejected the Marxist doctrine of the class war. The influential Christian socialist, R. H. Tawney, pinned his hopes on education and the development of a new social consciousness.

Yet there was an intellectual fuzziness at the core of this ethical socialism. A thorough-going Marxist analysis was implicitly rejected, but there was little in the way of a convincing alternative theoretical foundation for socialism. Ethical socialism was long on commitment and evangelical fervour, but short on economic and social analysis. Foote's verdict (1985, p. 37) is brutal: 'It was basically a withdrawal from the world, and as such, it was impossible to translate into the practical politics of government.' While the ethical socialist vision could win converts, and thus help win power, it offered little guidance in using power. Visions of the socialist millennium were little help in coping with the pressing problems of the present.

Fabian socialism

The Fabians were in many respects the antithesis of the ILP. If the imagery and rhetoric of the ILP was moralistic and quasi-religious, the Fabians prided themselves on their rational and scientific approach to economic and social issues (Greenleaf, 1983, Vol. II, p. 392). While the ILP recruited working-class activists and aspired to become a mass party, the Fabians began as a small group of middle-class intellectuals, with ambivalent attitudes towards working-class politics. The Fabian Society, founded in 1884, was named after a Roman General who defeated Hannibal by patient delaying tactics (effectively refusing to fight him), and it adopted the emblem of the tortoise on its early publications. Both name and emblem were symbolic of a commitment to gradualist, non-revolutionary socialism. Beyond that, there was no party line. The early Fabians contained a diversity of ideas and a rare array of intellectual talent, including two world famous authors, George Bernard Shaw and H. G. Wells, a celebrated children's writer, Edith Nesbit, an important if neglected social scientist, Graham Wallas, the neo-Malthusian, Annie Besant and the psychologist, Havelock Ellis. It was, however, Beatrice and Sidney Webb who were to become most closely identified with Fabian socialism (Greenleaf, 1983, Vol. II, p. 381).

Some would deny that the Fabians were socialist, although Sidney Webb (1859–1947) helped draft Clause IV of the Labour Party's constitution in 1918, with its commitment to the common ownership of the means of production, distribution and exchange. Critics of the Fabians have focused on their gradualist parliamentarian strategy for achieving socialism rather than their objectives. The Webbs believed, like Marx, in the inevitable triumph of socialism, but whereas Marx saw this as the result of class conflict and revolution, the Webbs viewed it as the irresistible endproduct of the steady growth of state intervention in society, the 'inevitability of gradualness'. Lovingly, Sidney Webb chronicled all the activities once 'abandoned to private enterprise', now controlled or regulated by the state. While some socialists saw the existing state apparatus as the enemy, Webb assumed the advance of the state was synonymous with the advance of socialism.

The Webbs believed the trend towards collectivism was irreversible, because state provision was manifestly more efficient than private provision. Good government was essentially a matter of applying the appropriate expertise, based on scientific research and professional training (Greenleaf, 1983, Vol. II, p. 397 ff.). The Webbs themselves were indefatigable researchers; they saw their socialism as essentially dispassionate, rational and scientific. It was also paternalist and elitist. The Fabians were imbued with middle-class attitudes, and despite their early involvement in the Labour Party, initially had little faith in trade unions or the working class. Socialism was to be applied from the top down for the benefit of the working class, rather than won by pressure from below. The Fabian vision of socialism involved scientific administration by disinterested, properly qualified civil servants, and owed more to the British utilitarian tradition than to continental socialism. It was to be achieved by rational persuasion – the Webbs hoped their ideas would permeate society, including the current political establishment, and before the First World War they pressed their recommendations on leading Liberal and Conservative politicians.

Fabian rational, scientific and paternalist socialism was very different from the evangelical and populist socialism of the ILP. Yet their ideas were not wholly incompatible. Both had their roots in strands of liberalism – the Fabians in utilitarianism, the ILP in nonconformist radicalism. Both wished to transcend the radical liberal tradition and the labourism associated with trade unionism. Yet both rejected Marxism. Both were parliamentarist, and, despite the millennial rhetoric employed by the ethical socialists, essentially gradualist. Their role within the Labour Party was, until 1918 at least, complementary rather than competitive. The ILP was the recruiting agent, winning the working-class for socialism, the Fabians were more an intellectual think-tank, carrying out policy-oriented research.

After 1918, and the establishment of a national organization for the Labour Party, with individual membership, the ILP lost its distinctive role in recruitment and effectively became a party within a party. With the influx of the 'Red Clydesiders' in the 1920s they also became more revolutionary, at least in terms of rhetoric. The resulting tension between a reformist parliamentary leadership and an increasingly critical and radical left ILP ultimately led to disaffiliation from the Labour Party in 1932. Its influence was subsequently marginal. By contrast, the Fabian Society, eclectic and undoctrinaire, has continued to provide a forum for ideas and a research capacity for the Labour Party until the present day.

State socialism and alternatives to state socialism

The ideology of the Labour Party was the product then of four main influences – radical liberalism, trade unionism, Fabianism and ethical socialism. In terms of sheer numbers, organisational strength and financial support, trade unionism was by far the most significant of these contributory elements. Yet, on wider political issues the trade union wing of the labour movement was generally content to defer to the leadership of the parliamentary party, and at this level other influences predominated. Thus the dominant figures in Labour's early history, Keir Hardie its first leader, Ramsay MacDonald its first Prime Minister, and Philip Snowden its first Chancellor of the Exchequer, all came up via the ILP. However, both Hardie and MacDonald had also been members of the Fabians. Nor should the influence of radical liberalism be underestimated.

MacDonald's early links with Liberals through the 'Rainbow Circle' were reinforced by his association, after 1914, with anti-war Liberals, many of whom subsequently joined Labour. Significantly, ex-Liberals figured prominently in MacDonald's governments (Figure 4.1).

Socialists disagree as much over means as ends, and the British Labour Party has perhaps attracted more criticism over its strategy than its values. The circumstances in which the Labour Party was founded involved a clear commitment to electoralism and parliamentarism. In contrast with Marxism, syndicalism and anarchism, Labour assumed that the state was benign (Barker, 1978, p. 48), and accepted without question most of the apparatus of the British state. Socialism was to be achieved by winning and using power through the ballot box. This implied a centralised state socialism, imposed from the top downwards.

Alternatives to this centralised state socialist model were advanced. The roots of early British socialism lay in grassroots working-class

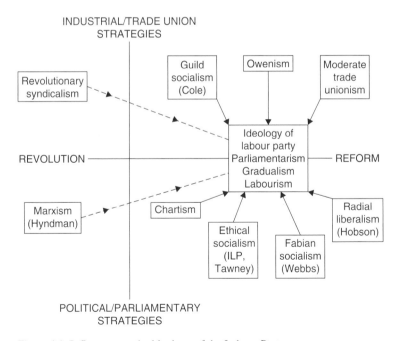

Figure 4.1 Influences on the ideology of the Labour Party

self-help. The socialism of Robert Owen and, later, William Morris, was bound up with the life and work of ordinary people, not with the state. The co-operative movement, in which Owen had played a leading part, was an effective practical demonstration of what could be achieved by mutual action. Socialists were also actively involved in local government from the late nineteenth century onwards, pursuing socialism at the grassroots or municipal level. Subsequently, both the co-operative ideal and municipal (or local) socialism became absorbed within the labour movement and effectively subordinated to the mainstream goal of securing a parliamentary majority and control of central government. When some Labour councils tried to pursue radical socialist municipal policies, notably at Poplar in the 1920s, 'Poplarism' was outlawed by the courts and effectively disowned by the Labour leadership (Branson, 1979).

Labour in power? MacDonaldism

One reason why these rival socialist currents of thought ultimately made little headway was because Labour's rapid advance seemed to confirm the wisdom of the Westminster-centred electoral strategy. Labour overtook the Liberals in 1922 to become the second largest party in Parliament, and the official opposition. Unexpectedly, they soon exchanged opposition for office. In 1924 and again from 1929–31, MacDonald headed minority Labour governments. It was questionable how far office involved real power; Labour was constrained by the lack of a parliamentary majority, and this alone ruled out radical socialist reforms. Yet there were few signs of radical intentions. MacDonald and his colleagues were keen to reassure the political establishment of their moderation. Their socialism remained an article of faith, but it was a distant aspiration. For the present they had to operate within the existing capitalist system.

It was Labour's misfortune to be in office from 1929 when the whole western economic system was in a deepening crisis. From a Labour perspective this was a crisis of capitalism. Theoretically, the remedy was socialism, but there was no electoral mandate and no parliamentary majority for socialism. Distant visions of a socialist millennium appeared irrelevant to the urgency of the immediate situation for which Labour had no remedy. Thus the government was helpless in the face of rising unemployment, and finally broke up in 1931 in disagreement over the spending cuts demanded by business and financial interests (Skidelsky, 1967; Marquand, 1977). MacDonald agreed to stay on as

Prime Minister to head a (largely Conservative) National government, and parted company with his party, which was decimated at the ensuing general election.

For some socialists, 1931 confirmed Communist criticism of Labour and parliamentarism and led to a revival of interest in the Soviet route to socialism, ironically at a time when the Stalinist tyranny was at its worst, culminating in purges and show trials. Others, like the majority of the ILP, rejected both communism and Labour's gradualist parliamentarism, seeking an alternative 'revolutionary' route to socialism which was never too well-defined (Brockway, 1977). Yet such defections ultimately had little impact on the Labour movement, for whom MacDonald and his associates were convenient scapegoats. Thus MacDonald's treachery only demonstrated to his embittered former supporters that he had never really been a socialist. In truth, MacDonald's ideas were only too typical of the socialism of the Labour Party, which combined the cautious rational pragmatism of the Fabians and the ethical socialism of the early ILP. The Labour split in 1931 was not essentially ideological. Purged of MacDonald, the new party leadership remained committed to his version of socialism and his gradualist parliamentary strategy – 'MacDonaldism without MacDonald' as Miliband (1972) described it.

Labour in power – the Attlee government

The Second World War and Labour's role in the coalition government from 1940–45 helped to revive the party's fortunes and interest in socialist ideas. The war involved state planning of output, partly presided over by Labour politicians, while alliance with the Soviet Union also rendered central planning more fashionable. Moreover, war both accustomed people to high levels of state activity and state spending and taught them to look to the state to meet peacetime needs. Thus, hopes for post-war reconstruction and social reform assumed a large measure of state direction and control. All this was highly consistent with the ideas of the Labour Party, which was well-placed to realise public hopes and expectations after 1945, when it won a landslide parliamentary majority.

Both at the time and for a generation afterwards it was the record of the 1945–51 Attlee government that seemed to embody what the Labour Party meant by socialism – both what it was and what it was not. Labour's continuing commitment to a reformist parliamentary strategy rather than the alternative Soviet approach was clear from its foreign policy, in which it showed strong support for NATO and the American alliance in the developing Cold War with the communist world. The Attlee government's domestic policy involved the establishment of a welfare state, nationalisation of key industries to promote a mixed economy, Keynesian economic planning, and the promotion of industrial harmony through partnership with the trade unions. These policies provided the basis of a new political consensus which was to last into the 1970s and essentially involved not the replacement of the capitalist economy by a socialist planned economy, but a modification of capitalism and a qualified acceptance of it.

This was most obviously true of the adoption of Keynesian economic theories, which were thoroughly consistent with Labour's gradualist state socialism. Keynes himself was a committed Liberal, never a socialist. Although critical of many aspects of capitalism, he was in the last resort a defender of the capitalist system. Keynesian macro-economic planning involved governments attempting to influence aggregate demand through fiscal and monetary policy, without involving detailed planning of output. Moreover, for a long time it successfully delivered full employment, a goal that had eluded inter-war governments. Yet Keynesian planning was effectively a substitute for, rather than a step towards, full socialist planning as it had previously been understood.

The establishment of a welfare state providing a system of social security 'from the cradle to the grave' drew on socialist values, although it built on reforms achieved by Liberals and Conservatives and on proposals developed under the wartime coalition government. The new system of national insurance derived from the 1942 report of William Beveridge, a lifelong Liberal whose commitment to individual responsibility was embodied in the insurance principle. However, Aneurin Bevan's National Health Service, funded largely from taxation and initially free to all users, was rather more socialist in inspiration.

Under the Attlee government, trade unions were incorporated into the political establishment. Yet this was a process which had been begun as early as the First World War (Middlemas, 1979), and had been promoted by Churchill's coalition government. Whether the arrival of trade union leaders like Ernie Bevin into the heart of government heralded a socialist revolution is, however, to be doubted. It involved rather the high point of a trade unionist or labourist ideology. The trade union movement acquired power and influence on the tacit understanding that this would be exercised moderately, in the national interest. Thus, trade unions co-operated in wage restraint policies, as they were to do again in the 1960s and 1970s.

The Labour government's nationalisation policies derived more obviously from socialist inspiration, and specifically from Clause IV of the party's constitution. Even so, pragmatic rather than ideological arguments were advanced for the nationalisation of specific industries, while the government made clear that its nationalisation programme was limited to the 'commanding heights' of the economy – mainly fuel and transport. Finally, under the guidance of Herbert Morrison, nationalisation took the form of wholly state-owned public corporations, run by appointed managers rather than the workers. Although a significant section of industry was now publicly owned, implying a 'mixed' rather than a capitalist economy, socialist critics argued it involved 'state capitalism' rather than socialism.

Yet the Attlee government's achievement proved durable, lasting substantially for a generation. Labour's values were effectively incorporated into a cross-party consensus, sometimes described as social democratic. Even so, the Attlee government's very success left an awkward legacy for the Labour Party. From the perspective of the leadership, Labour's programme was essentially completed by the 1945–51 government. It was not the first instalment of a socialist transformation of Britain's economy and society, but the culmination of that mixture of radical liberalism, trade unionism and Fabianism that was the essence of British socialism. Attlee, Bevin and Morrison had fulfilled their strictly limited socialist revolution, leaving their successors with little more to do than defend that achievement. A problem that only became apparent later was the extent to which it depended on its least socialist element, Keynesian economic theory. The apparent breakdown of Keynesian analysis and prescription in the 1970s not only challenged much of Labour's case for government economic intervention and a mixed economy, but also undermined the viability of the welfare state.

Revisionism, fundamentalism and pragmatism

Theoretical justification for Labour's policies lagged somewhat behind practice, although several Labour politicians and thinkers such as Morrison, Dalton and, from a younger generation, Evan Durbin and Douglas Jay contributed to the evolution of Labour ideas in the 1930s and 1940s (Foote, 1986, ch. 9). However, it was only after Labour was once more in opposition from 1951 that a comprehensive attempt was made to update the party's ideology to bring it more in line with what a Labour government had actually tried to do.

The most significant contribution to this reappraisal was Tony Crosland's *The Future of Socialism* (1956), which sharpened, although it did not inaugurate, a developing ideological schism within the Labour Party between social democracy and a more fundamentalist socialism. The schism effectively began with Nye Bevan's resignation from the Attlee government in 1951 over the introduction of health service charges. It developed into a personalised division between the supporters of Bevan and those of his arch-rival on the party right, Hugh Gaitskell. This split survived the deaths of both the leading protagonists to become a long-running and deep-seated struggle between left and right factions for the soul of the party from the 1960s through to the 1980s.

'Revisionism' is a term widely employed, especially by Marxists, to describe efforts to moderate or water down socialism, yet Crosland was 'revising' a party ideology which had never been Marxist, and only moderately socialist. He was dismissive of Marxism. 'In my view Marx has little to offer the contemporary socialist either in respect of practical policy, or of the correct analysis of our society, or even of the right conceptual tools or framework' (Crosland, 1956, p. 2). He argued that capitalism in its old nineteenth century sense no longer existed. It had been transformed out of all recognition by progressive taxation, welfare reforms and state enterprise, but above all by the divorce of ownership from effective control of industry. Ownership of industry was no longer critical. What was required was professional management, coupled with effective influence and control in the public interest. Crosland's redefined socialism was not about nationalisation but the pursuit of equality, through universal social benefits, progressive taxation and the redistribution of the product of economic growth.

Although this revisionist socialism substantially reflected Labour's record in office, it was less compatible with the party's explicit Clause IV commitment to common ownership. Modernisers believed that this commitment to nationalisation alienated voters, so following a third successive election defeat in 1959 the party leader, Hugh Gaitskell, campaigned to drop Clause IV, and even canvassed a change of the party name (Jenkins, 1991). Gaitskell's attempt to change Labour failed, yet his old supporters continued to act as a faction within the party through to the 1980s when some of them broke away to form the Social Democratic Party (SDP). Retrospectively, it could be said that they always stood for social democracy rather than socialism within the Labour Party, although Crosland continued to proclaim his socialism until his death in 1977.

In the 1970s, the Labour left renewed its attempt to commit the party, in line with Clause IV, to an extensive further programme of national-isation including the banking and building industries, and the encour-agement of workers' co-operatives. The most bitter conflicts between the Labour left and right were not, however, ostensibly over rival inter-pretations of socialism, but over party organisation, and over defence and foreign policy issues. Disputes over party organisation reflected dif-ferent interpretations of internal party democracy, but ultimately were about power to control the party agenda and leadership. Bitter divisions over nuclear disarmament in part stemmed from a strong moralistic and quasi-pacifist tradition which Labour inherited from the Liberals, although behind the issue of the bomb were also differences over the western alliance which reflected contrasting assumptions about the objectives of the superpowers, the USA and the USSR. Yet the most bitter issue dividing left and right in the 1970s and early 1980s was the European Community. It was not initially so, when supporters and opponents of EC membership could be found on both wings of the party. Subsequently, Europe became the crucial test of allegiance, with the social democratic right championing membership and the socialist left demanding withdrawal.

Between the left and right were those who sought balance and com-promise in the interests of party unity. As a 'broad church', the Labour movement has always contained a range of interests and tendencies, including social reformers, both moderate and militant trade unionists, and various kinds of socialists. Moreover, Labour could only achieve power in Britain's parliamentary system if it could retain the commit-ment of both its socialist left and reformist right. The preservation of some ambiguity over ultimate values and objectives was necessary to keep different factions happy. Thus Labour leaders Wilson, Callaghan and Foot all tried to preserve a pragmatic balance between left and right.

Critics argued that Harold Wilson, in his 1964–70 and 1974–76 Labour governments, was more concerned with day-to-day party man-agement and presentation than longer-term socialist objectives. Wilson's death in 1995 assisted a more positive reappraisal, already underway, of the achievements of his governments, which secured a significant expansion in educational opportunities and presided over modest pro-gress towards a more equal and tolerant society (Pimlott, 1992). Even so they did little to advance or further define British socialism, but involved an increasingly desperate defence of the 'social democratic consensus' established by the Attlee government which, by the 1970s, was under threat. Keynesian economic management no longer appeared effective. Industrial compromise had broken down and the union alliance had become an electoral liability. The nationalised industries and the whole concept of a mixed economy were under ideological assault. Even the welfare state appeared to be failing in important respects and to be under threat, with taxpayers increasingly unwilling to meet its escalating costs.

Democratic socialism and social democracy

If the political ideas of the old Labour Party are characterised as more labourist than socialist, Callaghan, Wilson's successor, embodied both the strengths and limitations of labourism. He was the last Labour leader who had not attended university; he had emerged from a working-class and trade-union (albeit white-collar), background. As such he belonged neither socially nor intellectually to the old Bevanite left represented by Wilson, Crossman, Castle and Foot, nor to the revisionist Gaitskellite right around Crosland and Jenkins. Instead, Callaghan was, generally, the authentic voice of the old 'contentious alliance' with the trade unions (Minkin, 1991, p. 112). As such he led the opposition to Wilson and Castle's plans to reform industrial relations in 1969 and eagerly pursued incomes policy and the social contract with the unions when he became Prime Minister in 1976. He related to Labour's old male, working-class base. He was less interested in either the progressive liberal reforms over which Roy Jenkins had presided as Labour's Home Secretary, or Barbara Castle's enthusiasm for equal opportunities and child benefit. The collapse of his government in 1979 in the face of 'the winter of discontent' associated with trade union strikes in retrospect marks the death of old labourism. The future appeared to lie either with a more committed left-wing socialism or with a revisionist social democracy.

The old tension between left and right turned into open warfare within the party after the 1979 election defeat. The breach was provoked by a swing to the left within Labour (Seyd, 1987; Shaw, 1994). This was symbolised by the election of the old Bevanite and unilateralist Michael Foot as leader, but also involved changes to the party's constitution and a policy commitment to withdraw Britain from the EEC (Bradley, 1981; Kogan and Kogan, 1982; Stephenson, 1982). Four former Labour Cabinet ministers, Roy Jenkins, Shirley Williams, Bill Rodgers and David Owen then set up a new party, the Social

Democratic Party, soon joined by another two dozen Labour MPs (Jenkins, 1991; Crewe and King, 1995). 'Social democrat' had long been a convenient label for describing reformist or revisionist Labour politicians. Now the social democrats were effectively split between those who joined the new party, and those, like Dennis Healey and Roy Hattersley, who stayed with Labour. Weakened by defections, social democrats within the Labour Party had a difficult time. Healey came close to being defeated in the deputy leadership contest by Tony Benn, heading a broad left alliance. Despite this slight setback the left seemed firmly in control of the party's programme up to the 1983 election.

While Labour was weakened and divided, for a time the SDP thrived, performing well in parliamentary by-elections and opinion polls. The new members they attracted were enthusiastic about a wholly new party with a new style and approach. Yet the SDP was never essentially new, but effectively a 'Mark II Labour Party' (Crewe and King, 1995, pp. 125–8). Indeed, they claimed to be the true heirs of Attlee and Gaitskell. Their leaders alleged that they had not left the Labour party, but that the Labour party had left them, implying a marked ideological shift to the left by Labour. However, most Labour 'moderates' in parliament, and the vast bulk of Labour councillors, active members and trade unionists declined to join the SDP, whose preoccupation with past battles within the Labour party bedevilled any project to establish a broad centre party with a new philosophy and programme. Ultimately, the SDP failed to break the mould of British politics, partly because of the handicap of the British first-past-the-post electoral system. Most SDP MPs lost their seats in the 1983 election. Having failed to win over most Labour moderates, or to forge a distinctively new political ideology, the SDP majority voted to merge with the Liberals (Crewe and King, 1995, pp. 385–410).

The left's apparent dominance within the Labour party, which had provoked the SDP breakaway, proved short-lived (Seyd, 1987), although whether the formation of the SDP assisted or delayed the return of the Labour Party to 'moderate' consensus politics is contentious (Healey, 1989; Jenkins, 1991; Hattersley, 1995). A more potent influence on Labour was Mrs Thatcher's brand of conservatism. Four successive Conservative party election victories from 1979 altered the political landscape and compelled some rethinking of Labour's philosophy and commitments. The party could no longer simply defend the Attlee inheritance. They could seek to restore it, or jettison parts no longer considered relevant, or forge new policy proposals. Preservation of the *status quo* was no longer an option. Realisation of this compelled an extensive policy review (Shaw, 1994, pp. 81–107) and some ideological reassessment, beginning under the leadership of Kinnock, and continued by first Smith and then Blair (Ludlam and Smith, 2001).

Thus Labour subsequently abandoned virtually all the commitments which led to the establishment of the SDP. The 1983 manifesto commitment to withdraw from the European Community was among the first casualties of this new realism, and since then Labour has become positively enthusiastic about Europe. Following the 1987 defeat, the commitment to nuclear disarmament, with which Kinnock had been closely associated, was quietly abandoned as part of the policy review. After the more unexpected 1992 defeat, Labour avoided any commitment to raise spending and taxation.

The international context: the Cold War and collapse of Communism

Although Labour's ideology has long been peculiarly insular, influenced largely by British politicians and thinkers, it has inevitably been significantly affected by developments in the wider world. From 1945 the 'Cold War' between the west and the Soviet Union particularly shaped and constrained Labour's thinking. The Cold War divided socialists. Labour, along with social democracy in Europe, was aligned with the USA, the standard bearer of capitalism, against the alternative 'really existing socialism' of the USSR. Indeed, the Labour leadership remained as committed to Britain's presumed 'special relationship' with the USA as the Conservatives. This periodically caused severe strains within the broad labour movement, parts of which were never keen on NATO and the American alliance. Thus, there was opposition to German rearmament in the 1950s, to the nuclear deterrent in the 1960s and to US policy in Vietnam and elsewhere in the 1960s and 1970s. Such issues split the party and also provoked Conservative accusations that Labour was 'soft on Communism'.

The end of the Cold War removed the presumed Soviet threat and marginalised Labour's previous problems with defence policy. Yet at the same time the collapse of the USSR confirmed the supremacy of the free market and discredited planning. Whatever its deficiencies in the eyes of western socialists, Soviet communism represented an apparently flourishing alternative to western capitalism – living proof that it was possible to organise an economy on different lines (Hobsbawm, 1994). Its collapse removed the alternative, and the constant threat it presented to capitalism. Socialism everywhere suffered a psychological defeat, while a triumphalist capitalism felt less obliged to make concessions to the interests of labour. Dahrendorf (1990) emphatically declared that socialism in all its variants (including social democracy) was dead. Socialists naturally refused to accept this verdict but recognized that they were now purveying their message in a 'sceptical age' (Miliband, 1994).

The longer-term consequences were less clear. The transition to a 'New World Order' of liberal capitalism in the former Communist block has not been smooth. Dahrendorf's announcement of the death of social democracy proved premature. By the year 2000, the largest EU member states, Germany, France and Italy, as well as Britain, all had governments which might be described as social democrat (although the Italian 'Olive Tree' coalition, the French socialists and the German social democrats have since suffered electoral defeats).

Yet social democrats now had to recognise that they operated in a transformed global environment. Socialism in one country was no longer a feasible option (if it ever had been). Even the British Labour party, with its long insular tradition, had to face up to the realities of the diminished power of nation states in the global economy, and rethink its relations with the wider world. Among other developments this assisted a more positive evaluation of the European Union at the very time when Conservatives were becoming increasingly Eurosceptic.

The road to New Labour – the end of labourism?

Fundamental to the changes in the Labour Party after 1992 has been a rethinking of the relationship with the trade unions, begun under the leadership of John Smith (1992–94), and maintained by Blair. This involved the end of the old trade union block vote and the introduction of one member, one vote (OMOV). While the importance of the union link was reaffirmed, in practice the Labour leadership increasingly distanced itself from the unions. It was soon clear that Labour would not reverse the bulk of the Conservative union reforms. Organisational reforms within the Labour party reduced union influence over party policy.

This accentuated a trend away from Labour's past identification with trade unions and the manual working class that has been under way for over half a century. Thus, firstly, most of the parliamentary party and even the bulk of constituency activists have long ceased to be of the working class (Hindess, 1971). Secondly, and partly perhaps reflecting these social changes within the party, the policies pursued by Labour have not always appeared to benefit the old working class. Moreover, in recent years Labour has been represented as more interested in promoting equal opportunities for women, blacks or gays than defending the interests of their traditional (and formerly largely male) working-class clientele. Such perceptions may be exaggerated or misconceived, but help to explain why many white, male, manual workers no longer see Labour as 'their' party.

The manual working class is itself relatively smaller, and more divided – for example between public and private sector employees, between council tenants and owner occupiers, and on gender and ethnic grounds. Some workers have become relatively affluent consumers and property owners, while others have lost jobs and seen their living standards eroded. Such changes have weakened working-class solidarity. As the working class appears less homogeneous, it is not surprising that there is less of a common working-class culture. Labour began as an explicitly class party, with a programme pitched deliberately at the working class, although it always enjoyed some middle-class support and active involvement. The reduction in size and the fragmentation of the old manual working class meant that Labour had to broaden its appeal towards 'middle England'.

This was deemed to require the ditching of Labour's commitment to public ownership, symbolically secured through by the rewriting of Clause IV, pushed through by Tony Blair after he succeeded to the leadership following the unexpected death of John Smith. Blair succeeded where Gaitskell had failed in 1960 partly because circumstances had changed. Most of the former nationalised industries had been privatised, and it was increasingly recognised that wholesale renationalisation was politically and economically unrealistic. Blair argued that Labour's principles and values remained the same, but required updating because the world had changed. 'Let us say what we mean and mean what we say' (Blair Conference speech, 1994). The replacement statement of values, backed by a three to one majority, was broader but less memorable than the old. Labour's proclaimed ideology was adjusted to accord more closely with Labour practice.

While it was Blair who was substantially responsible for rebranding the party as 'New Labour', it was Gordon Brown, whose own leadership ambitions had been frustrated in 1994 who, as shadow Chancellor and then Chancellor from 1997 to 2007, helped shape much of the domestic agenda of the government. Moreover, it was Brown who banished for a decade the old negative perception that Labour could not be trusted with the management of the economy. The much publicised differences between Blair and Brown were always more personal than ideological. While some of Blair's critics inside the party fondly imagined that Brown's sympathies were 'old Labour', when Brown succeeded Blair as Prime Minister there was little discernable difference in policy or underlying political philosophy. Despite all the turmoil inside the party from 2007 onwards, there did not appear to be any real alternative to New Labour on offer.

New Labour has been variously identified as purely cosmetic, as a thinly disguised continuation of Thatcherism, as a 'third way', or as revived social democracy. Each of these verdicts contains at least a grain of truth, but hardly the whole truth. Thus, New Labour certainly involved a strong emphasis on presentation or 'spin' but also significant policy substance. Some of that substance involved an acceptance of aspects of Thatcherism, including privatisation, competition in the provision of public services and trade union reforms. However, it also included major constitutional reforms, a minimum wage and other measures to reduce poverty, and substantial increases in spending on health and education, much of which was the antithesis of Thatcherism. Such a mixture gives credence to the notion of a 'third way', a term used for a time by Blair (1998). It is a term with a long and not entirely reputable history, which can only be given a measure of precision by spelling out exactly what it is a 'third way' between.

Blair himself implied that the third way was a middle way. 'The solutions of neither the old Left nor the new Right will do. We need a radical centre in modern politics' (Blair, 1996, p. 38). This is reminiscent of the appeal of the old SDP, and Blair initially spoke of the need to rebuild the centre–left coalition of Labour and the New Liberalism, citing approvingly Marquand's (1999) 'progressive dilemma'. Anthony Giddens (1998, 2000) fleshed out the concept of the third way in more detail. He has since (in Beech and Lee, 2008, p. xv) redrawn attention to the subtitle of his 1998 book on the third way, 'the renewal of social democracy', claiming 'that for me is what the third way always meant.' Indeed, much of the Blair and Brown programme was consistent with the ideas expressed earlier by British social democrats, both inside the old Labour Party and the former SDP (some of whom had since rejoined Labour).

Was New Labour the end of socialism? The accusations of selling out on socialism have been frequently levelled at past leaders, from MacDonald onwards, yet, as we have seen (above) some would deny that Labour has ever been a socialist party. It all depends, of course, on what

is meant by socialism. In the same speech in which Blair announced proposals for a new Clause IV he also talked of his socialism:

> A belief in society, working together, solidarity, co-operation,
> partnership – these are our words. This is my socialism – and we
> should stop apologizing for using the word. It is not the socialism of
> Marx or state control. It is rooted in a straightforward view of soci-
> ety: in the understanding that the individual does best in a strong and
> decent community of people, with principles and standards and com-
> mon aims and values. It is social-ism. We are the party of the individ-
> ual because we are the party of the community. Our task is to apply
> those values to the modern world. (Blair, Labour Conference speech,
> 1994)

Critics would argue that Blair's rhetoric is short on specifics, and might
further fairly allege that he dropped any reference to socialism in
speeches and writing subsequently. Even so, Blair in this speech clev-
erly re-emphasised key buzz words which had been part of Labour's
vocabulary since the party's establishment: 'society', 'solidarity',
'co-operation', 'partnership', 'community'. He went on to talk about
'opportunity', 'responsibility', 'fairness' and 'trust'. Such words would
not have been out of place in the mouth of any of Labour's previous
leaders, although, as always, there is considerable scope for argument
over interpretation and application. Was there any theoretical substance behind the rhetoric? Three strands of thought associated with
Blair's leadership in opposition and early in his government have been
emphasised – Christian socialism, communitarianism, and stakeholding.
    Tony Blair, like his immediate predecessor as Labour leader John
Smith, was (and remains) a practising Christian who derived his political convictions from his Christianity, reflecting a long tradition of
Christian and ethical socialism within the Labour party. That tradition
has involved strengths and weaknesses (see above). While moral fervour increased the party's appeal, the implications for analysis and policy were less clear. Moreover, there is an additional problem today that
did not exist when Christian socialism was at its most influential, before
the First World War. Then, Britain was still substantially a Christian
country. Today, Christian imagery no longer has the same resonance for
the majority, and may alienate those attached to other faiths, or none.
Aware of the pitfalls, Blair's director of communications, Alastair
Campbell, declared tersely 'We don't do God.' While Blair himself
clearly did 'do God', he later referred more sparingly to his religious

convictions, and discreetly delayed his long-anticipated conversion to Roman Catholicism until after his resignation in 2007. His successor, Gordon Brown, has been more reticent about his religious beliefs, but as a 'son of the manse' (his father was a Scottish minister) the ethical basis of his own political convictions has always been equally manifest.

Both Blair and Brown have also laid considerable emphasis on the concept of community that links closely with the socialist values of fraternity, solidarity and co-operation, and contrasts with the extreme individualism associated with the New Right and neo-liberalism. Communitarianism is a political philosophy that has been intellectually fashionable on both sides of the Atlantic (Mulhall and Swift, 1996), and has been successfully popularised (Etzioni, 1995). Community suggests an inclusive concern for all members of society, rather than the divisive politics of class. It fits comfortably within the mainstream tradition of British socialism and broadens Labour's electoral appeal. It also implies a concern with the small scale and a more decentralised, participative approach to socialism which is useful for a party trying to avoid its past association with bureaucratic centralised state socialism. However, the term remains imprecise, and can be used in connection with almost any kind or size of human organisation or association. Its common use as an all-purpose sanitising term, promiscuously available across the political spectrum, renders 'community' a somewhat insubstantial foundation on which to base a remodelled socialist philosophy.

Another allied concept, 'stakeholding', became fashionable following its advocacy by Will Hutton (1995, 1997), and its endorsement by Blair (speech to Singapore Business Community, 8 January 1996; John Smith Memorial Lecture, 7 February 1996), and by Tony Wright in the pre-election publication *Why Vote Labour* (1997, pp. 53–4). The term 'stakeholding' has been used at the level of business companies to emphasise the 'stake' workers, customers and the local community, as well as shareholders, have in the organisation. At the level of society and the national economy, stakeholding similarly asserts the importance of employees, consumers and the wider public interest under capitalism. Hutton himself defined stakeholding in terms of 'a mutuality of rights and obligations, constructed around the notion of economic, social and political inclusion' that 'places limits on the operation of unfettered markets' (Hutton, in Kelly *et al.*, 1997, p. 3). In practice, however, the language of stakeholding was employed sparsely after 1997. Favoured German and East Asian alternatives to the Anglo-American model of capitalism increasingly seemed less attractive, and the broad inclusive agenda of stakeholding has been displaced in the business world by a renewed emphasis on 'shareholder value'. Thus, according to some observers, the dominance of the City and financial interests has been reasserted and 'Will Hutton's stakeholder economy seems more remote than ever' (Roberts and Kynaston, *New Statesman*, 17 September 2001, pp. 25–7).

New Labour in power

Much of the early analysis of New Labour necessarily depended on ideas and policies propounded in opposition or soon after Labour took office in 1997. It is only after more than a decade of Labour in government that a much fuller analysis can be made of the application of party ideology. Key areas of the performance of New Labour include management of the economy, the alleviation of poverty and redistribution, the delivery of public services, constitutional reform, and last, but by no means least, foreign and defence policy.

Management of the economy

It was Labour's management of the economy, presided over by Chancellor Gordon Brown from 1997 to 2007, that long seemed the most impressive aspect of the government's performance, transforming Labour's previous negative association with economic crisis. The immediate transfer of control of interest rates to the Monetary Policy Committee of the Bank of England, coupled with initially maintaining firm limits on government spending reassured the City and business community. For ten years the British economy showed steady growth, low inflation, and relatively full employment, a record previous Chancellors would have died for. With some credibility, Brown claimed to have ended 'boom and bust' (Smith, in Seldon and Kavanagh, 2005; Lee, in Beech and Lee, 2008).

Social justice and redistribution

From a socialist perspective New Labour's record in tackling poverty and redistributing income and wealth is rather more critical than its competence in overall management of the economy. Here, Brown introduced a raft of measures, including a national minimum wage, a 'new deal' to get the unemployed into training or work, the working families tax credit to improve minimum income, and a national child care strategy. These and other measures have done something to reduce child poverty and pensioner poverty, although not sufficiently to meet ambitious government targets (Toynbee and Walker, 2005, pp. 47–84). Overall, however, there has been no significant redistribution of income and wealth, partly because the government has declined to introduce higher rates of tax for the better-off (Stewart, in Seldon and Kavanagh, 2005). Although Brown brought in a lower ten pence level of income tax to help those on low incomes, he subsequently abolished it, to help pay for a reduction in the standard rate of tax in his last budget, a move that has undermined Labour's claim to look after the poor.

Delivering public services

While spending limits in Labour's first term only permitted modest increases in public services, there was subsequently a substantial increase in public expenditure on health and education, especially in Labour's second term (2001–5). This had some measurable impact on services. New hospitals and more doctors reduced waiting times and improved performance in the health service, while new schools and more teachers led to smaller classes and improved exam performance in education (Toynbee and Walker, 2005, pp. 11–46, 85–123). However, these successes were partially overshadowed by damaging scandals over hospital cleanliness and management of school exams, while critics denied that taxpayers had secured value for the extra money. From a socialist perspective, while the extra money was welcomed, further reforms in the management of health and education, involving more competition and increased private sector involvement, were deplored as creeping privatisation (Driver, in Beech and Lee, 2008, pp. 59–60). Increased reliance on targets and league tables, although arguably important in measuring performance, attracted widespread criticism, providing further evidence of Labour's bureaucratic, centralising tendencies, despite the government's claim to be devolving and decentralising power and decision-making to staff in hospitals and schools. Although some anticipated that Brown might reverse or modify some of the reforms in the management of public services introduced under his predecessor, he has maintained support for the reform agenda.

Constitutional reform

The most radical reforms introduced by the Labour government were not to do with the economy, nor with Labour's traditional interest in social justice and public services, but with the British constitution. Constitutional reforms have included devolution for Scotland, Wales, and Northern Ireland, reform of the Lords and the judiciary, new electoral systems for the European Parliament and devolved assemblies, and the incorporation into UK law of the European Convention on Human Rights. All this amounts to little less than a constitutional revolution, although one that remains incomplete, with the final outcome unclear. It was not, however, central to the New Labour project, and nor has it helped the party. Some constitutional reforms were a legacy of past commitments – of the Wilson and Callaghan governments' commitment to devolution, reaffirmed by John Smith. Some were partly a by-product of Blair's passing interest in rebuilding the progressive alliance with the liberals (for constitutional reform in the past has always been more a Liberal, and Liberal Democrat, cause than a Labour cause). Critics suggest that the constitutional reforms have been introduced piece-meal with no coherent overall vision. Moreover, it was soon clear that the government had lost control of some of the reform process (notably Lords reform), faced rebuffs on others (elected assemblies for English regions) and suffered significant party losses in its old strongholds in Scotland and Wales. Only the settlement in Northern Ireland currently seems a clear success, but one that hardly helps Labour's own ideological and electoral problems. One commentator (Evans, in Beech and Lee, 2008, p. 87) has compared Blair to the sorcerer's apprentice 'desperately trying to stem the unintended consequences that flow from constitutional reform'. Whether these unintended consequences will include ultimately the break-up of Britain that devolution was meant to avoid remains to be seen. Although Brown committed himself to a new constitutional settlement and the maintenance of the Union, in his first speech as Labour leader, prospects remain uncertain, particularly following the establishment of a nationalist government in Scotland.

International record

While the British Labour Party had long been affiliated to the Socialist International, and ostensibly had broader global concerns than their Conservative rivals, in practice Labour's ideology was often insular in its influences and concerns. The Labour government that took office in 1997 promised a more internationalist outlook. A new Department of International Development headed by a Cabinet minister was set up, symbolising New Labour's commitment to tackle global poverty and reduce the gap between rich and poor. The government also signed up to the Kyoto agreement, and a range of targets to tackle climate change.

It implemented a pledge to incorporate the European Convention on Human Rights into British law. New Labour also seemed far more committed to the European Union than the party had been in the past, signing up to the Social Chapter from which Major had negotiated British exemption at the Maastricht Treaty. Blair also indicated that British entry to single European currency (the Euro) would follow when the time was ripe. Beyond all this, Robin Cook, Labour's new Foreign Secretary in 1997 proclaimed an ethical foreign policy.

Some of this more internationalist perspective persists. Thus, while ambitious targets on world trade, aid and the environment may not be met, Britain's record is better than many other leading western powers. Gordon Brown as Prime Minister has strongly reaffirmed the commitment to tackle global poverty. The Human Rights Act remains in force, sometimes to the embarrassment of ministers found to be in breach of it. However, Brown as Chancellor effectively frustrated Blair's apparent support for British membership of the Euro, and the issue seems effectively dead. This has not by itself prevented Labour from taking a positive role in Europe, although Labour's foreign policy has since contributed to divisions within Europe. Robin Cook's ethical foreign policy met with difficulties over, particularly, the sale of arms and the interests of Britain's own arms industry. When, no longer Foreign Secretary, he resigned from the Labour government over the Iraq War in 2003, this perhaps reflected more effectively his own ethical convictions.

Ironically, Blair, whose determination to invade Iraq had provoked Cook's resignation, was also pursuing what he regarded as an ethical foreign policy, one that he had earlier pursued in Sierra Leone and Kosovo and later defended (speech in Chicago, 2004) on the grounds of 'humanitarian' or 'liberal' interventionism. Blair's liberal interventionism has been compared with that of Gladstone, another leader who espoused intervention on ethical grounds. In practice, the motives for intervention appeared mixed (particularly over Iraq), and liberal intervention was not universally pursued, because of the risks of attacking nuclear-armed states (Plant, in Beech and Lee, 2008). Whatever the arguments, 'Blair's wars' (Kampfner, 2004) have done more than anything else to cause disillusion with New Labour among many erstwhile Labour supporters and Liberal Democrat sympathisers.

Labour under Brown

Gordon Brown succeeded Blair as Prime Minister in 2007 with neither a contest for the Labour leadership, nor a General Election. Thus he lacked a party mandate as well as a national mandate, which some perceived as a problem. He clearly contemplated going to the country in the autumn of 2007, but his indecision damaged an otherwise promising start to his premiership. Instead, the 'election that never was' effectively finished his friend Menzies' Campbell's brief leadership of the Liberal Democrats (who would not have risked a leadership contest with an election imminent). More seriously from a Labour perspective, it boosted the standing of David Cameron, whose leadership of the Conservatives had been criticised, but who performed strongly in what was widely perceived as a pre-election party conference in 2007, in contrast with Brown's own rather lacklustre speech at the Labour conference. The initiative swiftly switched to the Conservatives, whose opinion poll ratings rose steadily as Labour's declined, while Brown's government grappled with a series of problems and, to critics, appeared indecisive and lacking in coherent purpose.

Brown faced increasing opposition within his own party, from 'Blairites', the left and those concerned about their own electoral prospects. The damaging long-running feud between Blair and Brown still had echoes among their respective followers. Some of the leading Blairites, particular those now out of office, became outspoken critics of the performance of the new Prime Minister. Yet, paradoxically, those on the Labour left who had hoped that Brown's premiership would herald a return to Old Labour values and policies, and a repudiation of Blair's New Labour, were disappointed with the continuity between the Blair and Brown governments in both domestic and foreign policy. Thus, although Brown's friends claimed 'Gordon does not do wars', there was little discernible difference in British foreign policy after the change of premiers. Regardless of their views on policy, all those Labour MPs whose parliamentary majorities were less than substantial feared for their seats following opinion polls pointing to a Conservative landslide perhaps larger than that which had brought Labour to office in 1997.

Thus by the spring and summer of 2008, 'New Labour' appeared tired and old, in the face of a reviving Conservative challenge under David Cameron, Alex Salmond's popular Scottish Nationalist government in Brown's own backyard, and Liberal Democrats alienated by Iraq and no longer potential partners in a 'progressive alliance'. In these circumstances, there was increasing talk in the spring and early summer of 2008 of a formal challenge to, or a Cabinet putsch against, Brown. Several backbench Labour critics went public, while there were numerous 'off the record' hostile briefings attributed to members of the government. Various plotters and potential political assassins were cited in the media. David Miliband, Labour's young Foreign Secretary (and the son of the late Ralph Miliband, a leading academic Marxist critic of 'labourism') was widely considered to be on the point of a leadership challenge. Other potential alternatives to Brown were discussed. Yet it is perhaps true to say that issues of personality, presentation and government management loomed larger than issues of policy and ideology. There was no credible alternative leader in sight on Labour's left.

Ironically, what seems to have saved the Brown premiership (in the short term at least) was a financial and economic crisis that might have been expected to destroy it. Labour's unprecedented run of election victories had depended substantially on Brown's successful management of the economy as Chancellor of the Exchequer. Brown had presided over ten years of steady economic growth with relatively high employment and low inflation. Plausibly he had claimed to have ended the former cycle of 'boom and bust'. The collapse of Northern Rock in 2007, the wider banking crisis of 2008 and the ensuing economic recession appeared to have damaged irretrievably Brown's (and Labour's) new hard-won reputation of economic competence. Indeed, old speeches by Labour's former Chancellor provided plenty of damaging quotations for his political enemies. Yet in spite of all this, Brown himself seemed reinvigorated by the crisis, and his party substantially united behind him. The Conservative poll lead dropped sharply in the second half of 2008, until it was at least possible to conceive of a fourth Labour election victory, or (more likely perhaps) a hung parliament or relatively narrow defeat.

Partly it could be argued that the crisis played to Brown's strengths. Whatever criticisms had been levelled at Brown's past management of the economy (such as inadequate regulation of the financial sector and complacency over the expansion of credit), his unrivalled experience in managing the domestic economy and his extensive contacts with world finance gave him renewed authority. As Brown and his Chancellor, Alastair Darling, repeatedly emphasised, this was a global economic crisis, not a purely domestic one, with the implication that a global crisis required the attention of an experienced global statesman. It was not the time for a novice, as Brown warned (referring clearly to David Cameron) at the 2008 Labour Conference. The leading role of Brown at a series of international meetings to promote co-ordinated action presented him as a man taking charge of the crisis. Although the official opposition did their best to lay a sizeable share of the blame for the crisis at Brown's door, for once the public had another target besides politicians on which to vent their fury, the bankers. Moreover, in so far as governments could be blamed for the huge expansion in banking and credit and for 'light touch regulation', this implicated not only Labour but also the Conservatives (who had presided over the 'big bang' in the City and the demutualisation of former building societies).

Whoever bore responsibility for the crisis, it was Labour who in some respects were more ideologically equipped to deal with it. A generation of earlier Labour politicians, including Douglas Jay, Hugh Gaitskell and Tony Crosland, had embraced the theories of Keynes enthusiastically. Despite setbacks in the 1970s, many Labour politicians on the party's right and centre, as well as those who left Labour for the SDP, remained, at heart, Keynesians. They still believed in active government intervention in the management of the economy, and were partial and unwilling converts to the claimed benefits of unregulated or lightly regulated free markets. Moreover, some on the party's centre and left had only reluctantly acquiesced in the revision of the party's Clause IV, which had committed the party to common ownership.

When Brown's government finally recognised in 2008 that there was no viable alternative to the nationalisation of the failed Northern Rock, and went on in the autumn of the same year to part-nationalise other banks in the wake of the wider banking crisis, many Labour members actively welcomed this development. Nationalisation, apparently buried by Blair, was remarkably disinterred to rescue failing banks. The longer term consequences for the ideology of the Labour Party, and other ideologies, remain to be seen. Most commentators were almost certainly right in judging this did not mark a return to old Labour, still less Marxism. It was, however, widely heralded as a retreat from lightly regulated free market capitalism and a return to Keynesianism and social democracy.

Thus it was the economic theories of Keynes, rather than the more fundamentalist socialist ideas associated with Labour's Clause IV, that were really back in fashion (Skidelsky, *New Statesman*, 22 December 2008, 68–71). Keynes had provided a justification for deficit finance in a recession. Brown's government could commit itself to both tax cuts (including a reduction in VAT) and increases in public spending over and beyond the massive injection of cash into the banking system, entailing a substantial increase in public sector debt. Other western governments took similar measures. All this substantially followed Keynes' prescriptions for kick-starting an economy in recession. Labour supporters who knew their history, argued that such measures should have been taken by the Labour leadership in 1931, instead of the public spending cuts they were persuaded to adopt. Thus Labour broadly welcome the reincarnation of Keynes. It was more difficult for the Conservatives who had more emphatically repudiated Keynes, and could hardly turn their backs on the neo-liberal free-market economics they have professed for a generation. Thus, although the two major parties still advanced some fairly similar policies to deal the crisis, there was a widening rhetorical and ideological divide between them.

For good or ill, the credit crunch and economic crisis so dominated politics that other issues were relatively marginalised. The government quietly dropped its controversial proposals for 42 days detention without trial of terror suspects, and there has been less political and media focus on the so-called 'war on terror'. Although there were important continuing issues over health, education, and law and order they were less central to political debate. Some feared that the parties' commitment to pursue green policies would be adversely affected by the apparently paramount need to stimulate consumption and save jobs. In practice, the government has brought forward both energy-saving measures and other new investments in power stations and transport infrastructure (new roads, airport runways) with contentious environmental implications.

Meanwhile, Brown has also moved to unite his party and end the long-running feud with those close to his predecessor (Nicholas Watt, *Guardian* G2, 13 January 2009, pp. 4–7). Thus 'Blairites' have been brought back, including, most surprisingly, Peter Mandelson. Mandelson had attracted the odium of his former friend Brown and his supporters back in 1994 by endorsing Blair for the Labour leadership. He was widely credited with, or blamed for, the creation of 'New Labour', and the systematic development of new techniques of political communication or 'spin'. Following his second resignation from Blair's Cabinet in 2001 and his appointment as a member of the European Commission, he had played no part in British domestic politics. His return to the Cabinet as Business Secretary in 2008 was perceived as controversial and risky. However, it not only helped to heal the breach with Blairites, but also brought much needed additional experience of European and global trade and finance to government, as well as reinvigorating Labour's communication techniques.

A modest Labour revival may prove short-lived. A strong demand for change remains after an unprecedented long period of Labour rule, and this may ultimately be decisive. Sooner or later the political pendulum will swing, and Labour will return to opposition. Yet in retrospect it may be the extent of Labour's dominance, rather than its eventual defeat, that requires explanation. Labour's succession of general election victories in 1997, 2001 and 2005 was a feat that had eluded not only previous Labour governments but the reforming Liberal administrations of Gladstone and Asquith. Left of centre administrations in the past had represented relatively brief interruptions to normal Conservative rule.

What has Labour achieved while it has been in power? Writing before the financial crisis, Simon Lee (in Beech and Lee, 2008, pp. 191–2) suggests that despite three election victories, Labour has not won the 'battle of ideas'. In so far as it had succeeded electorally, this was not by establishing a 'modernised social democracy', as Blair himself had argued, but by occupying 'ideological territory defined by its political opponents'. Thus, Lee argues, the key ideological battle will be for Brown 'to convince the electorate that he rather than David Cameron or Nick Clegg is the most authentic voice of liberalism.' Others would argue, by contrast, that it is the Conservatives who have been constrained to accept much of Labour's agenda, including delivering social justice, maintaining public services, and responding to global challenges on the environment and poverty (see Beech, in Beech and Lee, 2008, pp. 9–13).

Yet, despite its electoral success and dominance of parliament and government the so-called 'People's Party' ultimately failed to engage with or enthuse the people. For all Labour's rhetorical emphasis on community, devolution, participation and inclusion, the reality is falling electoral turnout, falling party membership and, apparently, the increased alienation of the public from the political process. This is not a problem confined to Britain, nor within Britain is it confined to Labour, although it is particularly problematic for a party which has always placed a strong emphasis on an active engaged membership and citizenry.

Further reading

Crick's (1987) useful, if idiosyncratic, introduction to socialism includes short extracts from British texts, while Wright (1983) has introduced and edited a one-volume reader. Two commentaries on the development of British socialist thought can be recommended, Foote (1986) and Callaghan (1990). Davies (1996) has written a readable history of the Labour Party. Sassoon (1997) provides a stimulating overview of the history of the west European left which helps to place British socialism in context.

From the massive literature on specific aspects and periods the following are worth a mention (in rough order of subject matter): Thompson's (1980) classic but controversial account of the rise of the English working class in the early nineteenth century, Pierson (1973) on Marxism and British socialism, Pelling (1965) on the early history of the Labour Party, Miliband (1972) on parliamentary socialism, Saville (1988) on labourism. Minkin remains indispensable on the *Contentious Alliance* with the trade unions (1992) on the labour–trade union link. Morgan (1992) contains insights into Labour politicians. Among specialised biographies Marquand (1977) on MacDonald, Pimlott (1992) on Wilson, Morgan (1997) on Callaghan, and Seldon (2001) on Blair are particularly useful. Biographies of Brown appeared before and soon after he became Prime Minister (e.g. Bower, 2004), and largely do not cover recent developments.

For the internal problems of the Labour Party in the 1980s Seyd (1987) and Shaw (1994) provide an overview. Crewe and King (1995) provide the most authoritative account of the rise and fall of the SDP, while Jenkins (1991) and Owen (1991) provide contrasting personal reminiscences. Williams (1982), Owen (1981, 1984) and Rodgers (1982) all contributed to the debate on social democracy from an SDP perspective, and Hattersley (1987) from Labour's ranks.

On the emergence of New Labour, see Blair's (1996) collection of speeches, insider accounts by Mandelson and Liddle (1996), and Gould (1998), and other perspectives from Anderson and Mann (1997), Brivati and Bale (1997), Driver and Martell (1998), and Fielding (2003). Freeden (1999), Bevir (2000), Ludlam (2000), Temple (2000) and Wickham Jones (2000) have all written useful journal articles. See Marquand (1999) for his interpretation of the *Progressive Dilemma* and subsequent observations on the 'Blair paradox'. Hutton (1995, 1997) and Kelly *et al.* (1997) have written on stakeholding, and Giddens (1998, 2000) on the Third Way, but on the latter see also Rhodes (1997), Le Grand (1998) and a brief retrospective view by Gamble in Seldon and Kavanagh (2005) and by Giddens in Beech and Lee (2008). For communitarianism see Etzioni's (1995) populist interpretation.

Analysis of New Labour in government includes Ludlam and Smith (2001 and 2004), Seldon (2001), Seldon and Kavanagh (2005), Toynbee and Walker (2005), Beech and Lee (2008). On the transfer from Blair to Brown see Giddens (2007) and the symposium on Gidden's book in *Policy Studies Review*, Vol. 6, No. 3, pp. 277–313, (2008). Recent speeches, policy statements and so on can be found on the party website www.lab.org.uk.

Some past judgements will need revising in the wake of the 2008 financial crisis, and this will be reflected in the academic literature, although in the immediate aftermath there was little available besides analysis in newspapers and periodicals. Robert Skidelsky, the biographer of Keynes, has contributed a useful short article (2008) on his relevance today. The same author's *Politicians and the Slump* (1967) is still worth consulting on the earlier 1931 crisis.

5

Nationalism

Introduction

Nationalism is theoretically thin, and it has even been questioned whether it amounts to an ideology (Freeden, 1998). Yet if ideologies are 'action-oriented', nationalism has demonstrably influenced political behaviour over the last two centuries, more so perhaps than supposedly 'mainstream' ideologies. Men and women have been prepared to die for their nation, and to kill for it. Today, the nation state and nationalism face contrasting pressures towards globalisation on the one hand, and devolution of power downwards to regions and local communities on the other. Yet nationalism continues to confound predictions of its impending demise, retaining and even increasing its appeal in advanced industrial or post-industrial countries, in former communist states, and in the developing world.

Britain's status as a mature nation state long seemed uncontroversial. The nationalist principle was something to be applied to others: to Greece, Italy, Hungary, Rumania or Poland. Although British governments were increasingly forced to confront Irish nationalism and, subsequently, nationalist movements in Britain's overseas empire, nationalism within Britain itself remained largely unproblematic, until around the 1960s and 1970s. Then the demise of empire, the resurgence of Irish nationalism in Northern Ireland coupled with the growing strength of Scottish and Welsh nationalism and the issue of Britain's relations with Europe all combined to raise issues of national identity and the future of the British or UK state. The programme of devolution implemented from 1997 and the revived controversy over the European Union are in large part the product of these pressures. They raise further issues of allegiance, power and sovereignty that are fundamental to the future politics and government of these islands and their relationship with their neighbours. Nationalist ideas, in some shape or form, are now of paramount importance for political institutions and behaviour in Britain, as they have long been elsewhere.

What is nationalism?

Nationalism presupposes the existence of nations, but it is not easy to define a nation. It is essentially a community of people, bound together by some characteristic such as a common language, religion, culture or ethnicity. Yet, in the last resort there are no satisfactory objective criteria – a nation exists where a people feel they constitute a nation. Nations exist in the minds of their members. They are 'imagined communities' (Anderson, 1983).

The concern here is with nationalism as a political doctrine. Some writers distinguish between political and cultural nationalism. The celebrated early German nationalist, Herder, was concerned with German language and culture, not political institutions. Yet where the nation is regarded as the natural focus for pride and loyalty this almost inevitably has wider political implications, involving demands for some autonomy and, more usually, full independence as a sovereign state. Thus Ernest Gellner (1983) succinctly defines nationalism as 'a political principle which holds that the political and the national unit should be congruent.' In other words, nations should form states, and states should consist of nations. This is commonly taken to mean an independent sovereign state, with a monopoly of coercive powers within its own borders, and free from external interference. However, nationalist sentiment may sometimes perhaps be satisfied with a form of devolved government that falls short of sovereign independence.

Nationalism is an ideology that can have a general application. The Italian nationalist Mazzini (1805–1872) argued that the world (or at least Europe) was divided naturally into nations, which should each form states, and coexist in international peace and harmony. The American President Woodrow Wilson likewise hoped that applying the principle of national self-determination would end the wars caused by aggressive competing dynastic empires and inaugurate a new era of world peace.

Yet most nationalists have been less concerned, if at all, with nationalism as a general principle, and have concentrated almost exclusively on the rights and qualities of a particular nation. Indeed, for Breuilly (1993, p. 2) a basic assertion of nationalism is that the interests and values of the nation take priority over all other interests and values. The implication is that loyalty to one's own nation should override all other interests and loyalties – to self, family, tribe, class or religion. Success in competition with other nations, in the military, economic or even the sporting arena may provide gratifying confirmation of the particular merit or virtue of the nation, strengthening national loyalty and pride.

When and why nationalism developed

Nationalists commonly maintain that nations are ancient, their origins lost in prehistory, and that nationalist demands developed naturally as peoples became conscious of their national identities and their right to self-determination. Academics generally perceive nations as of comparatively recent origin. According to Greenfeld (1992, p. 14), 'The original modern idea of the nation emerged in sixteenth-century England, which was the first nation in the world' and, she adds, 'the only one for about two hundred years.' Others would discern national consciousness developing early elsewhere (Smith, 1991; Kellas, 1991). However, most accounts of the ideology of nationalism see it originating in the late eighteenth or early nineteenth century (Hobsbawm, 1990; Gellner, 1991; Breuilly, 1993; Alter, 1994).

Kedourie (1993, p. 1) bluntly declares 'nationalism was a doctrine invented in Europe at the beginning of the nineteenth century'. The French revolution was the catalyst. The revolutionaries denied the conventional assumption that states were the property of their ruling dynasty, and claimed instead that supreme power or sovereignty was derived from the people, the French nation. Such a principle could be applied to governments generally. The French revolution directly encouraged Italian and Polish nationalism and helped stimulate German, Spanish and Russian nationalism, both in imitation of, and in reaction against, French nationalism.

Some critics would argue that nationalism spread through elite manipulation rather than through growing popular consciousness of national identities. Kedourie (from the right) blamed the subversive propaganda of liberal intellectuals, while alternatively some socialists argued that dominant classes fomented nationalist ideas to divert the workers (who 'had no country') from their common economic interests and class loyalty. There is something in the insinuation of elite manipulation. Particular nationalist causes involved much reinterpretation and sometimes invention of history, and the creation of new national myths and symbols. Moreover, new nation states were commonly forged by relatively small intellectual elites, and a mass national consciousness fostered subsequently. Gellner (1983, p. 55) tartly observes, 'It is nationalism which engenders nations, and not the other way around.' Thus the Italian nationalist d'Azeglio (1792–1886) declared 'We have made Italy; now we must make Italians' (Hobsbawm, 1991, p. 111).

Yet the importance of nationalist ideas and propaganda may be exaggerated. Gellner (1983, p. 125) explicitly criticises Kedourie for treating nationalism 'as a contingent, avoidable aberration, accidentally spawned by European thinkers'. Eric Hobsbawm, working within a broadly Marxist theoretical framework, makes a similar point. It is not ideas, like nationalism, which change history; instead, new ideas are articulated in response to historical change. Nationalism was the consequence of industrial modernisation, which required the breakdown of traditional and local restraints on trade, a mass, fluid and mobile society, and the development of a national economy. It also required, as previous agrarian societies had not, mass education and mass literacy involving in turn a standardisation of language, officially recognised and taught, in place of the essentially local or regional dialects and cultures which predominated earlier. Indeed, nationalism has been attributed to a revolution in the technology of communication (Deutsch, 1966), an argument supported by Gellner (1983, p. 127): 'It is the media themselves, the importance of abstract, centralized, standardized, one to many communication, which itself automatically engenders the core idea of nationalism.'

Compatible with the linking of nationalism with industrial modernisation is a quasi-sociological/psychological explanation of nationalist feeling. This points to the needs of individuals in a modern atomised mass society to find some identity or allegiance to which they can attach themselves, following the breakdown of traditional ties and communities under modern industrial capitalism. Thus nationalism is the consequence, not the cause (as Kedourie implies) of the breakdown of other allegiances.

One implication of identifying the rise of nationalism with a particular phase of historical development is that another phase might see its decline or extinction. Indeed, just as nationalism has been identified with modern industrial society, so it has been suggested that it is incompatible with post-modern, post-industrial global economy and society. This may eventually prove to be the case, but there are few signs as yet of nationalism's imminent demise. Its continuing appeal in changed circumstances suggests it may answer some psychological need in modern humanity.

Varieties of nationalism

For two centuries the simple core principle of nationalism has been that nations should form states. Even so, the ideas with which nationalism has been associated have changed quite considerably. Indeed nationalism has a chameleon quality, taking colour from its ideological context. Thus, while most other political ideologies can be readily placed on the conventional left–right political spectrum, nationalism has been promiscuously associated with ideas across the spectrum. Accordingly, Freeden (1996, p. 7; 1998) suggests that nationalism is not a distinctive ideology but a component of other ideologies. Here it is argued that nationalism is a distinctive ideology in so far as it prioritises the nation over other interests and values, although it is acknowledged that it can take a wide variety of forms.

It began as a revolutionary doctrine, posing a profound threat to the prevailing social and political order in Europe in the early nineteenth century. The idea that political authority should derive from the nation was particularly damaging to foreign dynasties, or those who ruled over multi-national states. Nationalism threatened Russian rule in Poland and Finland, Austrian rule in north Italy, Hungary, Czech Bohemia and elsewhere. Much of this rule was associated with absolutism and reaction and thus opposed by liberals who sought individual political freedoms and constitutional reform. Thus liberalism and nationalism in the early nineteenth century were closely linked. Individual self-determination appeared to go hand in hand with national self-determination. Popular sovereignty entailed both the extension of political rights and the creation of states by national communities.

A distinction is sometimes drawn between unification nationalism and separation nationalism. Where a nation was divided into several independent states (for example, nineteenth-century Italy and Germany), nationalists sought unification to form a single nation state. Where a nation was part of a multi-national state (for example the Hapsburg empire) nationalists sought separation. Application of the principle of self-determination thus depended on circumstance.

Yet early liberal nationalists tended to assume limits to the establishment of independent nation states. States had to be economically, politically and militarily viable, which implied a certain minimum threshold size and defensible frontiers, as well as a developed national consciousness. Very small states seemed inconsistent with economic modernisation and cultural progress. Mazzini envisaged a Europe divided into no more than 12 nation states (of which Ireland was not one). John Stuart Mill's support for the nationalist principle in general did not extend to Bretons and Basques, who, he argued, benefited by being brought within 'the current of ideas and feelings of a highly civilised and cultivated people – to be a member of the French nationality.' Progress involved the extinction of the Breton nation. Almost parenthetically, Mill suggested that the same was true of Scottish Highlanders or the Welsh, with reference to Britain (Mill, 1861, 1972 edition, p. 395).

This 'threshold principle', as it has been termed, was subsequently largely abandoned (Hobsbawm, 1990, 1994) and self-determination was applied to some relatively small and poor nations, most notably in the Balkans, leading to the derogatory expression 'Balkanisation' to describe the proliferation of small, potentially unstable states. Yet there were never any clear criteria to determine limits to the process. Thus the American President Woodrow Wilson was confronted with demands for self-determination from peoples of whom he had never previously heard, in his attempts to apply the principle to Europe at the end of the First World War.

A more intractable problem was the inter-settlement of peoples and the continued existence of national minorities within new nation states. The application of self-determination is necessarily an untidy affair at best, with undesired consequences for the resulting minorities. The national principle often proved inimical to the individual rights which liberals championed. Thus, the creation of new nation states could involve the denial of minority rights and sometimes expulsions, forced transfers of population, and even extermination, or 'ethnic cleansing'. To the disillusion of some early liberal nationalists, rival national interests within and between states subsequently appeared a spur to conflict and war rather than international co-operation and peace.

But if some liberals became disenchanted with nationalism, some conservatives increasingly found it useful as a political creed that could be harnessed in the interests of the existing social order. While in the early nineteenth century the concept of the nation was invoked against the state, once nation and state were conflated, an official state-sponsored nationalism could be utilised against radicals and socialists preaching class conflict and revolution. Patriotism appeared to transcend class loyalties. Moreover, in the increasingly important struggle for working class votes, nationalism proved a cheaper and more effective alternative to social reform (see, for example, Beer, 1982, p. 272).

Much of the nationalism of the late nineteenth century and early twentieth centuries was also more assertive and aggressive than the earlier essentially liberal nationalism of Mazzini and others. Instead of proclaiming the universal rights to self-determination of all national communities, it involved advancing the claims of particular nations, often at the expense of other national interests. Behind it there were more competitive assumptions, bound up with Darwinian notions of the survival of the fittest in international relations. Strong nations could, and indeed should, flourish at the expense of their weaker adversaries. Economic, diplomatic and military success could be attributed to the superior virtues of the nation. To the dismay of those liberals and social-ists who championed international brotherhood, the mass of workers in all western European countries demonstrated the overriding strength of their national allegiances in 1914.

The nationalism of western European countries was also closely bound up with colonialism and imperialism. The rights to self-determination proclaimed for peoples in Europe were rarely applied to peoples in Africa and Asia. They were 'lesser breeds without the law', incapable of self-government. Indeed, such comforting assumptions of cultural and racial superiority enabled Europeans to see imperialism as an idealistic crusade – a 'white-man's burden' to bring good government, religion and civili-sation to 'primitive peoples'. The easy acquisition of colonial empires (secured with modern weaponry) confirmed for Europeans the superior-ity of the white man in general, and their own nation in particular (see also Chapter 6).

Both assertive nationalism and imperialism were closely (although not exclusively) associated with the right and conservatism. The con-cept of national community fitted comfortably with an organic theory of state and society, advanced by some conservative thinkers in oppos-ition to the atomised individualism of liberalism. Although nation-alism is a product of the modern world, it derives much of its appeal from the past. Thus the history of the emerging nation is portrayed in terms of key defining moments, of brave struggles by national heroes, of potent historical myths and symbols. Even ruling dynasties of for-eign descent could, through the rediscovery or invention of appropriate traditions or ceremonies, hope to identify themselves with the national spirit. In Britain, coronations, jubilees and other more routine ceremo-nial occasions, such as the trooping of the colour or the state opening of parliament, helped to promote a nationalist sentiment steeped in tradition, even if some of that 'tradition' was of relatively recent origin (Cannadine, in Donald and Hall, 1986).

However, if nationalism could become associated with such (real or imagined) traditional values, in some countries such as Japan and Turkey it was aggressively employed as an instrument of modernisation by a ruling order determined to overcome traditional practices and loyal-ties which were seen as an obstacle to progress. Here a state-sponsored nationalism deliberately rejected traditional culture and dress, encour-aging alien western ways as part of a process of national regeneration. This confirms further the chameleon character of the ideology.

Both the traditional and modernising implications of national-ism were present in fascism, which was perhaps the most extreme manifestation of the ideology, employing racist ideas to establish the superiority of specific national communities over others. German nationalism from the late eighteenth century was based particularly on German language and culture, but some German nationalists went on to claim that the German *volk* were a distinctive race which could be marked off from Slavs, or Latins or Jews. (Fascism and racism are explored further in Chapter 6.)

Although nationalism became closely associated with the right, and particularly the far right, in Europe in the late nineteenth and the first half of the twentieth century, there were also nationalist movements which were supported by socialists, particularly those which involved resistance against colonialism and imperialism. At first sight, socialism and nationalism appear incompatible. Socialism essentially involved a reaction against, and an alternative to, capitalism. For a socialist, the fundamental divisions in human society were economic class divisions, and the common interests of the working class transcended national boundaries. Socialism, in theory at least, proclaimed the universal brotherhood of man.

Yet socialists had to provide some explanation for nationalism and imperialism. Lenin neatly linked the phenomenon of imperialism with another problem for Marxists – improved living standards for the working classes in advanced capitalist countries, which ran counter to predictions of increasing proletarian misery which would ultimately provoke revolution. For Lenin, imperialism enabled advanced capitalism to postpone the collapse predicted by Marx. Exploitation of peoples and resources in other continents allowed western capitalist states to avoid intensifying the exploitation of their own working class, who instead would reap some of the rewards of imperialism.

Yet for Marxists, and indeed most socialists, imperialism involved exploitation that should be opposed and resisted. Thus they supported anti-colonial movements, which, in demanding freedom and independence from the colonial power, inevitably borrowed the terminology and ideas of European nationalism, using against them their own slogans of freedom, equality and self-determination. They often also employed the language of socialism that could be readily applied to their own situation. Their leaders, largely western-educated, imbibed western socialist teaching, particularly Marxism, although some also discerned a distinctive form of socialism in their own native cultures. Thus socialism and anti-colonial nationalism became closely linked.

The extent to which socialism and nationalism are ultimately compatible remains contentious. If nationalism requires an overriding loyalty to the nation (Breuilly, 1992, p. 2) this presents problems for the general assumption that socialism is international and transcends national borders. As Hobsbawm (1989, p. 125) has tartly observed 'any Marxists who are not, at least in theory, prepared to see the "interests" of their own country or people subordinated to wider interests, had best reconsider their ideological loyalties'. Yet other socialists, and even Marxists, have seen no incompatibility between their nationalist and socialist convictions (Nairn, 1981, 2000). The argument partly depends on the definition of nationalism, and the extent to which nationalism is, or is not, exclusive.

A distinction is sometimes drawn between civic nationalism and ethnic nationalism. Civic nationalism is related to liberal nationalism; it is inclusive rather than exclusive in the sense that 'all permanent residents fully enjoy the human rights conferred by citizenship, irrespective of ethnic criteria'. It is also compatible with other identities and loyalties, both within and outside the nation. Ethnic nationalism by contrast relates the nation to a specific ethnic group (which might be based on race, tribe, language or culture). Thus it excludes from the nation residents who lack the appropriate ethnic qualification. Ethnic nationalism commonly also requires an overriding loyalty to the nation which subordinates or excludes other identities and loyalties. In its more extreme manifestations it is chauvinist, xenophobic, ethnocentric and racist (Griffin, in Eatwell and Wright, 1999, pp. 154–5).

While it has been argued that the concept of the sovereign nation state is increasingly obsolete in an era of intensifying globalisation (Ohmae, 1996), nationalism shows little sign of weakening. On the contrary, there has been an expansion of separatist pressures the world over, but particularly in eastern Europe (Table 5.1). Thus, most of the former constituent republics of the Soviet Union have proclaimed their independence, and these pressures have extended into areas of Russia itself, where there are pressures from non-Russian ethnic minorities. The former Czechoslovakia has divided into a Czech and Slovak state, while the former Yugoslavia has broken up as its former constituent republics proclaimed their independence. Yet few of these new states are themselves ethnically homogeneous, but often contain new minorities seeking their own national self-determination. Thus, the west has effectively assisted Kosovan Albanians to pursue independence from Serbia, while in states such as Georgia there are minorities who seek independence, or union with Russia. There are often cross-border complications. The Iraqi Kurds seek at least autonomous status, but Kurdish nationalism also has implications for neighbouring Turkey and Syria, with their own

Table 5.1 Varieties of nationalism

Type of nationalism	Associated ideas	Countries	Politicians/thinkers
Revolutionary nationalism	Popular sovereignty, national sovereignty	Revolutionary France and client states	Rousseau
Cultural nationalism	Language and culture	Germany early 19th century Wales 19th century	Herder
Liberal nationalism	National self-determination, constitutionalism, free trade Threshold principle	Unification nationalism – Germany, Italy Separation nationalism e.g. Greece, Belgium, Ireland	Mazzini John Stuart Mill
Conservative nationalism	Patriotism, social integration, national unity, fatherland, imperialism, social Darwinism, protection, autarchy	German empire (1871–1918), Tsarist Russia, late 19th century Britain and France	Bismarck, Disraeli, Joseph Chamberlain
Modernisation nationalism	Modernity, industrialisation, westernisation, breach with tradition	Japan from 19th century Turkey in 20th century	Kemal Attatuck
Fascist and Nazi nationalism	Totalitarian state, New Roman Empire racism, anti-semitism, genocide	Fascist Italy Nazi Germany facist movements elsewhere	Mussolini Hitler Oswald Mosley
Anti-colonial nationalism?	Imperialism higher stage of capitalism, Movement for Colonial Freedom	South America, south east Asia, India, Africa	Lenin, Ho Chi Minh, Gandhi, Mandela
Modern separation nationalism	Language, culture, national identity	Scotland, Wales, Baltic, Balkans	MacDiarmid, Nairn

Kurdish minorities. The principle of national self-determination often conflicts with the widely acknowledged right of independent sovereign states to preserve their own territorial integrity and resist external interference in their internal affairs.

These nationalist pressures are not confined to the world's trouble spots. Even some of the mature nation states of western Europe, such as Spain, France and Italy have faced significant separatist movements. Here, ethnic nationalism is sometimes complicated by economic inequality or 'uneven development' within the state, and the reaction of a relatively deprived 'periphery' against a more prosperous 'core'. This kind of nationalism is thus sometimes described as 'peripheral nationalism'. However, there are also sometimes political pressures from more prosperous regions for separation from less developed areas, regarded as a drain on national resources and living standards. Thus, some from the relatively prosperous north of Italy wish to establish a separate state of Padania, free from the incubus of the south.

Nations and states in Britain

If nationalism requires that nations should form independent states and states should consist of nations, there is an immediate difficulty in applying the ideology to Britain, where the very identity of state and nation is clouded in ambiguity. The state is officially the United Kingdom of Great Britain and Northern Ireland, but is often referred to as the UK, Great Britain or simply Britain while part of the state, England, is commonly confused with the whole. It is sometimes suggested that this political unit constitutes a nation state, implying a single 'British' nationality. Yet the historian Norman Davies (1999, p. 870) categorically maintains, 'The United Kingdom is not, and never has been, a nation-state.' More commonly, the United Kingdom is reckoned to include four nations, English, Scots, Welsh and Irish. Some of those living within the United Kingdom claim a dual national allegiance – British and Irish, or British and Scots, while others arbitrarily describe themselves as English or British depending on mood or circumstances. There are also recent immigrants belonging to ethnic minorities who are full citizens of the United Kingdom, but whose national identity and allegiance is doubtful in the eyes of others, and sometimes perhaps to themselves.

Many of these difficulties surrounding national identity are derived from the history of the British Isles and its changing political units (Davies, 1999). England was politically united from the tenth century, with strong links with Scandinavia until the Norman conquest, and then with France until the fifteenth century. From the sixteenth century, under the Tudors, an English national consciousness developed (Greenfeld, 1992). Wales was politically subject to the English crown from the thirteenth century and Wales was formally united with England in 1536 in the reign of Henry VIII. The Welsh themselves had little say in the process of absorption under English rule. They retained their own language and culture, but this seemed under threat by the nineteenth century. Ireland was more erratically controlled by the English monarchy from the twelfth century, but unlike Britain remained obstinately Catholic, apart from Ulster, which was forcibly settled by Scottish Protestants from the seventeenth century. In 1801 it was politically united with England under an Act of Union.

It was rather different with Scotland which existed for several centuries as an independent state with its own crown, parliament and legal system, although it had a troubled relationship with its powerful southern neighbour. It might, like Wales, have been brought under English rule from the reign of Edward I had not the exploits of William Wallace and Robert the Bruce preserved Scottish independence, eloquently asserted in the Declaration of Arbroath of 1320, for another three centuries. While Scottish nationalists have derived powerful inspiration from these early indications of a separate national consciousness, it is not clear how far it extended beyond a tiny elite. Moreover, Scotland was internally divided almost throughout its history, with clan rivalry in the highlands and conflicts between rival noble families in the lowlands on top of old ethnic and linguistic divisions. To these divisions was added religious conflict in the sixteenth century, when John Knox converted most of Scotland to Protestantism and transformed Scotland's external relations from the 'auld alliance' with France against England to a common Anglo-Scottish interest in resisting Catholic France and Spain. The succession of James VI of Scotland to the English throne in 1603 ensured that Scottish and English interests remained closely entangled throughout the seventeenth century. The combination of Scottish presbyterianism and English puritanism effectively destroyed the government of Charles I, while Scottish and English interests were involved in both the restoration of the Stuarts in 1660 and the 'Glorious Revolution' of 1688.

The Union with Scotland in 1707 created a British state, symbolised by the figure of Britannia on coins, and celebrated in Thomas Arne's patriotic anthem, 'Rule Britannia'. The next century saw the establishment of a new British national identity (Colley, 2003) which, however, was never fully accepted. Scottish nationalists have generally regarded the Act of Union of 1707 as a craven betrayal of Scottish interests by the old Scottish Parliament (see for example Nairn, 2000, pp. 93–9). However, many educated Scots willingly acquiesced in their new designation as North British and the incorporation of the cross of St Andrew into the Union Jack. Advocates of the Union in Scotland saw positive benefits in terms of peace, security for the Scottish religion, a degree of political freedom, and, most of all, trade. Subsequently, although not necessarily as a consequence of Union, Scotland enjoyed a flowering of economic, intellectual and cultural life in the eighteenth century.

Nationalism in nineteenth-century Britain

Thus nationalism, in its early nineteenth-century liberal form as a political doctrine asserting the right to national self-determination, appeared to have little relevance to Britain. Britain was already a nation state that did not need to be freed from foreign rule or united. Nationalism was a principle to be applied to others. British politicians and intellectuals gave enthusiastic support to a whole range of nationalist causes abroad – notably Greek, Belgian, Hungarian, Polish and Italian nationalism. There was in the nineteenth century no significant movement for Scottish or Welsh independence. Ireland of course was a very different matter, although Britain's rulers continued to regard Ireland as an integral part of the Union until Gladstone became converted to Irish Home Rule in 1886.

Nationalism in its later nineteenth-century version was a political doctrine that asserted the primacy of national loyalties over other loyalties, and gloried in the superiority of one's own nation over other nations. It was deliberately stimulated in Britain – by the revival or invention of ritual, through the arts and popular culture (particularly the music hall) and through education. British nationalism and imperialism became key ingredients of conservatism from the late nineteenth century, but was also enthusiastically endorsed by large sections of the Liberal and Labour Parties. British colonial acquisitions, and British victories in wars, provided convincing confirmation of national superiority.

All this implies a conscious attempt by the rulers of the British state to secure the full political integration of its once separate elements. Indeed, the new officially sponsored British identity never succeeded in obliterating older national loyalties. Ireland, in particular, obstinately maintained a distinctive Irish national identity, which was intensified rather than destroyed by the Act of Union of 1801. A sense of Scottish nation-hood also persisted. The writer Sir Walter Scott had helped to foster an influential romantic tartan culture, which was enthusiastically adopted by the British royal family and did much for the tourist trade, but had little to do with any incipient separatist Scottish nationalism. Indeed, Britain's ruling class came to appreciate that a 'state-fostered cult of a depoliticised Scottish identity' was a more reliable tactic for secur-ing Scotland's allegiance than cultural integration (Crick, 1991, p. 91). Significantly, also, the most numerous participants in the British state maintained an attachment to 'England' which was proudly or sentimen-tally celebrated by poets from Blake to Tennyson and Rupert Brooke.

Scottish and Welsh nationalism

While Irish nationalism was clearly a significant political factor throughout the nineteenth century, and led ultimately to the 1916 rising and the creation of a separate Irish state from 1922, Scottish and Welsh nationalism then appeared less threatening to the United Kingdom. A strong consciousness of separate national identities persisted which had some basis in real differences, a distinctive religious, legal and edu-cational system in Scotland and a surviving Welsh language and cul-ture. However, this national consciousness did not in the nineteenth and early twentieth centuries involve widespread demands for national inde-pendence as it had done in Ireland and over much of the continent of Europe. Indeed, most Scots and Welsh then seemed content with their participation in the industrial growth and imperial expansion of the British state, from which, it could be argued, they profited economically and politically. Substantial support for nationalism, in the sense of full independence for Scotland and Wales, is relatively recent. Plaid Cymru was only founded in 1925 and the Scottish National Party (SNP) in 1928 (Marr, 1992, pp. 63–7) and neither achieved much electoral success before the late 1960s.

The British or UK state made some concessions to national senti-ment in Scotland and Wales. Thus Scotland, which already had its own system of courts, local government and education, acquired a Secretary for Scotland from 1885, while Scottish administration was progres-sively reorganised and rationalised under a largely autonomous Scottish Office in the course of the twentieth century. Wales, which had (and still has) similar administrative legal and educational systems to those in England, did not acquire a minister until 1951, and a full Secretary of

State with a separate Welsh Office only in 1964. Yet from the late nine-teenth century onwards, there were also concessions to Welsh national feeling on religion, temperance, education and the use of the Welsh lan-guage in administrative and judicial proceedings, and on television.

The rapid loss of empire and great power status after the Second World War relegated Scotland and Wales to the declining periphery of a shrunken British state. Moreover, partly because of their peripheral location, both suffered disproportionately from the decline of the United Kingdom's manufacturing industries. The decline of textiles, shipbuild-ing and coal mining hit the Scottish economy, while South Wales was similarly damaged by the rundown of iron and steel and mining. 'UK Ltd' no longer appeared a successful enterprise. British decline was doubtless one factor in stirring nationalist currents in Scotland and Wales.

Welsh nationalism, however, was not essentially a question of eco-nomics. It has not flourished in the valleys of South Wales which were hardest hit by industrial decline, but in the core Welsh-speaking areas of the north-west where preservation of the Welsh language and culture has been the key concern. Education in Welsh, Welsh television, and Welsh as the language for legal and administrative business have been important issues, although supplemented to a degree by concerns over English immigration, which is partly related to the protection of Welsh culture but also has an economic dimension (particularly in terms of housing). Yet Wales is essentially divided rather than united by the lan-guage issue, which helps to explain both the consistency of support for Welsh nationalism, but also its failure to grow, at least until the 1999 Assembly elections.

Support for nationalism in Scotland has been stronger but also more volatile. There, language is a negligible issue, enabling the SNP to make a wider appeal based on national sentiment and Scottish economic and political interests. The negative part of this appeal is a perceived neglect of Scottish issues by a remote and (in 1979–97) politically alien United Kingdom government, responsible for the imposition of the poll tax and privatisation measures strongly opposed in Scotland. At the same time, the SNP could plausibly claim that an independent Scotland would be economically better off because of North Sea Oil. 'It's Scotland's Oil' became a potent election slogan, although the force of it diminished with the depletion of oil reserves and the fall in world oil prices.

Such naked appeals to Scottish self-interest provided some ammu-nition for critics who denounced the nationalists as narrow and mater-ialist. Since then the SNP have sought to counter charges of narrow chauvinism by campaigning on the platform, 'Scotland in Europe', aligning themselves with progressive tendencies favouring closer European integration. This involved a marked policy reversal from earlier opposition to EC membership, yet it is logical that Euro-federalists and separatist nationalists should make common cause against the entrenched power of existing European states.

There were formerly some significant differences in the location of Scottish and Welsh nationalism on the political spectrum. Whereas Plaid Cymru was firmly associated with the left and socialism, a common gibe by Labour opponents of the SNP used to be that they were 'Tartan Tories'. The rapid growth of the SNP from the 1970s, and the defection to it of some erstwhile Labour politicians, has weakened that charge, although it is still true that the SNP covers a wider range of views on domestic and economic policy than Plaid. Yet it is now easier for socialists like Nairn (1981, 2000) to identify Scottish and Welsh nationalism with progressive civic nationalism rather than a more exclusive ethnic nationalism.

Nationalism and devolution

British politicians and parties from time to time proposed some transfer of political power to Scotland and Wales. The notion of Home Rule for Scotland and (to a more limited extent) Wales, began to appear on the political agenda in the late nineteenth century, largely as a consequence of the bitter controversy over Irish Home Rule. 'Home Rule all round' was one attempt by Liberals to popularise a cause which did not greatly appeal to the British electorate, and they and their Liberal Democrat successors have fairly consistently supported it. Labour's record has been more erratic. They favoured Home Rule up to 1945, then opposed it, only becoming reconverted in 1974 when they promised Scottish and Welsh Assemblies (a promise that initially failed in 1979, but was finally implemented after 1997). The Conservatives occasionally flirted with some concession to nationalist feeling but remained in name and spirit an Unionist party opposed to 'home rule' or 'devolution' (although they have since recognised Scottish and Welsh devolution as an accomplished fact).

The SNP, and to a lesser extent Plaid Cymru, made a political break-through from the late 1960s and early 1970s. The SNP won 30.4 per cent of the vote and 11 seats in October 1974, when the Welsh nationalists won over 10 per cent of the Welsh vote and three seats. By the mid-1970s there were, for the first time almost since its establishment, serious doubts about the long-term survival of the British state, with Northern Ireland already in turmoil and nationalism on a steep upward curve in Scotland and Wales (Birch, 1977). It was this that converted the Labour party to devolution, although the government was unable to implement its proposals, which the Welsh rejected and too few Scots supported, in separate referendums in 1979.

After the failure of Labour's devolution plans the separatist tide briefly appeared to recede. The SNP lost votes and particularly seats in the 1979 General Election. British nationalist sentiment was arguably stimulated by the 1982 Falklands War, a generally more assertive foreign policy and a reaffirmation of commitment to the Union under the premiership of Margaret Thatcher. John Major strongly opposed the Labour and Liberal Democrat commitment to devolution in 1992 and 1997, arguing that this threatened the break-up of the United Kingdom, a point also made by some Labour dissidents like Tam Dalyell (Marr, 1992; Harvie, 1994).

Yet the fundamental problems of the British state remained, involving uncertain and changing internal loyalties, as well as questions over the United Kingdom's external relationships, particularly with Europe. Labour's landslide victory in 1997 led to the rapid implementation of plans for devolution conceived in opposition. A Scottish Parliament and Welsh Assembly were instituted following referendums in 1997 and elections in 1999. Meanwhile, a devolved assembly and executive was rather more precariously established in Northern Ireland.

Labour, already the dominant party in Scotland and (especially) Wales, hoped that they would benefit further from devolution, and reduce the nationalist threat. Yet the additional member electoral system they agreed with the Liberal Democrats for elections for the devolved assemblies substantially conceded proportional representation and made it difficult for Labour to win an overall majority. In the event, a Labour–Liberal Democrat coalition took control of the Scottish executive and, briefly, the Welsh executive, after a period of Labour minority rule following elections in 1999. Both the SNP and Plaid Cymru attracted strong support and became the second largest parties in Scotland and Wales. However, the nationalist parties lost support in the elections of 2003, enabling the Labour–Liberal Democrat coalition to continue in power in Scotland, and Labour to rule alone in Wales.

This appeared to confirm the hopes of the unionist parties that devolution would weaken support for Scottish and Welsh nationalism and independence. Yet there were some built-in problems with devolution, seen as an unsatisfactory half-way house by nationalists. In so far as devolved government appeared to work, this provided an argument for further devolution of powers. In so far as devolved government disappointed, this, it could be argued, was because not enough powers had been devolved to make it effective. Thus all the pressure was one way, towards further devolution. Moreover, the combination of a Labour government at Westminster and Labour controlled or dominated governments in Scotland and Wales, while reducing without eliminating, the scope for tension between UK and devolved government, caused additional problems for the governing party. Thus, Scottish and Welsh Labour felt the effects of increased opposition to the UK government of Blair (particularly over foreign policy) and subsequently Brown, while Labour's reputation was further tarnished by internal divisions and scandals within the Scottish and Welsh parties.

After a third round of elections in 2007, Labour lost its precarious majority in Wales, and formed a coalition administration with Plaid Cymru, while in Scotland the SNP emerged as the largest party and formed a minority administration with its leader, Alex Salmond, as First Minister. Thus nationalist parties, whose ultimate goal is independence, now govern Scotland and have a share in the government of Wales. Meanwhile, and more remarkably, a new power-sharing executive had been formed in Ulster, headed by a coalition of formerly irreconcilable opponents from the Democratic Unionist Party and the republican Sinn Fein. Nationalism has thus made a significant advance in each of the three smaller nations belonging to the United Kingdom.

There is also increasing dissatisfaction in England with the post-devolution system of government. A continuing anomaly is that Westminster MPs elected for Scottish constituencies can and do vote on issues that now largely affect England (e.g. health and education), while English MPs no longer have any power over issues devolved to Scotland. This is the celebrated West Lothian question, originally posed by the dissident former Labour MP for the old constituency of West Lothian, Tam Dalyell. Dalyell asked why he, as a Scottish MP, could vote on education in England but not in Scotland, where control of education was devolved to the Scottish Parliament. The anomaly has increased since the General Election of 2005, when Labour lost its majority in England, and depended on the votes of Scottish and Welsh MPs to win votes at Westminster. It was intensified further when Brown succeeded Blair in 2007, and a Scottish Prime Minister, with other Scots prominent in the Cabinet, assumed responsibility for the government of the United Kingdom, of which 86 per cent of the population live in England.

Various solutions have been proposed. One, given some support by Conservatives, is that Westminster MPs sitting for parts of UK where powers had been devolved should not be able to vote on purely English issues. An objection is that this would create two classes of MPs at Westminster, those with full and those with more limited voting rights and responsibilities. More to the point, it would result in unstable or deadlocked government. Another partial solution, favoured by Labour, was regional devolution for England, but this was rejected in the only region (the North East) where a referendum was held. Another proposal is for a separate English Parliament, to balance devolution elsewhere, and create a fully federal state. Yet it would be a very unbalanced federation with 86 per cent of the UK population living in one state, and inevitably there would be tension and overlap between the UK and English Parliament.

The nationalist solution is, of course, the break-up of the United Kingdom, an outcome long predicted by the Scottish nationalist Tom Nairn (1981, 2000, 2001). Changes in the European political map since 1989 make it easier to contemplate a Scottish or Welsh state. If Slovakia, Slovenia and Latvia, why not Wales? At present there does not seem to be a majority for independence in Scotland or Wales, but it could happen, perhaps sooner rather than later. The SNP did not campaign on an immediate programme of independence in 2007, but promised a later referendum on the issue. Their longer term chances of success have been increased by early approval for the minority SNP government in Scotland, coupled with intensifying problems for Labour both at Westminster and Edinburgh. They could be improved further if and when Scotland has to deal with a Conservative government at Westminster.

Indeed, a critical issue could be the future policy of the Conservative party. It has always been the party of the union, as its official title continues to proclaim. Yet increasingly this seems against its own electoral interests, especially with regard to England. Elsewhere in the United Kingdom its fortunes have declined. In 1955, Conservatives held the majority of seats in Scotland, but in subsequent General Elections they lost votes and seats until in 1997 no Conservative MPs were returned for Scottish or Welsh constituencies. In the meantime, the Ulster Unionists in Northern Ireland had broken their links with the Conservatives in 1974. Thus the party of the union had become, over time, an overwhelmingly English party. Indeed, the party's electoral interests might now be best served by a total reversal of past policy, capitalising on English resentment of devolution and a government led by Scots to embrace English nationalism. So far this has not happened. David Cameron has proclaimed his party's continued support for the union and even encouraged the resumption of the alignment of diminished Ulster Unionists with the Conservatives in 2008. However, if subsequent elections deliver a clear a majority of Conservative MPs in England but no majority at Westminster the pressures for a party rethink could intensify. A Conservative and Unionist party that has long boasted of its pragmatism could abandon the union, as it was earlier obliged to abandon empire.

Nairn (1981, 2000) argues that the break-up of Britain could have a progressive, beneficial effect, enabling all its former constituent parts, including England, to rediscover or develop separate national identities and a civic republican nationalism which could coexist and co-operate fruitfully in a European or global environment. Hobsbawm (1989, pp. 134–5) considers reactionary consequences more likely. One possibility is a narrow exclusive chauvinism, which would discriminate against non-Welsh speakers in Wales, English settlers in Scotland, and all kinds of ethnic minorities in England, with bitter inter-state disputes over assets, debts, off-shore fishing and mineral rights. Interpretations and expectations rest heavily on different perspectives on the nature of nationalism.

Europe, regionalism and nationalism

The growth of the European Union is one development that runs counter to traditional nationalist assumptions. European integration appealed to many precisely because it would transcend and render redundant the old national rivalries within Europe that had culminated in two world wars. It involved a different vision and a distinctive political programme. From the beginning, the founders of the European Community envisaged a political as well as an economic union, which implied the development of a European consciousness and identity, at the expense of nationalist rivalries.

Yet, despite the hopes of Euro-enthusiasts and the loudly voiced fears of British Euro-sceptics, the European Union is hardly yet a 'superstate'. Some of its key institutions involve, in embryo, the framework of a sovereign state – an executive in the shape of the European Commission, a legislature (potentially at least) in the European Parliament, and a judiciary in the Court of Justice in Luxembourg. However, these institutions coexist with others, such as the European Council and Council of Ministers, which reflect the national interests of the constituent member states. These increasingly seem more influential in decision-making despite formal progress towards integration.

In the long debate over British membership of the European Community from the early 1960s onwards, there has been some discussion on the implications for British national sovereignty, an issue that was early raised by opponents of UK entry such as Enoch Powell. Similar concerns have recently been articulated by leading members of the Conservative party, and in more extreme form by the British National Party and a new British political party, UKIP, the United Kingdom Independence Party, that has achieved some success in recent elections for the European Parliament. Supporters of British membership, both at the time of accession and since, have largely played down the political implications, and emphasised instead the economic advantages. In so far as they addressed the issue of sovereignty, it was to deny that it was affected.

The term sovereignty is used to describe two linked concepts – sovereignty, or independence, in relation to other states, and supreme power within the state, involving 'parliamentary sovereignty' in the case of the United Kingdom. Both have been affected by British membership of the European Union. As with membership of other international associations, such as the United Nations or NATO, membership of the European Union effectively constrains UK freedom of action in relation to other states. It also has implications for the traditional constitutional doctrine of the sovereignty of Parliament, as European law overrides state law and is automatically applied within member countries. It may be argued that parliamentary sovereignty is unaffected, as a vote of the Westminster Parliament took Britain into Europe and a similar vote could take Britain out again; yet as the real possibility of withdrawal recedes, the argument weakens.

The European Union thus has considerable consequences for existing European states, and for the ideology of nationalism. The idea that nations should constitute independent sovereign states pursuing their national interest does not sit easily with the concept of European unity in which such sovereignty may be 'pooled' or 'shared'. Nationalism may be reconciled with a relatively loose and weak form of political association – a 'Europe des Patries' in De Gaulle's formulation, or 'confederalism' rather than federalism, a solution which some British politicians have implicitly or explicitly favoured. Thus, strong independent sovereign states co-operate with other members, but retain the right to protect their own separate state interests.

Equally, a rather stronger form of European unity involving a federal structure is quite compatible with a form of nationalism that does not necessarily demand full sovereign independence. Indeed, the European Union may give some tacit encouragement to 'peripheral nationalism' within existing member states. The existence of the European Union weakens old objections to such nationalism on the grounds of lack of viability or economic dependence. Moreover, it enables nationalists to avoid accusations of narrow chauvinism; they can proclaim their national and European loyalties together, as in the (relatively recent) SNP slogan 'Scotland in Europe'.

Even if the European Union does not give overt encouragement to 'peripheral nationalism', there are certainly some institutional pressures towards regional devolution which have implications for existing states and nationalist assumptions (Keating, 1998). Both local and regional governments have long sought direct links with Brussels, and regional subsidies have become a growing element of the European budget. The Committee of Regions set up by the Maastricht Treaty further institution-alizes this strong regional element in European policy-making. Regional institutions potentially bypass the national state level, which is thus eroded from above and below. The principle of 'subsidiarity', used to justify tak-ing decisions at the national rather than European level, can equally be employed to devolve decision-making further to regional or local bod-ies. Thus there is some commonality of interest between those advocat-ing closer European union and more devolution of decision-making within states.

So far it has been assumed that the European ideal is incompatible with older more aggressive and exclusive forms of nationalism within Europe. However, the debate over the European constitution and EU enlargement has revived some awkward questions about European identity. In 2004 the European Union admitted ten more states from eastern and central Europe, and in 2007 Romania and Bulgaria joined, bringing the total number of member states to twenty-seven, with negotiations with other applicants (including Turkey) ongoing. This major and on-going enlargement raises not only economic concerns but more fundamental issues over Europe's boundaries and identity, not dissimilar in essence from issues raised by traditional nationalism. The 'natural frontiers' of Europe suggested by geography may not be the same as those indicated by language and culture. While the European Union has always been multi-lingual, questions remain over the very nature of European culture and civilisation. Some assume that to be European is to be white, an assumption which would, implicitly or explicitly, exclude the substantial black or Asian minorities from the European dream. A Christian Europe would rule out Muslim states or communities. European unity, like national unity, poses questions of identity that can be interpreted in an exclusive or inclusive way. The

European ideal has not been wholly successful in overcoming the narrow nationalist assumptions it theoretically transcends.

Globalisation, decentralisation and the future of nationalism

The movement towards European unity is just one among many trends in the modern world which appear incompatible with nationalist doctrines. Just as the rise of nationalism was connected with industrial modernisation and associated economic developments, so it can now be argued that in the modern post-industrial globalised economic and political environment nationalism is outdated. Global markets on the one hand, and pressures towards decentralisation on the other, have combined to render nationalism potentially redundant. It is increasingly clear that nation states can no longer immunise themselves from the international economy (if indeed they ever could). Movements in money or security markets in New York or Tokyo have immediate repercussions for London, and the operations of multinational corporations have massive implications for domestic economies, as became manifestly clear in the global banking crisis from 2007 onwards. The alleged greater vulnerability of small states to international financial crises has become a key argument in the debate over an independent Scotland. Unionists point to the collapse of Iceland and the need for UK government loans to rescue Scottish banks in 2008 to indicate the risks of independence. Salmond and the SNP respond that they could run the Scottish economy more effectively, and that other small states like Norway are surviving the crash. This is an argument that will be further debated if and when Scotland has a chance to vote on independence.

Similarly, developments in communication technology are rapidly creating a global culture. Just as industrialisation in the nineteenth century helped create a national culture instead of diverse regional and local cultures in many European states, so post-industrial society has created cultures that transcend national boundaries. Much popular music now finds an international audience. Television programmes may have a global market, particularly with the development of satellite and cable television. Regimes determined to preserve a distinctive national culture find it more difficult. While France still tries to restrict Anglo-American imports into its language and culture, former Communist regimes and the former apartheid regime in South Africa both failed to immunise their people from alternative perspectives and implicit promises held out by the western media.

But if nationalism is apparently being undermined by globalisation, it is also threatened by decentralisation. 'Fordist' assumptions about economies of scale, mass production and standardisation have given place to a 'post-Fordist' economy and society, where small is once again beautiful, and where the emphasis is on flexibility and meeting customers' requirements. Government and public services as well as the private sector are affected. In some European countries there has been a significant devolution of power from central government to regional and local authorities. In Britain and other western countries the introduction of increased competition and quasi-markets into the public sector has transformed patterns of service delivery. Whether power is really devolved to consumers is questionable, but there has been some decentralisation of decision-making to institutions, managers and professionals away from centralised bureaucracies. The 'free economy' has after all undermined the 'strong state' despite the Thatcherite attempt to combine them (Gamble, 1988). On the left, few desire a return to bureaucratic central control, or older models of centralised state socialism, despite continuing criticism of market individualism. More emphasis instead is placed on the values of community and locality.

The implications for mainstream nationalist ideology should be manifest. Nationalism suggests that national communities should have their own political and governmental framework in the form of sovereign independent nation states, perceived as the only level of government which ultimately counts. Yet increasingly the trend is towards multi-level governance where different levels of public institutions work with private and voluntary organisations, 'steering' or 'enabling' rather than 'rowing' (Rhodes, 1997; Pierre and Peters, 2000). Multi-level governance may be mirrored by multiple identities as 'a natural feature of the human condition' which increasingly may involve dual or multiple national, regional and civic loyalties (Davies, 1999, p. 874). Such developments reflect changes in the economy, society and technology that may prove irreversible. On this analysis, nationalism, the most potent political ideology of the nineteenth and twentieth centuries, is doomed to extinction.

Yet there is now little sign of the impending demise of nationalism. On the contrary, nationalism seems as vigorous as ever in most parts of the world, and has flourished in extreme forms particularly in former communist countries where a counter-ideology stressing universalism and international working-class solidarity has been inculcated for half a century or more. 'Peripheral' or 'separation' nationalism continues to thrive in parts of the western world and remains manifest over much of the third world also. While nationalism appears logically redundant in the post-modern, post-industrial, post-Fordist world, it continues to defy predictions.

However, if nationalism still seems extraordinarily potent, it remains a distinctly limited ideology. It provides a potential answer to just one, admittedly very important, political question facing humanity, the borders and authority of states. This may have some further implications for power and resources. Thus it may help transform a previously disadvantaged ethnic minority into a majority, yet equally it may create new minorities who complain they are now relatively disadvantaged. Beyond this, the ideology of nationalism provides little guidance on the conduct of international relations, on economic and social policy, taxation and expenditure, issues of personal morality and religion, gender issues, or issues affecting natural resources and the environment. Whenever a nationalist movement is successful, all these questions remain for the new nation to attempt to deal with.

Further reading

The literature on nationalism is extensive and growing. A useful if now dated critical survey is provided by Calhoun (1997). Contrasting interpretations are offered by Kedourie (4th edn, 1993), Gellner (1983), Anderson (1983), Breuilly (2nd edn, 1993), Hobsbawm (1990), Smith (1991), Greenfeld (1992) and Alter (1994). Extracts from nearly all these and much else besides can be found in a reader on nationalism by Hutchinson and Smith (1994). Hobsbawm's (1989, 1992, 1994) four volumes on modern history also contain valuable material on nationalism. Schwarzmantel (1991) illuminates the troubled relationship between nationalism and socialism, while Hutchinson (1994) is good on nationalism in the modern world.

It is more difficult to find books that can be confidently recommended on nationalism in Britain. Davies (1999) provides a stimulating corrective to Anglo-centric history. Colley (2003) is required reading on the making of the British nation in the eighteenth century. On the issue of national identity Crick (1991) has edited a collection of essays, while there has been a spate of books on English identity (for example Paxman, 1998). On Scottish nationalism McCrone (1992), Marr (1992) and especially Harvie (1994) are useful on the older background, while Nairn (1981, 2000, 2001) provides a provocative nationalist commentary on past history and recent developments. There is also now McGarvey and Cairney (2008) on Scottish politics. For nationalism and devolution in the UK, see short articles by Hall (2004) and Goodlad (2005), an edited book by O'Neill (2004), and chapters by McLean (in Seldon and Kavanagh, 2005) and Evans (in Beech and Lee, 2008).

On the European Union there is a huge literature. On the more specific questions relating to Britain and Europe see Young (1998), George (1998) and Gamble (2003). Globalisation also involves a large and growing literature – see Scholte (2005) for an overview and Ohmae (1990, 1996) for one view of the implications for nation states.

6

Racism and Fascism

Introduction

It may be questioned whether racism qualifies as an ideology and whether it rates a separate chapter in a book on political ideologies in Britain. It depends on how ideology is defined, itself a contentious issue (see Chapter 1). If, however, ideologies are 'action-oriented', their significance may be assessed more in terms of their implications for political behaviour than their degree of intellectual sophistication. Racism is an ideology with very significant political implications manifest in other societies past and present where overtly racist doctrines have been extensively promoted, sometimes officially by the state as in Hitler's Third Reich (Kershaw, 1993), or under the apartheid regime in South Africa.

In contemporary Britain, by contrast, overt racism has been long-excluded from elite political discourse. Mainstream politicians and respectable organs of opinion publicly repudiate racism, and public and private-sector organisations officially pledge themselves to combat racial prejudice and discrimination. Some forms of racist expression are punishable by law, and the accusation of racism is a serious charge to be hotly denied.

Yet although overt racism is an ideology which is officially 'beyond the pale', racist beliefs are widely held. In a 1997 survey, 32 per cent of British people described themselves as very or quite racist (Parekh, 2000a, p. 227), while politicians who publicly denounce racism have sometimes employed coded language to appease (or appeal to) racist sentiment, and pursued policies which are racist in effect and intention. However, it is the incontrovertible evidence of the persistent and extensive discrimination and disadvantage suffered by ethnic minorities which continues to provide the clearest evidence of the deeply-rooted prevalence of racism in Britain. For many blacks and Asians, racial prejudice and discrimination is a routine and inescapable element of their everyday lives.

In so far as racist ideas are examined at all in general surveys of political ideologies, it is commonly as a component of other ideologies, particularly fascism. Racism seems intellectually threadbare, partly because the concept of race no longer appears to have scientific validity, while fascism offers more substance for analysis. It was once presented as a serious and comprehensive ideology, with pretensions to offer a middle way between liberal capitalism and bolshevism. Its culmination in the horrors of the holocaust may have totally discredited fascism for the bulk of humanity, but also provided a dire warning of where racism can lead.

Yet to examine racist ideas largely or exclusively within the context of fascism is to risk underestimating their importance. Racism existed before fascism (and was not even a key element of Mussolini's fascism originally) and survived fascism's defeat. In Britain, the full fascist ideology was an alien creed which never presented a serious threat to the political mainstream. British fascists did not create racism, although they sought to exploit racist feelings and exacerbated racial tensions. Yet, ultimately, it is racism rather than fascism which remains a significant feature of domestic British politics. In this chapter, therefore, the main focus will be on racism, and fascism will be examined in connection with racism.

Racist ideology: critical issues

Racism has been very variously defined, but virtually all definitions stress the implications of racist beliefs for behaviour. Thus, on one formulation, racism is 'any political or social belief that justifies treating people differently according to their racial origins' (Robertson, 1993, p. 404). Racist doctrine does not bear close examination, for it is now accepted that there is no scientific basis for the division of humanity into distinct races. Even so, many people still cling to racist assumptions and for some 'race' remains the key political divide that informs their whole political outlook and behaviour.

Moreover, the study of ideologies is not only concerned with the consequences of political convictions, but how people come to hold those convictions. Even if racism is regarded as intellectually untenable and morally repugnant, it is still important to analyse how and why people come to hold racist views. Is racism the consequence of the deliberate stirring of racial, ethnic or religious fears by politicians (mainstream or fascist) for their own ends, or the by-product of religious convictions or prejudices (such as anti-semitism, Islamophobia), or the legacy of imperialism and slavery, or the consequence of inequality and deprivation? Is racism essentially about 'colour' prejudice, or can racial conflict involve communities with similar skin colours? Is it largely or exclusively a white problem (as has sometimes been suggested), or can blacks and Asians be racist?

Different explanations for racial prejudice clearly may have different policy implications. There are important questions about the efficacy of outlawing discrimination, about the scope and limits of educational policy, over the rights of ethnic minorities and the advisability of 'positive discrimination' in their favour. More fundamentally, there has been a shift from past 'colour-blind' policies designed to promote the integration and assimilation of ethnic minorities, towards the acceptance of difference and the perceived benefits of multiculturalism (see Chapter 7).

The origins and development of racism – physical, cultural and religious differences

Theories of the division of humanity into distinctive races were not elaborated until the eighteenth and nineteenth centuries. However, from the earliest times human societies have observed distinctions between themselves and others, particularly when they came across people with different physical characteristics, such as skin colour, hair or height. Such physical differences were easily identified, but perceptive observers, such as the ancient Greek historian Herodotus, also noted that other peoples held markedly different beliefs and behaved differently. Thus, from the start, perceptions of peoples involved both physical and cultural distinctions. Other civilisations sometimes evoked interested curiosity and even admiration, but more commonly differentiation was accompanied by negative evaluation, and sometimes fear. Ancient Greeks and Romans looked down on, but also feared, 'barbarians' outside their Greco-Roman civilisation, with some reason because of the military threat they presented, but they did not normally perceive other cultures or more specifically other religions as a threat. Indeed, the gods worshipped by other peoples were commonly seen as different versions of their own divinities.

Yet many of the great religions which came to dominate the world were rather more exclusive in the demands they made of their followers, and 'other peoples' might often exhibit a mix of different physical and cultural characteristics, generally evaluated extremely negatively. Thus medieval Christians scorned and feared 'heathens', Jews and Moslems. 'The Islamic Other was portrayed as barbaric, degenerate and tyrannical, and these alleged characteristics were considered to be rooted in the character of Islam as a supposedly false and heretic theology' (Miles, 1989, p. 18). Yet Christianity and Islam were competing creeds and the threat from Islam was real enough to Christians in parts of Europe, while Christian crusades posed a similar threat elsewhere to Islam. By contrast, the threat from Jews was almost wholly imaginary. Jews were targeted as an 'enemy within' partly on religious grounds (the rejection and crucifixion of Christ), but also partly because of their involvement in banking and finance, which rendered them both useful but resented. Fantastic stories of secret Jewish practices fed anti-Jewish feeling. This periodically led to persecution and violent attacks on the Jewish community in many countries, including Britain.

Colonialism and imperialism

Exploration and trade brought Europeans into more extensive contact with other peoples and civilisations, particularly from the fifteenth century onwards. This led to negative and pejorative assessments of other people as 'cruel', 'savage' and 'heathen', although there was also a minority, more positive assessment, sometimes associated with notions of 'lost innocence' and the 'noble savage'. Exploration and trade often led in turn to colonisation and western imperialism. While this phase in European history is now almost universally condemned, it is important to recognise the diversity of the colonisation process. Some European settlers were 'asylum seekers' – victims of religious persecution in their country of origin – and sought a new life of freedom in the 'new world'. Some were convicts deported as a punishment. Some were 'economic migrants' driven by relative poverty and lack of opportunity. Some were adventurers on the make. Some even saw imperialism as a noble and inspiring cause – a 'white man's burden' to bring the benefits of western law, religion and education to less fortunate peoples (although the reality was generally otherwise). The attitudes of colonists to indigenous peoples likewise varied. Some were regarded as heathen savages, who might be exploited or even enslaved, but equally might, more paternalistically, be 'converted' and 'civilized'. Other cultures (for example India) were sometimes initially treated with more respect (Saggar, 1992, p. 17).

White racism is often plausibly attributed to the past history of European colonial exploitation, and more particularly slavery. Thus, it is suggested, slavery was both a product of western assumptions of black racial inferiority and reinforced those assumptions. Moreover, the ideology of imperialism and the linked assumption of white superiority was spread and reinforced through education and popular culture in the nineteenth and early twentieth centuries. Today, the sizeable black and Asian minorities in the UK population are clearly a legacy of empire (or the 'colonial diaspora'), in that most of them are descended from immigrants from the 'new commonwealth' or old empire. To that extent, tensions between the majority white population and ethnic minorities might also be fairly regarded as a product of empire. Yet it is questionable whether modern white racism in Britain today is largely the product of past imperialist assumptions rather than contemporary experiences and misconceptions. Britain's former empire is now recalled with more shame than pride, but is generally shrouded in collective amnesia.

Thus it seems misguided to relate racism largely or exclusively to imperialism. Racist attitudes preceded the European colonial period and have survived its collapse. Anti-semitism, one of the most persistent and extreme forms of racism, owes nothing to colonialism and the past domination of blacks and Asians by whites. Some contemporary racism is directed against peoples who were never colonised in the conventional sense – against Turkish *Gastarbeiter* (guestworkers) in Germany and eastern European asylum seekers in Britain. Moreover, as these examples suggest, although 'colour prejudice' is a familiar form of racism, racist attitudes are not always linked to distinctions based on skin colour. Anti-Irish prejudice and derogatory observations on the Irish 'race' have a long history in Britain, although this 'anti-Irish racism' has often been ignored or downplayed (Mac an Ghaill, 1999, pp. 77–80). The linked contention that racism is largely or exclusively a 'white' characteristic also seems untenable in the face of fairly extensive evidence of prejudice between, for example, blacks and Asians (Phizacklea and Miles, 1980, pp. 181–3). Rather, it seems that what would now be called racism is a long-standing and widespread aspect of human beliefs and behaviour, although its precise form is clearly influenced by specific historical experiences.

'Scientific' racism

Much of this racism was, however serious its effects, not extensively rationalised nor related to any systematic theory of racial difference. Indeed, in so far as attempts were made to explain observable differences between peoples in physical appearance or behaviour, these were commonly linked to environmental factors such as climate rather than attributed to innate biological differences. A commonplace division of humankind into different races in the early modern period was based on observed differences in skin colour – white, brown, yellow, red and black, although these colours were always crude and inaccurate descriptions of the subtle range of pigments of human skin.

This changed with the development of 'scientific racism' from the late eighteenth century onwards. The application of science to the previously rather arbitrary and imprecise concept of race led to extensive measurement, classification and theorising. Much of this work seems to have been inspired by genuine scientific curiosity, rather than aimed merely to legitimate racial prejudice. There were observable physical differences between peoples, and cultural differences also, and it seemed a reasonable object of scientific enquiry to determine more precisely the extent of these variations and the links between them, and to produce a more comprehensive scientific theory of racial differences. Some of this work initially appeared to confirm that there were a number of distinctive human races whose differences were innate. Scientific theorising was extensively supported by measurements of head shapes, hair colour and structure, eye colour and, most significantly, cranial capacity, which implied some races might naturally be more intelligent than others. Unsurprisingly perhaps, 'science' seemed to confirm the expectations of European investigators, and was used to support some of the racist doctrines that were beginning to circulate, including the notion of a Nordic/Aryan master race that was destined to rule over other 'inferior' races.

Later in the nineteenth century, Darwin's theory of evolution was misapplied to indicate that some races had evolved to reach a higher level than others, although Darwin's work really made nonsense of the whole notion of fixed and innate biological differences which underpinned scientific racism (Miles, 1989, p. 36). Darwin's concept of the survival of the fittest was misused to serve racist ideas by its adaptation to justify a necessary and inevitable struggle between human races for supremacy in which victory validated claims to superiority. Thus the race or people who conquered in war, or secured the largest empire, 'proved' they were the highest race. In this way 'social Darwinism' served to justify imperialism.

The assumption that there were distinct races hierarchically ordered also implied that a superior race might be damaged or weakened by intermingling with an inferior race. This reinforced pre-existing prejudices against immigration. Thus, the purity of the Anglo-Saxon or Aryan race might be undermined by the increasing presence in their midst of Jews, Irish or eastern Europeans. Among the consequences of these fears, apparently legitimated by science, were increasing restrictions to immigration on implicitly and often explicitly racist grounds, such as the Aliens Act passed in Britain in 1905.

By the time scientific racism was to receive its most complete endorsement in Hitler's Third Reich, the scientific world was retreating fast from the whole concept to the extent that race was declared a pseudo-scientific term. Scientists concluded that classification of people by racial type was subjective rather than objective, and 'race' did not determine mental or physical ability, or behavioural characteristics. After the Second World War scientific or biological racism was totally discredited. Yet this did not mean the end of notions of race and racist ideas, which had existed before scientific racism, and survived its refutation.

Fascism and Nazism

Any analysis of racism can hardly avoid some reference to fascism and Nazism, as it was notoriously Hitler's Nazi regime that most systematically adopted and applied racist doctrine. The horrors of the 'final solution' have become so inseparably linked with fascism to marginalise other elements of the ideology.

Yet fascism, in Mussolini's original form, was not particularly racist; it was always a strange amalgam of ideas. Linz (in Laqueur, 1979, p. 15) has referred to 'the essential anti-character of its ideology and appeal', and indeed it is easier to describe it in terms of what it was against rather than what it was for. Thus fascism can be seen as involving a reaction against the rationalism, individualism, liberalism and parliamentarism which constituted the mainstream European tradition from the eighteenth-century Enlightenment onwards (see Chapter 2). It stood for national loyalty rather than class loyalty, the state rather than the individual, action rather than intellectual debate, leadership, discipline, order and military virtues rather than the mundane liberal democratic values of bargaining and compromise. It looked back to an imagined heroic past which emphasised traditional values, but it also gloried in and exploited modern technology, particularly the modern mass media. It claimed to offer planned economic growth and higher living standards through a 'middle way' between liberal capitalism and revolutionary communism, in which labour and capital would be brought together in corporations to serve the interests of the whole state and people.

In practice, the boasted achievements of fascism were more cosmetic than real, and Mussolini's regime was always a rather squalid dictatorship which involved the silencing of opposition by brutal intimidation and violence. However, while Mussolini was certainly an aggressive nationalist, he was not in the usual sense of the term a racist, and indeed, he initially referred rather contemptuously to the racial doctrine of the German Nazis, and spurned the eager admiration of Hitler (who came to power a full decade later). Fascism was Mussolini's creation and he regarded imitators with some suspicion. Yet, effectively, Nazism has absorbed fascism in the public mind. Although some academics would still prefer to distinguish between fascism and Nazism, the two terms have come to be used interchangeably.

While Hitler's Nazism certainly shared many of the key characteristics of Mussolini's fascism, its distinguishing feature was the racist theory and practice with which it will ever be associated. Hitler took on board the 'scientific' racial theories of the nineteenth century, such as the Frenchman Comte de Gobineau. Gobineau discerned not only differences in physical characteristics, but also in intelligence, attitudes and behaviour between Aryans (Europeans, or more specifically northern or Nordic Europeans) and the yellow (Asian) or black (African) races. Men were not all equal. Some races were inferior to others. Moreover, the mixture of races would lead to degeneration. Hitler adapted Gobineau's typology of races to promote the notion of a pure Aryan master race, destined to rule not only over those with different skin colours but over Slavs and other inferior races in Europe. Yet although Hitler's racism was directed against all non-Aryans, his hatred was concentrated particularly on the Jews.

The Jews had faced persecution for centuries in Europe, largely on religious grounds, although hostility to Jews often persisted even against those who converted to Christianity and sought to assimilate. It was only in the nineteenth century that negative evaluations of Jews came to be related to their supposed race, the Semites (who incidentally included both Jews and neighbouring Arab peoples). Anti-semitism was the theme of several books published in Germany and France in the late nineteenth and early twentieth centuries. One writer in particular influenced Hitler, the Englishman Houston Stewart Chamberlain, who argued that the future of civilisation depended on a life and death struggle between the chosen Aryan people and the evil Semites. Hitler absorbed and developed these ideas which he expressed in *Mein Kampf*, and later sought to implement in Germany and subsequently in Europe. After the Nazis came to power in 1933 racism and anti-semitism became the ideology of the Third Reich, taught in schools, (where biology textbooks showed pupils how to distinguish the physical characteristics of Jews) and embodied in German law. While other inferior races could be exploited for the benefit of the master race, the 'final solution' of the Jewish question involved extermination. Against the deliberate policy of the wholesale genocide of the Jews, other elements of fascist ideology have paled into insignificance (Kershaw, 1993). It was ultimately Hitler's version of the ideology that came to define what fascism was about. Fascism became racism, and racism pushed to hitherto unimaginable extremes.

While fascism and Nazism did not create racism and anti-semitism, the pre-existing conscious and unconscious racial prejudices of many were legitimated, encouraged and employed in the service of a state in which racism was the official orthodoxy. Anti-semitism had certainly been a feature of German society before Hitler came to power, but Germans had not been markedly more anti-semitic than Poles, Russians, French or British. Indeed, the German Jewish community had appeared more fully and successfully integrated into German society than Jews in many other countries. The apparent ease with which the Nazis applied race hate, and ultimately genocide, in an apparently advanced and civilised country suggests that other societies might be equally vulnerable. This was demonstrably true in many of the countries occupied by the Nazis, where willing collaborators helped round up Jews for transportation to death camps, and sometimes were directly involved in atrocities.

The defeat of the Axis powers in 1945 did not completely destroy the fascist and Nazi ideologies. These had an afterlife in watered-down form in parts of South America (where some surviving Nazis fled) and, in small extremist parties, in parts of the European continent. One apparent surviving exception to the defeat of fascism in Europe was the Iberian peninsula, where Franco's regime survived until his death in 1975. Yet although Franco's victory in the Spanish Civil War owed a debt to Mussolini and Hitler, and he imitated some aspects of Italian fascism, he remained essentially an old-fashioned military dictator. His regime was conservative, authoritarian, nationalist and (in contrast with the Third Reich) religious, rather than fascist. Elsewhere in Europe, neo-fascist or neo-Nazi parties fitfully flourished from time to time on the political fringe, usually by exploiting concerns over immigration and prejudice against ethnic minorities. But although racism survived and thrived, the full ideology of fascism was confined to a generally insignificant lunatic fringe.

Fascism in Britain

Had Britain been defeated in the Second World War there is little doubt that collaborators with the occupying forces would have been found, particularly perhaps from those in Britain who had openly espoused fascism, or who had expressed sympathy for Hitler. Yet although fascism had attracted some support in the early 1930s even before war was declared with Nazi Germany, it was already a spent force. It has never attracted a significant political following since.

The roots of British fascism lay in a number of small extreme right-wing nationalist and racist groups founded before, during and immediately after the First World War (Thurlow, 1987, pp. 1–61). Some of them were established to campaign against immigration, particularly of Jews from Eastern Europe, which led to the racist Aliens Act of 1905. Prejudice against Jews, long a feature of British society, became particularly virulent amid fears of relative British decline and the degeneration of the Anglo-Saxon 'race'. During the First World War those perceived to be of foreign origin (including both Jews and Germans), were suspect as potential traitors. After the war there was a ready market for international Jewish conspiracy theories, commonly inspired by forged documents such as the notorious *Protocols of the Elders of Zion*. Jews were convenient scapegoats, indiscriminately blamed for the excesses and failures of capitalism on the one hand and Bolshevism on the other, for fears of the 'socialist menace' were another major concern (Benewick, 1972, ch. 2; Thurlow, 1987, pp. 62–91). Some right-wing groups in Britain labelled themselves 'fascist' following Mussolini's rise to power in 1922. However, the British Fascists consciously or unconsciously followed Mussolini in being 'insufficiently anti-Semitic' for the taste of some right-wing nationalists (Thurlow, 1987, p. 53). Another organisation, the Imperial Fascist League, was strongly anti-semitic from the start.

It was only when an already established politician with a national reputation was converted to fascism that it was briefly taken seriously. Oswald Mosley had pursued a chequered career across the party political spectrum, starting as a Conservative MP before crossing the floor to become briefly a Labour Minister, and finally the leader of the New Party, soon converted into the British Union of Fascists (BUF). This quickly absorbed most of the tiny older fascist groups (Skidelsky, 1990). Mosley's capabilities have perhaps been exaggerated, but he was certainly (like Mussolini and Hitler) a gifted platform orator, capable of whipping up a crowd. Yet although the activities of Mosley and the BUF for a time alarmed the authorities, they never, in retrospect, represented a significant threat to the British political scene. It would be comforting to assume that the BUF's increasingly strident anti-semitism was unacceptable to most Britons, but the relative failure of British fascism was more down to other factors. Unlike Germany, Britain had not been defeated and humiliated in the 1914–18 war. As compared with Italy or Germany, parliamentary democracy was longer and more securely established, society less deeply divided, economic difficulties, although severe enough, less catastrophic. A particular problem was that fascism drew on extreme nationalism, but in Britain the fascist role models, Germany and Italy, were increasingly viewed as national enemies. Support for fascism (never very significant) crumbled once it appeared incompatible with British patriotism, particularly after war with Germany was declared.

Yet if fascism never caught on in Britain, racist ideas were (and remain) widespread in British society. In so far as fascism achieved any temporary appeal it was not because of the attractions of totalitarian-ism, elitist theory, the corporate state, autarchy, or other elements of fascism as propounded by Mussolini's tame philosophers, but because of its anti-semitism and racism. Mosley himself does not seem to have been particularly anti-semitic or racist in his earlier political career, and even in his fascist phase generally avoided openly racist or anti-semitic language. Yet his leading henchmen were far less restrained and his movement became increasingly anti-semitic and racist, in imitation of the Nazis, because this played well in areas such as the East End of London where there was long-established hostility to the Jewish com-munity. But it was not British fascism that created racism, rather it was pre-existing racism which sustained, for a time, British fascism.

The same is true after the Second World War, when Mosley himself formally renounced the fascist label, although his new Union Movement was little more than a renamed BUF, and his reformed creed, which included support for European unity, was not unreasonably described as 'Euro-fascism'. His occasional forays into British politics owed little to these refinements of his political message but essentially involved exploiting racism – against 'coloured immigrants' rather than Jews – in the East End and areas such as the West Midlands.

Similarly, although some of the leading activists of other far-right parties such as the National Front or the British National Party (BNP) endorsed the full fascist ideology and at one time showed a predilection for dressing up in Nazi uniforms, their appeal was essentially confined to racism (Walker, 1977; Taylor, 1982). Indeed, the fascist and Nazi associations were a distinct handicap, as anti-racists recognised when they set up the Anti-Nazi League and campaigned on the effective slogan 'The National Front is a Nazi Front'.

In so far as the British National Party, under its leader Nick Griffin, has more recently secured a slightly larger share of the vote than earlier far right parties, it has been by cultivating a more respectable image and exchanging the trappings of fascism for smart suits, although it is immigration and race that remain central to the party's electoral appeal. Yet its support remains fairly modest compared with racist or neo-fascist parties on the European continent. In 1997 the average vote secured by 57 BNP candidates was only 1.3 per cent. In 2001 the party put up fewer candidates (33) but these gained a higher average vote of 3.9 per cent (Butler and Butler, 2007, p. 70). In 2005 the party put up many more candidates, double the number in 1997 and almost four times as many as in 2001, and managed to save its deposit by winning more than 5 per cent of the vote in 34 seats (Peele in Dunleavy *et al.*, 2006, p. 209). Of course, such figures involve considerable variations between individual constituencies. The party secured 17 per cent of the vote in Barking, 13 per cent in Dewsbury and 9 per cent in Keighley after a highly publicised campaign featuring the BNP leader (Geddes in Geddes and Tonge, 2005, pp. 289–90). Even so, the party remains a long way from winning a single parliamentary seat.

Immigration and race in modern Britain – a new racism?

Yet the extent of racism in Britain should not be measured by the support attracted by far right overtly racist parties. Indeed, racism remains widespread in Britain, despite the discrediting of the whole concept of race as 'an idea that should be explicitly and consistently confined to the dustbin of analytically useless terms' (Miles, 1989, p. 72). Miles, indeed, only uses the term 'race' in quotation marks, and insists that the focus of analysis should be on the ideology of racism and the process of racialisation rather than the bogus concept of race. He further argues that the official use of the term in Britain in, for example, 'Race Relations Acts', legitimises differences which have no scientific validity. Thus racism is unwittingly reinforced by policies ostensibly designed to combat it. Some have continued to use the term 'race' as a concept familiar in modern everyday usage, but linking it primarily with culture rather than biology. Others have preferred the broader, more culturally oriented term 'ethnicity', but while this avoids the bogus scientific overtones of race, it lacks precision (Kohn, *New Statesman*, 30 July 2001, p. 12).

However, much of the official public debate in the decades after the Second World War did not refer to the forbidden discourse of 'race' but to immigration. Britain had, over centuries, experienced waves of immigration, so it was hardly a new phenomenon or a new concern. Moreover, legal controls over immigration had been introduced in the first half of the twentieth century through a series of Alien Acts and Orders from 1905 onwards (Solomos, 2003, pp. 43–4). However, renewed concerns were raised by the increasing numbers of immigrants from the British Empire and Commonwealth who were officially UK citizens with a right of entry to the 'mother country' (Saggar, 1992, pp. 66–85). Immigration controls pursued by both Conservative and Labour governments from 1962 onwards were effectively and intentionally racist (Solomos, 2003, pp. 56–9). Ostensibly the concern was with the *numbers* of immigrants entering Britain in the post-war period, but as ministers privately admitted, they were not worried about immigrants from the old (white) Commonwealth but only about immigrants from the 'new' (or black and Asian) Commonwealth. The real concern was over what was then termed 'coloured' immigration, and the resulting 'racial tension' that could result (Solomos, 2003, pp. 51–6).

An uglier populist and explicitly racist rhetoric lurked behind the bland elite debate. A Conservative candidate won a seat against the general Labour swing in the 1964 election on the slogan 'If you want a nigger neighbour, vote Labour' (Butler and King, 1965, p. 361; see also Solomos, 2003, pp. 59–60). Yet measures to outlaw racial discrimination and to promote good 'race relations' and integration accompanied controls on immigration. This 'twin-track' approach reflected a bipartisan political consensus on race issues for much of the 1960s and 1970s. The Conservative politician Enoch Powell challenged that consensus. He dramatically prophesied 'rivers of blood' from continuing immigration in 1968. Although Powell acquired a populist following, he effectively destroyed his own political prospects as he was sacked from the Conservative Shadow Cabinet by Ted Heath (Saggar, 1992, pp. 109–13).

Subsequently, some leading Conservative politicians employed more coded language to express sympathy with the fears of 'ordinary people' that increasing numbers of 'immigrants', 'ethnic minorities' or 'asylum seekers' threatened their own traditional values and ways of living. Thus Margaret Thatcher in 1978 referred to a 'fear' that the 'British character' might be 'swamped' by 'those coming in', while Norman Tebbit aroused concerns over the allegiance of ethnic minorities through his 'cricket test', which asked whether blacks and Asians supported England or from countries where their families had lived cricket teams, such as the West Indies, India and Pakistan (Kingdom 1999, p. 189). More recently, William Hague's Conservative Conference 2000 vision of a future Britain as a foreign land was widely linked to fears of asylum seekers, although the speech was more obviously directed against a European 'superstate'. Michael Howard's election campaign in 2005 made a central issue of immigration, which was mentioned fifteen times in the Conservative manifesto. Some Conservative candidates raised the issue more bluntly. Thus, Robert Spink (in Castle Point) asked 'What part of send them back don't you understand, Mr Blair?' (Geddes and Tonge, 2005, p. 286).

The racism which has been more recently, covertly or overtly, expressed in Britain has sometimes been termed a 'new racism', based not on biology but on perceived differences in culture between communities. The new racism reflected an assumption that humans naturally seek to form bounded communities or nations, which they perceive as different from other communities or nations, and which they wish to protect (Barker, 1981, p. 21). This new racism is linked closely with a form of nationalism. 'Its focus is the defence of the mythic "British/ English way of life" in the face of attack from enemies outside . . . and within' (Solomos and Back, 1996, p. 18). Thus 'Peter Simple' of the *Daily Telegraph* lamented that

> the people of England ... have seen everything that is distinctively English suppressed and derided... They have seen their decent manners and customs corrupted... They have seen part of their country colonised by immigrants and been forbidden by law to speak freely of the consequences. (Quoted in Paxman, 1998, pp. 70–1)

Yet although the new racism is supposed to relate to cultural rather than physical differences, the two are often implicitly or explicitly linked. Indeed, most idealised images of Britain, and more particularly England, relate to a past not shared by ethnic minorities, so that 'Englishness' and a black skin seem almost mutually exclusive. Powell denied that a 'West Indian or Indian' born in England could become English: 'In law he becomes a United Kingdom citizen by birth; in fact he is a West Indian or Asian still' (quoted in Saggar, 1992, p. 113). Thus, according to Miles (1993, p. 75) 'English nationalism encapsulates racism'. Miles denies that modern racism is essentially new, arguing, firstly, that crude 'scientific' racism survives in contemporary expression despite its official discrediting, and, secondly, that cultural racism is still underpinned by implicit notions of biological inheritance and physical differences.

Racism and class

Racism has been persuasively associated with economic deprivation and class relations under capitalism (Phizacklea and Miles, 1980). Although some 'Asians' (particularly Indians and East African Asians) are middle-class and relatively integrated and successful in British society, the majority of the black and Asian ethnic minorities are employed in manual work, and many live in racially segregated and economically deprived urban areas. As a 'fraction' of the working class, they are perceived to be competing for jobs, houses and services with members of the white working class inhabiting the same deprived urban environment. Both working-class white racism, and the aggressive response of young black and Asian males to racism can be seen as the consequence of economic decline and deprivation. 'Racial' conflict is a symptom rather than the cause of the problem.

Such an (essentially Marxist) analysis provides a convincing explanation not only of the recent 'race riots' in British towns and cities, but also of working-class anti-semitism in the East End of London, and much anti-Irish racism over the last two centuries in Britain. Moreover, such examples underline the point that it is not necessarily colour, or other observable physical differences, or even necessarily clear cultural differences which drive racism. Yet if economic conflict and deprivation provides a substantial explanation for racism, it hardly provides a sufficient explanation. While anti-semitism flourished in working-class areas, it was also common among the middle classes (who often attempted to exclude Jews from their golf clubs and other social institutions) and particularly among the upper classes.

Racism, religion, and religious fundamentalism

Differences in religious observance were obviously an element behind this cross-class anti-semitism. They have become an increasingly evident aspect of racism directed against 'Asians' today. Much of the early post-war racism in Britain was directed against black West Indian immigrants who shared many aspects of British culture, including Christianity. In the 1950s and 1960s the 'Asians' who 'kept themselves to themselves' were less often perceived as a 'cause of trouble' and were less conspicuously victims of white racism. By the late twentieth and early twenty-first centuries it was the 'Asians' who had become the main target for white racists, and relations between whites and Asians became the focus of much anguished analysis. In part, this simply reflected the growth in numbers of Asians as opposed to Afro-Caribbeans, and the particularly severe economic problems of industries and towns into which Asian migrants had been drawn, but it was exacerbated by increasingly manifest religious differences. Relatively few Asian immigrants were Christian. Many were Muslim, Hindu or Sikh, and temples of an oriental appearance became a feature of the urban landscape where Asians had settled in any numbers. There were conspicuous differences in dress and diet also that marked the adherents of some of these religions from their fellow citizens. Muslims appeared particularly distinctive, and over the last decade or so Islamophobia has become a marked aspect of anti-Asian racism.

An early catalyst for Islamophobia was the Rushdie affair that served to reinforce some existing prejudices, but also alienated many liberals. The publication of Salman Rushdie's *The Satanic Verses* in 1989 was perceived by many Muslims as an insult to their faith and their identity. Angry Muslim demonstrations in Britain and elsewhere culminated in the declaration of a *fatwa* (effectively a death sentence) by the Ayatollah Khomeini, and Rushdie went into hiding under police protection. The issue drew attention to Islamic fundamentalism. A *Daily Telegraph* editorial observed 'there must be increased pessimism about how far different communities in our nation can ever be integrated or want to be.' (*Daily Telegraph,* 17 May 1989, quoted by Solomos, 2003, p. 214). The Rushdie affair severely damaged relations between the Muslim community, the British establishment and the wider public. As Solomos (2003, p. 215) observes 'many on the left found it impossible to sympathise with the arguments of the radical Islamic groups.' Muslims everywhere found themselves regarded as dangerous fundamentalists. As one Muslim has sardonically observed:

> while 'Asian' and 'Indian' suggest amorphous yet containable differences, 'Muslim' describes a specific and volatile difference. Muslims are not simply a brand of believers: they are rampant, dangerous and impenetrably different believers. (Sardar, *New Statesman*, 30 July 2001, p. 16)

Yet this may exaggerate the capacity of many 'whites' to discriminate between 'Asians'. Indeed, 'Asian' and 'Muslim' have become so associated in popular consciousness that it is sometimes assumed that an 'Asian' is a Muslim, when they may be Hindu, Sikh or Christian. Religion, rather than skin colour, has become the defining mark of the community, although colour provides a ready, if highly misleading, means of identification. Thus for some, brown skin means 'Muslim', and 'Muslim' means 'Islamic fundamentalist', regardless of distinctions between and, indeed, within faiths.

This became more evident after the attack on the World Trade Centre on 11 September 2001, followed by Britain's involvement in the Afghanistan and Iraq wars, and the subsequent terrorist attacks in London on 7 July 2005, perpetrated by British Muslims, leading to 'revenge attacks' on the predominantly moderate British Muslim community and even on non-Muslim Asians. Religious differences have become bound up with racism and have fuelled prejudice. That religion can be an element in racism or ethnic conflict has long been evident from anti-semitism, as well as the experience of northern Ireland and many other parts of the world.

Racism, asylum seekers and Europe

Most of the immigration into Britain until the 1990s involved economic migrants from the British Commonwealth and former empire. Relatively few were driven out from their country of origin, although East African Asians were one conspicuous exception. These were an early wave of a phenomenon, refugees seeking asylum, which has become more familiar of late. Some of those who sought asylum came from former British colonies, such as Kenya or Hong Kong, and British governments acknowledged a particular responsibility in these cases. Yet increasingly, Britain, along with many other countries, was also accepting political refugees from other non-Commonwealth trouble spots, in accordance with international obligations. Moreover, there were also numbers of illegal immigrants, some escaping persecution, others simply poverty and hopeless prospects in the countries they had left.

'Asylum seekers' became the new pejorative term freely used by the tabloid press, extremist groups and some mainstream politicians to categorise these new immigrants. Commonly, the adjectives 'bogus' or 'illegal' were routinely added, to further demonise them. It was widely alleged that the number of asylum seekers was large, rising and out of control. Yet, while there was widespread condemnation of the numbers of asylum seekers, bogus or otherwise, entering Britain, there was also, paradoxically, often strong local community support for individual asylum seekers threatened with deportation back to their country of origin. Also, some asylum seekers had some claim on British hospitality as it might be reasonably suggested that their plight was a direct or indirect consequence of British policy (for example, some Iraqi refugees).

Alongside increased numbers of asylum seekers, there were also many quite legal migrants from the European Union. The expansion of the European Union in 2004 and further expansion in 2007 brought in several relatively poorer countries from eastern Europe. The principle of the free movement of labour within the EU allowed economic migrants from these countries to seek work in the west, although some temporary controls were introduced by some states to moderate the numbers taking advantage. Britain, like other older members of the EU, received numbers of workers from eastern Europe. Some of these met skill shortages, such as the legendary Polish plumbers. Others took work such as fruit picking too poorly paid to attract British workers. In both cases, it could be argued that the British economy benefited, although there were allegations that some employers were ignoring minimum wage and/or health and safety regulations, and that the incomers were undercutting British workers.

Some of these European migrant workers may settle permanently in Britain, joining communities of previous Italian, Greek and Polish immigrants that have made a life here from the Second World War onwards. Others are only here for the short term, planning to return home later. Indeed, some, disillusioned with work and conditions in Britain, have already returned. Economic opportunities in Britain, as in other countries, have declined with the recent slowdown.

Institutional racism

It remains difficult to equate the relative absence of overt racism in mainstream British politics and polite society with the continued evidence of extensive discrimination and disadvantage suffered by ethnic minorities in their everyday lives. The concept of institutional racism provides one possible answer – racist assumptions are so embedded in society and societal institutions that racist outcomes result, even in the absence of overt racist attitudes. The concept was developed by race theorists in the United States, who suggested that racism was deeply ingrained in American society as a consequence of the historical experience of slavery and racial segregation. Thus, the dominant white group continued to exclude and disadvantage the black subordinate group, without necessarily deliberately intending that outcome.

Miles (1989, pp. 50–61) has argued that this interpretation of institutional racism involves 'conceptual inflation'. As institutional racism 'denies that intentionality or motivation are measures of the presence or absence of racism' it does not constitute an ideology in Miles' own understanding of the term. Miles himself (1993, p. 74) confusingly employs the term institutional racism to mean institutionally or officially recognised racism. Thus, he argues that British legislation on immigration involved an 'institutionalization of racism' by the British state which 'legitimated common-sense racism'. Yet for Miles this 'institutional racism' not only in practice discriminated on grounds of 'race' or 'colour', but intentionally discriminated on those grounds without acknowledging a racist purpose.

Other British scholars have employed the term 'institutional racism' in a sense broadly derived from the American use of the concept, but have sometimes applied it more narrowly to specific institutions whose practices might be 'unwittingly discriminatory' against black people. The term became more widely familiar as a result of the Macpherson Inquiry (1999) into the conduct of the police in response to the murder of the black teenager, Stephen Lawrence. An internal police inquiry found no evidence to support the allegation of racist conduct by officers, who 'roundly denied racism or racist conduct'. The Macpherson Inquiry agreed that it had not 'heard evidence of overt racism or discrimination' but did nevertheless conclude that the Metropolitan Police Service (MPS) was 'institutionally racist' according to the Inquiry's own definition of the term:

> The collective failure of an organisation to provide an appropriate and professional service to people because of their colour, culture, or ethnic origin. It can be seen or detected in processes, attitudes and behaviour which amount to discrimination through unwitting prejudice, ignorance, thoughtlessness and racist stereotyping which disadvantage minority ethnic people. (Macpherson, 1999, p. 28)

Other evidence to the Inquiry accepted that institutional racism was a feature of police forces elsewhere in the country and reflected 'racism which is inherent in wider society which shapes our attitudes and behaviour' (Macpherson, 1999, p. 31), a perspective which comes closer to the American use of the term. However, the Inquiry's conclusion that the Metropolitan Police Service was institutionally racist was widely interpreted in the media and the police service to mean that all police officers who belonged to the MPS were themselves racists, almost the opposite of the argument advanced in the report. Indeed, one criticism of the whole concept of institutional racism is that it too readily acquits individuals of responsibility for racist attitudes and behaviour. The acknowledgement that 'we are all guilty' often means in practice that no one is.

Anti-racism

Anti-racist ideas would not need to be articulated in a society that did not recognise racial differences nor discriminate on racial grounds. It is only the prevalence in British society of racist ideas that seriously and adversely affect ethnic minorities which has provoked the dissemination of a counter-ideology of anti-racism. Perhaps inevitably, the emphasis of anti-racism has been negative rather than positive – to attack politicians, groups or parties disseminating racist ideas, to root out racist discrimination and prejudice, and ban racist language. Anti-racism has been successful in securing formal commitments to anti-discrimination and equal opportunities policies from public and private-sector bodies, and the establishment of special committees and units to combat racism on local councils.

Yet it is questionable how far anti-racism has really changed ideas and lessened ethnic conflicts. Indeed, to many it is anti-racism rather than racism that is perceived as the problem. Because racism is so embedded in the majority culture, its manifestations are ignored or downplayed, while the expression of anti-racist ideas is widely noticed and criticised as unnecessary and exaggerated. An official anti-racist discourse has sometimes had the perverse effect of reinforcing a popular misconception (against all the evidence) that ethnic minorities are especially favoured by officialdom and thus secure more than their fair share of jobs and public services. In practice, although such positive discrimination is sometimes advocated to reverse the substantial persistent disadvantage and inequality suffered by members of ethnic minorities, it is actually illegal under equal opportunities legislation. Even so, the 'race relations industry' and 'politically correct' attitudes are routinely denounced and mocked in the tabloid press.

A more fundamental criticism of anti-racism has been its neglect of the importance of culture, identity and difference. Anti-racism tended to focus on what has been called 'black–white dualism' neglecting differences within the majority and minority communities, and ignoring racism that is not based on skin colour (such as anti-semitism or anti-Irish racism). Anti-racism similarly downplayed differences in culture and religion (such as Islamophobia) which did not fit its theoretical assumptions derived from the liberal universalism of the Enlightenment and the materialist class focus of classical Marxism. The anti-racist strategy was to deny racial differences in emphasising a common economic interest, as in the slogan 'Black and White Unite and Fight'. Anti-racism thus attracted criticism not only predictably from the New Right, but also from sections of the left for its neglect of differences within and between ethnic groups, and for its rationalistic rejection of felt identities (Mac an Ghaill, 1999, pp. 105–16). Some of this criticism was echoed within ethnic minority communities.

Ethnic-minority community mobilisation

Many of the anti-racist organisations such as the Campaign Against Racial Discrimination or the Anti-Nazi League were white-dominated, and ethnic minorities were sometimes slow to organise in their own defence. The first generation of immigrants from the West Indies or the Indian subcontinent often preferred not to 'cause trouble' by directly confronting prejudice or discrimination. Nor did they make much use of the formal political process to defend their interests. Although Asians in particular used their votes, they were not initially active within political parties and they long remained grossly under-represented in both the council chamber and parliament. When they did become more directly involved they often faced discrimination and prejudice. Some parties at the local level were openly racist and a few local Labour Clubs even operated a 'colour bar' in the 1960s. Later, black members were recruited and even actively sought. However, even then the local political culture was characterised as a 'patron-client relationship' in which white politicians looked after ethnic minority interests in return for their loyal support in the internal affairs of the local party (Solomos and Back, 1995, p. 74).

Later still, black party members became more assertive, often seeking to influence party policy directly and become candidates for the council or parliament, principally through the Labour Party. To become more effective some sought to organise black sections within the party, which became a major issue from the mid-1980s onwards (Solomos and Back, 1995, pp. 85–91). Although this battle was lost, an increasing number of black and Asian candidates were selected and subsequently elected to play a growing role in the mainstream political process. Even so, blacks and Asians remain grossly underrepresented at every level.

Alongside this growing involvement in the party and electoral process, ethnic minorities have also played an increasingly important role in pressure group politics. Organisations representing ethnic minorities have sought influence and often funding from the council and other public bodies, and have engaged in the policy networks which now characterise the modern local governance process. Yet this cannot conceal their relative lack of political clout both within organisations and in policy bargaining between them. Nor has it ensured that ethnic minorities secure a better deal at local or national level.

The children and grandchildren of black and Asian immigrants, born and raised in Britain and speaking English with local accents, appear less willing to accept the discrimination and prejudice which their parents and grandparents have more docilely suffered. Educated alongside white children, they are only too aware that they cannot compete on equal terms with them, particularly when it comes to seeking employment. Many live in deprived, segregated communities where education and employment prospects are poor, where they routinely suffer harassment and prejudice from the police, and where they are provoked by the racial taunts and violence of gangs of whites. It is hardly surprising that some are drawn into violent demonstrations and riots, which are almost guaranteed to provoke a serious political response and focus more attention on the problems of the area than years of patient consultation.

One reaction of disaffected members of ethnic minorities is to deny allegiance to the national community of which they legally form a part, and focus their loyalties on their own community. Thus, some blacks and Asians have sought to imitate the 'black power' movement in the United States, pursuing their own version of racial pride and loyalty and displaying a form of racist ideology which mimics that of the white majority. While some would see racism as solely a white ideology, reflecting the majority power of the white community, it is also clear that ethnic minorities can display prejudice and practise discrimination towards each other, as well as showing a more understandable 'racist' reaction against white prejudice.

A trivial but symbolically significant illustration of the latter has been expressed in the support of young British-born Afro-Caribbeans and Asians for West Indian, Pakistani or Indian cricket teams in matches against England. Faisal Bodi (*Guardian*, 21 June 2001, p. 28), a Muslim journalist, has argued that underlying the show of allegiance to Pakistan is

> a malaise of identity. Many of the revellers will never have been 'back home' . . . They are only nominally Pakistani . . . [but in supporting Pakistan] they are underlining and celebrating their alienation from mainstream society. Rejecting those who don't accept you is a common reaction of excluded groups.

Indeed, exclusion and separation, once forced on ethnic minorities, is now often freely chosen. This further reinforces a segregated pattern of housing, education and employment in which there is very little social contact across the 'racial' divide. Already it is claimed that there are virtual 'no-go areas' for both whites and ethnic minorities in some urban areas, and some physical barriers have even been erected between communities. The dangers of such segregation for intercommunal incomprehension, hostility and conflict hardly requires emphasis. If extremist racist 'solutions' are to be avoided, a viable alternative would seem to involve a willing acceptance of a non-racist multicultural society in which people's ethnic origins did not determine their life chances. (Multiculturalism is discussed further in the following chapter.)

Further reading

The literature on fascism and Nazism is formidably large. Kitchen (1976) provides a useful general introduction, while Carsten (1967) and Eatwell (1996) provide good brief histories. Kershaw (1993) is illuminating on Nazism. Laqueur (1979) has edited a thought-provoking collection of essays that discuss some of the main theoretical issues. On British fascism, Thurlow (1987) has written a useful general history that takes the story beyond Benewick's (1972) earlier illuminating study. For Mosley, see the scholarly but rather too sympathetic biography by Skidelsky (1990). Walker (1977) provides a good (if now dated) general account of the National Front, while Taylor (1982) is particularly useful on their ideology.

The literature on racism is similarly large and complex. Saggar (1992), Skellington (1996) and Solomos (2003) provide broad surveys of race and politics in contemporary Britain. Key texts that focus on theory from different perspectives include Rex (1986), Miles (1989, 1993), Solomos and Back (1996) and Mac an Ghaill (1999). Bulmer and Solomos (1999) and Back and Solomos (2000) have edited substantial readers on racism which include extracts from many key writers. Other required reading includes several landmark reports on racism in Britain that discussed theoretical issues including Scarman (1981), Macpherson (1999) and Parekh (2000a). There is a useful chapter by Geddes on the issue of immigration in the 2005 General Election in Geddes and Tonge (2005).

7

Multiculturalism

Introduction

Multiculturalism may seem an unusual choice of topic for a book on ideology. At one level multiculturalism is a shorthand term simply used to describe the extent of cultural diversity in many modern states and societies, including Britain. At another level it is a policy that accepts and promotes cultural diversity, as an alternative to past policies emphasising integration and assimilation in the interests of cultural homogeneity. Underlying that policy are assumptions and values that amount to a distinctive political perspective which contrasts markedly with many interpretations of nationalism (see Chapter 5) and, more obviously, racism and fascism (see Chapter 6). Multiculturalism additionally carries challenging implications for mainstream ideologies, particularly conservatism, although some liberal philosophers have also challenged the notion of minority group rights, with potentially damaging implications for the rights of individuals and universal human rights.

This chapter begins by exploring briefly the difficult concept of culture, and the range and types of distinctive cultures. It proceeds with an account of the development of a more culturally diverse, less homogeneous, society in Britain. It goes on to explore multiculturalism as a policy and philosophy, examining the arguments for it, and the contrasting conservative and liberal critiques of multiculturalism. It concludes with a brief discussion of some controversial issues.

Culture

Culture, according to Raymond Williams (1976, p. 76) is one of the most confusing words in the English language. It has been used in different senses over time, and is still understood in very various ways by different disciplines. However, for modern social scientists and political theorists, culture includes the attitudes, beliefs, values, and behaviour acquired from living in a specific society or community, as opposed to those attributable to universal human nature. Of course, how much of our attitudes and behaviour is derived from culture, and how much from nature is itself a controversial question. While liberals generally assume that human beings are much the same everywhere, and motivated by similar impulses, conservatives and nationalists commonly attribute a much larger role to cultural traditions. Socialists tend to share the liberal assumption of a universal human nature, and downplay the role of culture, (although they argue that particular human attitudes and behaviour may be influenced considerably by their economic circumstances).

Cultures

What constitutes a culture is also contentious. Sometimes the term is used very broadly to cover extensive geographical areas, as in 'western culture', 'European culture', or 'Asian culture'. Thus western or European culture and values may be contrasted with Asian culture and values (Parekh, 2000, pp. 136–41). The 'Clash of Civilizations' perceived by the American political scientist Samuel P. Huntington (1996) divided humanity into a number of distinctive civilisations or cultures (he uses both words almost interchangeably) based substantially on religion. Such broad conceptions of culture clearly transcend state boundaries, and involve the assumption that people may share a sense of common cultural identity across national borders.

This is a now familiar phenomenon. Thus in 1999 many Greeks wore targets on their clothes in protest against the bombing of Serbia by NATO forces over Kosovo, as if to say, 'Bomb us also'. On one interpretation, this Greek display of solidarity with Serbia reflected their common Orthodox Christian faith. Jews and Muslims also of course can similarly show solidarity with their co-religionists. Yet all these religions are far from homogeneous, and often deeply internally divided between rival practices and interpretations, that amount to separate cultures or sub-cultures. Thus Christianity was early split between Latin and Orthodox, and subsequently between Catholic and Protestant, with all kinds of further, often bitter, subdivisions, such as that between evangelicals and anglo-Catholics in the Church of England. The west is belatedly learning that there are similar divisions within Islam.

Such a sense of shared identity across state borders may be based on a common or similar language or ethnicity, as well as a common religion. There is an 'English speaking world', peoples who share a French language and cultural heritage, or a broad Hispanic culture. There are pan-Slav, pan-Arab and pan-African movements, reflecting some sense of a common culture. This has often had implications for foreign policy and alliances at one level, and at another level for sport and popular culture.

Yet at least over the last two centuries cultures have been particularly identified with nations. Although nations are variously defined (see Chapter 5) they are generally associated with a distinctive culture. The process of establishing nation-states and nation building commonly involved the deliberate establishment and encouragement of a homogeneous shared culture, and the discouragement of cultural diversity. Minorities were encouraged or compelled to assimilate to the majority culture, while any immigrants were expected to integrate. This helped to promote a dominant or exclusive loyalty to the nation over other cross-national or sub-national communities. Thus, in states such as Britain, France and Spain, minority faiths once faced not only discrim-ination but often persecution, while minority languages, such as Welsh, Breton or Catalan were discouraged and sometimes even officially prohibited (as was the Catalan language under the Franco regime in Spain). Yet despite such official discouragement (or possibly even because of it) many such minority cultures within states have patently survived, and today may be officially recognised, and perhaps granted some autonomy.

While modern social scientists and political theorists still acknowledge a strong association between the terms 'nation' and 'culture', they also increasingly identify many 'sub-cultures' within each nation. Thus minority religious communities, such as Catholics in Britain generally, or the 'Wee Frees' in Scotland, can be seen as sub-cultures, with their own distinctive values and behaviour. Some would also identify distinctive regional sub-cultures in, for example, Merseyside or Cornwall, or the Scottish highlands and islands. However, others lament the erosion of distinctive sub-national and even national cultures as one consequence of globalisation.

Other sub-cultures may not be associated with specific localities or religions, but cut across them. Some link culture and class. Thus while there is a 'dominant' or 'elite' culture shared by dominant or elite classes, there is also a 'subordinate', 'popular' or 'working-class' culture, as exemplified by different dialects and linguistic usages, different tastes and pastimes. Often there has been a further tacit or explicit assumption that elite culture is superior to popular culture – and indeed the very term 'culture' has been frequently associated with classical music, opera and ballet, 'serious' literature, and the visual arts displayed in galleries and museums. (Today, however, the relatively new subject of cultural studies commonly focuses more especially on mass or popular culture.)

Culture may also be linked with age groups (for example the notion of 'youth culture'), gender (masculine and feminine culture, emphasised especially in some feminist approaches), or sexual orientation ('gay culture'). Some special interest groups (such as bikers, football fans, or the hunting fraternity) have a strong sense of shared identities and tastes that amounts almost to distinctive sub-culture.

Ethnic minority cultures

Many of the sub-cultures described above are almost by definition 'minority cultures'. However, the sub-cultures that are identified and discussed most frequently in the media, are those linked with relatively recent migrants who constitute 'ethnic minorities'. Virtually all states have ethnic minorities, although certainly not all these are immigrants. Some, such as the Australian aborigines, the New Zealand Maoris, or the 'Indians' of the Americas are indigenous. They were there first. It was the white European settlers who were the immigrants, even if their descendants now constitute the majority of the population. (Within the United Kingdom the Welsh may perhaps be described as an indigenous minority, being largely descended from people who inhabited Britain before the Anglo-Saxon, Viking and Norman invasions.) Other ethnic minorities, such as American blacks, are largely descended from involuntary migrants who were victims of the slave trade. In Britain and some other European states, such as France, the Netherlands and Spain, there are ethnic minorities from former colonial empires. However, many who have arrived more recently in both Britain and other European countries are asylum seekers or economic migrants, not necessarily connected with former colonies.

Many of these ethnic minorities are culturally distinctive, including some who are also differentiated by skin colour and may appear to belong to a different 'race' from the majority (see Chapter 6). They may continue to use the languages of their country of origin. They may follow a non-Christian faith, or practise their Christianity in different ways, as part of distinctive Christian communities. Their clothes, food and customs may mark them out from the majority of the population. Yet even those prepared or willing to integrate have not infrequently encountered discrimination and prejudice and have understandably become more dependent on their own community. Moreover, the children of westernised immigrants have sometimes consciously sought to rediscover their roots, perhaps simply from curiosity, perhaps following experience of unequal treatment.

Yet many ethnic minorities in Britain are neither black nor Asian. Among older ethnic minorities are the Jews, their numbers swelled by immigrants facing persecution and worse in the first half of the twentieth century, and Irish, who continued to enjoy the rights of British citizens even after the establishment of the Irish Free State, and subsequently the Irish Republic. There have also been smaller numbers of Italian and Greek immigrants, and immigrants from Poland and other countries of eastern Europe once behind the Iron Curtain, following the Second World War and more recently after the enlargement of the European Union. Many of these immigrants settled in similar areas, and formed distinctive communities with their own culture.

Culture and identity

Our identity – who we think we are – is commonly closely bound up with culture. Parekh (2000a, p. 156) argues that 'membership of a cultural community … has two major consequences. It structures and shapes the individual's personality in a certain way and gives it a content or identity. It also embeds him or her within, and identified with, a particular group of people.' Yet, while such identities may be strong, they are not necessarily exclusive. Indeed, sub-cultures almost inevitably overlap, and we may feel we belong to several cultures, with multiple identities and allegiances. This is clear from the way in which British black and Asians talk about themselves (see Box 7.1). The multiple identities encompass nationalities, cities, regions, tastes and pursuits, and sexual orientation, although as Benjamin Zephaniah (Box 7.1) points out – identities are sometimes imposed by others.

Who we think we are can clearly change over time, under different circumstances. Thus, someone brought up in an Asian Muslim community who discovers he is homosexual may come to identify more with fellow gays (Asian, African or European, and of all faiths and none) than with fellow Muslims, particularly if those fellow Muslims cannot accept his sexual orientation. A similar shift of identity may be experienced by an individual brought up among evangelical Christians who 'comes out' as gay or lesbian. Migration to countries with different

---

Box 7.1   Self-identities of individuals from Black and Asian ethnic minorities in Britain

Tommy Nagra (television producer): I see myself as Brummie Punjabi British. I am comfortable with all three and don't feel it compromises whatever is meant by Britishness.

David Yip (actor): When I was a kid I was just a Liverpudlian. It was only when I got older that I began to think of myself as a British-born Chinese.

Kwame Kwei-Armah (playwright and actor): I define myself as black British, but most importantly as tri-cultural: Ghanaian, Grenadian and English.

Sham Sandhu (television controller): For me being a British East-African Asian is as important as being a thirty-something, single, gay Londoner.

Lord Ahmed (Labour peer): I am a Muslim Kashmiri but also a Yorkshire lad who loves his fish and chips and his curry and chapati.

Benjamin Zephaniah (poet): Race is an important part of my identity but I wish it wasn't. I'd like to identify myself as a martial artist, an Aston Villa supporter, or a hip-hop reggae person, but when a policeman stops me on the street it has nothing to do with that.

(Derived from *The Guardian*, 21 March 2005).

---

cultures and cross-cultural marriages can oblige individuals to reassess their own identities and allegiances. In some cases, they may feel constrained to abandon their former culture, or they may freely repudiate it, embracing another nationality, or another faith.

This process can be painful and even sometimes dangerous for those concerned. A high premium is sometimes placed on loyalty to a cultural community, such as a nation or a faith (Parekh, 2000a, pp. 158–62). Those who repudiate their nation may be regarded and treated as traitors. Those who abandon their faith have often faced similar fates, and some are still commonly regarded and treated as apostates, although to any western liberal the freedom to choose one's religion, and sometimes repudiate the faith in which one is brought up, is a crucial principle. Parekh (2000a, p. 162), by contrast, regards leaving a cultural community as quite different from leaving a voluntary association. 'We might, of course, avoid participating in its collective life, discourage its members from entertaining certain expectations of us, and marry outside it, but none of these can sever all our ties with its culture or other members.' Moreover, as Parekh goes on to point out, even those who have largely abandoned their culture may still find that others associate them with it. Thus, non-practising Jews who married Christians or atheists still found themselves treated as Jews by anti-semitic Nazis under the Third Reich in Germany.

From homogeneous national culture to a multicultural society?

As Gillian Peele (in Dunleavy *et al*, 2006, p. 199) among others has observed, there are both descriptive and prescriptive aspects to the term 'multiculturalism' although it is not always easy to separate the two. Thus, it is possible to argue over the extent to which Britain has already become a multicultural society, in the sense that many different cultural communities coexist within it. There is some scope for argument over interpretation of census and other data on cultural diversity, but this is essentially a matter of description. There are other more normative issues over how far we should accept and encourage the development of a multicultural society, how we should treat minority cultures and how far we should respect minority rights. The term multiculturalism involves a conscious shift in policy on the treatment of minorities away from the past emphasis on integration and assimilation in the interests of cultural homogeneity and national unity to an acceptance and even encouragement of difference and cultural pluralism. This shift in policy is contentious not only among politicians and the general public but for political theorists, and raises issues over other key principles and values. In a book on ideologies it is necessarily the normative issues that primarily concern us, as these constitute a fairly coherent political doctrine with implications for action. However, in this section we deal first with the descriptive aspects of multiculturalism, and postpone discussion of the more critical normative questions until later in the chapter.

How far Britain can be described as a multicultural society is a relative question. Britain may now be more multicultural and less homogenous than it used to be. The contrast with the past can be underlined by citing the judgements of older writers on British politics and culture. Sir Ivor Jennings (1966, pp. 8–9) wrote in a book first published in 1941, 'Great Britain is a small island with a very homogeneous population.

Few think of themselves as primarily English, Scots or Welsh. The sting has long been taken out of religious controversy.' Textbooks on British politics in the 1960 and 1970s still described British political culture in terms of homogeneity. It is questionable whether anyone would use the same language today. A once broadly homogeneous society (though with less visible or suppressed minorities) has become much more culturally diverse.

It also depends partly on what one counts as a culture, whether one concludes that Britain is already a multicultural society. The main focus of the debate tends to focus almost exclusively on the black and Asian ethnic minorities and non-Christian religious cultures described in the previous section. Undoubtedly, immigration, some very recent, has transformed particularly many of Britain's cities and urban areas. Unfamiliar mosques and temples have sprung up alongside older Christian churches. Distinctively dressed Muslims and Sikhs mingle with white British shoppers, along with exotic hairstyles and bright colours of older African and West Indian communities. Formerly unusual fruits, vegetables and other foods appear on the shelves of British supermarkets, and British palates have become accustomed to a wide variety of cuisine, both at home and eating out. British ears have also become more used to music from different cultures, and British eyes more familiar with art and design from other continents.

This makes Britain much more culturally diverse than a country like Greece, with very few non-white citizens, and very few who are not officially members of the Greek Orthodox church, and only a tiny remnant of a once substantial Muslim population. Yet Britain is far less ethnically and culturally diverse than the USA. There, forty-five per cent of children under the age of five are from ethnic minorities, and census predictions suggest that whites will no longer constitute the majority of America's population by 2042. Besides a substantial Black and Asian population, there is a rapidly growing Latin American population, constituting 12 per cent of the electorate in 2008). Barack Obama's substantial victory in the US Presidential election was won despite the fact he trailed among white voters (43 per cent to 55 per cent). He owed his victory substantially to overwhelming support among blacks (over 95 per cent) and the backing of nearly two-thirds of Hispanics and Asians.

By contrast, the entire non-white population of the United Kingdom is just over four million of a total sixty million. Official statistics indicate that the Muslim population of the United Kingdom is only around 3 per cent of the whole, while all other non-Christian faiths (including Hindus, Buddhists, Jew and Sikhs) only constitute a further 3 per cent. The overwhelming majority (71 per cent) continue to describe themselves as

Christian, (while 15 per cent claim to have no religion, with 8 per cent not stating a religion). Thus members of non-Christian faith cultures still constitute a small proportion of the population of Britain, however visible their presence in some British urban areas, such as Leicester, Bradford, Birmingham and parts of London.

Yet if a less narrow view of culture is taken, over a longer period, there can be little doubt that modern Britain is far more culturally diverse than in past centuries. Once those who did not conform with the beliefs and ritual prescribed by the Church of England, at best faced discrimination and were treated as second class citizens, and at worst suffered real persecution. Other religious communities survived, if at all, at first underground, and later in the face of legally-backed discrimination and both official and popular persecution. Subsequently, Protestant nonconformists, dissenters, Jews, Catholics and (last of all) atheists had their disabilities progressively removed. Other religious communities, once barely tolerated, are now respected, their leaders given a public platform to advance their respective creeds.

There were similar developments with regard to minority languages and sub-British national cultures. Thus Welsh, once discouraged, acquired official status, its own television channel, and is now taught to all children in Welsh schools, to such an extent that Welsh language and culture is now thriving. The same is increasingly true on a more geographically restricted scale of Gaelic in Gaelic-speaking parts of Scotland. Minority national communities now also have significant self-government, following the implementation of devolution, and this has given further impetus to Scottish and Welsh culture.

With regard to the United Kingdom as a whole, the high or elite culture of the minority no longer dominates national media channels as it once did. Indeed, popular or mass culture dominates the media of communication. Regional dialects, reflecting to a degree surviving regional cultures, are heard more on television and radio. Class bias is less obvious than it was. Working-class accents feature more regularly, and working-class characters are portrayed seriously in television plays and soap operas, not in the condescending comic caricatures familiar in old British stage plays and films.

Some of the biggest changes have been over different sexual orientations and alternative life styles. Homosexual acts between consenting adults were once criminal acts, punishable by substantial prison sentences until 1968 when they were decriminalised. It took much longer for public attitudes to change, and there are still significant impediments to gays and lesbians 'coming out' particularly in some communities, but there can be little doubt that the climate of opinion has altered substantially. There is now a thriving gay community, celebrated in gay pride marches, while gay and lesbian partnerships are not only widely accepted but can be officially recognised in civil ceremonies.

Families also are changing. Many more heterosexual couples now live together and have children, without feeling constrained to marry, as the stigma of illegitimacy has substantially disappeared. Varieties of unconventional families and life styles are now more widely accepted. Moreover, increasing number of Britain's black and Asian population are marrying and taking partners across ethnic lines, creating a growing number of mixed race children. While certainly not everyone approves of this greater diversity, there can be little doubt over its existence, and its significance for British culture and sub-cultures.

Some caveats still need to be entered, however. Cultural diversity has not necessarily created a genuinely tolerant open-minded multi-cultural society. Different cultures may co-exist in modern Britain but there often remains much mutual incomprehension and sometimes hostility between them. Thus in northern Ireland, Protestant and Catholic working-class communities inhabit proximate and similarly deprived streets in mutual antagonism, with little or no inter-communal contact in the worlds of schools, leisure or even work. There is still similar, although less violent and more muted, incomprehension and hostility between Catholic and Protestant communities in some other British cities, such as Glasgow and Liverpool. Racial conflict is unfortunately more a feature of some other deprived urban areas. One point made, following race riots in some northern cities, was that the white majority and Asian ethnic minorities might inhabit areas in close proximity, but pursue 'parallel lives' with little mutual contact or understanding.

The white majority in general may know little of the various minorities living among them. Writers from the ethnic minorities have pointed to the often facile generalisations made about 'blacks and Asians' and non-Christian faith communities, particularly Islam. Thus Ziauddin Sardar (2008, a and b) argues that there is no such thing as an 'Asian community' in Britain, and that this is a label arbitrarily imposed on former migrants (some long resident) from a wide variety of backgrounds. Thus British 'Asians' come from several national communities, India, Pakistan, Bangladesh and Sri Lanka (and, he might have added, East African Asians from Kenya and Uganda). They also come from very different provinces, with different languages and cultural traditions (Sardar cites Punjabis, Bengalis, Kashmiris, Gujuratis, Sindhis, Beharis, Tamil and Singhalese). They, more obviously, belong to different faiths, which are themselves internally differentiated between sects (as indeed is Christianity). In some towns and cities, like Leicester, these various communities are well integrated, while in others, such as Oldham, they do not mix. Indeed, Sardar notes that 'bi-culturalism' may be a more accurate label than multiculturalism to describe a situation where white and brown economically deprived Lancastrians with similar accents fight over scarce resources.

The case for multiculturalism

While it is difficult to deny that Britain, like many other western states, has become more of a multicultural society (despite the caveats entered above), some go on to argue that this development is positively beneficial. There are, it is claimed, advantages to be derived from respecting and preserving minority cultures and encouraging cultural diversity. Multiculturalism as a deliberate alternative to the past policy of encouraging cultural integration and assimilation developed in the United States from the 1960s as blacks and other minorities insisted on affirming their distinctive cultural identities. A multicultural approach was also adopted in Canada and Australia from the 1970s. Around this time, partly in imitation of approaches elsewhere, partly in response to the refusal of minorities (particularly Asian immigrants) to assimilate, British policy began to shift towards multiculturalism (Parekh, 2000a, pp. 4–5). Thus multiculturalism as a policy is rather longer established than some critics imagine.

The normative arguments for multiculturalism are contentious. They amount to a distinctive ideological perspective that is markedly at variance with not only the assumptions of many interpretations of nationalism, as well as racism, but runs counter to some aspects of mainstream conservatism. Moreover, some of the arguments for minority group rights and respect for minority cultures have also aroused criticism even among liberals and socialists. In this section we concentrate on the benefits and values claimed for multiculturalism. These may be grouped under three headings: the benefits derived by minority groups and cultures, the benefits to individuals, and the benefits to society as a whole.

The benefits to those who come from minority cultures may appear most obvious. For Parekh (2000a, pp. 142–78), it is culture that makes people who they are, establishes their own identity and gives value and meaning and a moral compass to their lives. They also derive stability, strength and mutual support from the cultural community to which they belong. Recognition and acceptance of their distinctive cultural traditions helps to preserve all this and give those who share in the minority culture respect and personal value, without which they would feel deprived and incomplete. Parekh accepts that minorities may need to reach some accommodation with the majority culture, involving some concessions, and he also acknowledges that cultures inevitably change and develop over time, partly as a consequence of contact with other cultures. While he argues the majority should acknowledge the rights of minorities whose cultural beliefs and practices are different, he also suggests that these minority cultures have within them the capacity to reform and progress, and it is arrogant to assume a need for western guidance and 'moral leadership'.

The Canadian political theorist Will Kymlicka (1995) has strongly advocated the rights of minorities, and most particularly the rights of indigenous minorities. Thus he argues that in Canada the rights of the Inuit Indians and the French-speaking Quebecois should be especially respected, as they were there before British settlers, and their property and other rights were infringed. Thus he argues there is substantial justification for granting them special rights and privileges, giving them significant autonomy, and even exempting them from some laws and obligations affecting the rest of the population. The argument can clearly be applied to indigenous minorities elsewhere, and perhaps extended to others from cultural communities whose rights were previously denied (such as descendants of victims of the slave trade).

However, for Kymlicka, indigenous minorities are a special case, and he does not thinks that such rights should be conferred on all ethnic minorities. Thus there is some obligation on voluntary immigrants into a state to assimilate. However, he urges that immigrant communities should be allowed to maintain their distinctive cultures through what he calls 'polyethnic' rights, including some exemption from general laws on, for example, school dress codes, or animal slaughtering. Some minorities may even need additional 'representation rights', to compensate for their under-representation in governmental and political institutions.

Nevertheless, doubts have been expressed by conservatives and even by some of those from ethnic minorities over the benefits of some special treatment, encouraging for example more emphasis on education in their own culture and language. Thus John Rex (1986, p. 120) has observed 'Unfortunately the right to be different can all too readily be conceded without allowing for equality of opportunity and perhaps positively reinforcing inequality of opportunity.' Thus those from minorities who are not fluent in the majority language are almost inevitably at a disadvantage in competing for employment with prospects.

The benefits from multiculturalism to all individuals in a society, including those belonging both to minority communities and the majority may be described in terms of increased effective freedom of choice. It is an argument that seems thoroughly compatible with John Stuart Mill's brand of liberalism. Mill valued individuality and diversity that can only freely flourish in a society in where there is extensive freedom of choice between a wide variety of creeds, values and lifestyles. Mill railed against the tyranny of the majority, obliging conformity with majority tastes and values. The toleration and encouragement of all kinds of minority views and practices must thus assist a far fuller freedom of individuals to choose how to live their own lives.

However, the extensive freedom of choice implied by cultural diversity may be considerably constrained in practice, as individuals brought up within a specific culture will be strongly influenced by it and feel bound by obligations to family and community, that may also discourage any apostasy or backsliding by sanctions. Some minority cultures may effectively restrict the freedom and rights of individuals in other ways (see the liberal criticism of multiculturalism, below) so it is possible that the 'tyranny of the majority' criticised by Mill may be replaced or supplemented by the tyranny of minorities. Yet, on balance, cultural diversity still offers wider life-style choices.

Enthusiasts for multiculturalism argue that society as a whole can also gain from cultural diversity. Multiculturalism involves a conscious rejection of the past emphasis on integration and assimilation that obliged minorities to subordinate their own cultural values to those of the majority in the interests of national and social unity. Multiculturalism suggests that those from other cultural backgrounds should not be forced to choose between cultures, but enabled to draw freely on both, and develop multiple identities and allegiances (as, for example, in Box 7.1). This may secure the more willing engagement of minorities in wider society.

Cultural diversity can certainly enlist a wider range of talents, and encourage new thinking and innovation to the advantage of the national economy and culture. Thus it has often appeared that specific minorities have brought considerable benefits to the whole community in terms of science, the arts, entertainment and sport, as well as specific skills that have filled conspicuous gaps in the British labour market. Britain's cities are arguably more colourful, vibrant and exciting places by virtue of their rich cultural mix, which would be weakened by pressure to integrate and assimilate in the interests of cultural homogeneity.

The conservative critique of multiculturalism

As we have seen (Chapter 3), most conservatives almost by definition are suspicious of innovation and change, and attach considerable
importance to preserving national culture and traditional institutions
and processes. Thus many conservatives fear that the encouragement of
multiculturalism may divide and weaken society, undermining national
unity and loyalty, even creating an 'enemy within', alienated from and
hostile to mainstream British culture and society. While Parekh (2000a,
p. 196) argues that multiculturalism strengthens the unity of society,
because respect for the culture of minorities 'earns their loyalty', this
claim was made before the attacks on the Twin Towers in New York
in 2001 and the London bombings of 2005, and now appears more
questionable.

The American political scientist Samuel Huntington (1996, 2002,
pp. 305–6) articulates some of these fears. Cultural diversity, he suggests, involves 'schizophrenic torn countries . . . not belonging to any
civilization and lacking a cultural core.' He claims: 'History shows that
no country so constituted can long endure.' He criticises immigrant
communities who reject assimilation 'and continue to adhere to and to
propagate the values, customs and cultures of their home countries',
instancing Muslims in Europe and Hispanics in the United States. He
blames influential intellectuals 'who, in the name of multiculturalism' have 'denied the existence of a common American heritage and
promoted racial, ethnic and other sub-national cultural identities and
groupings.' He warns 'If assimilation fails . . . America will become a
cleft country with all the potentials for internal strife and disunion that
entails.'

Huntington's attack on multiculturalism is surprising to an outsider,
as cultural diversity and hybrid identities ('Irish-American', 'Greek-
American', 'Polish-American', etc.) seem one of the more attractive
features of American society. The very establishment of the American
Republic with its federal constitution involved a (largely successful) attempt to combine unity with considerable diversity. More recent
attempts to remedy some of the past oppression and injustice suffered
by other ethnic groups, particularly American blacks, might appear
more worthy of commendation than condemnation. Yet the attacks of
11 September in 2001 and the ensuing 'war on terror' made Huntington's
Clash of Civilizations appear prophetic. The London bombings and
attempted bombings of July 2005 and the subsequent failed attack
on Glasgow airport in 2007 brought similar terrorism to Britain.

Of particular concern was the discovery that the London bombers were not foreigners, but British Muslims, born and brought up in Britain. To some it confirmed that Britain was (in Huntington's phrase) a 'torn country' with 'an enemy within'. It raised questions over the allegiance of Muslims in western countries with significant Islamic minorities, and to some it revived doubts over the whole policy and practice of multiculturalism.

The British Conservative Party has more recently distanced itself from the sometimes overt, but more commonly covert, racism of the past (see Chapter 6). Indeed, David Cameron has actively encouraged the adoption of candidates from ethnic minorities. However, while leading Conservatives may have rejected racism, many remain suspicious of multiculturalism. Thus the Conservative Party's shadow home secretary, Dominic Grieve, has argued that multiculturalism has left a terrible legacy. 'We have done something terrible to ourselves in Britain. In the name of trying to prepare people for some new multicultural society we've encouraged people, particularly the sort of long-term inhabitants, to say "well your cultural background isn't really very important"'. He attributed rising support for the BNP on the one hand, and Islamic extremism on the other, to the vacuum created. 'They're two very similar phenomena of people who are experiencing a form of cultural despair about themselves, their identity.' This leads some to 'latch on to confrontational and aggressive variants of their cultural background as being the only way to sort of reassure themselves that they can survive and have an identity' (interview at the Conservative Party conference, *The Guardian*, 27 September 2008).

The interview provoked a strong critical reaction from *Guardian* readers. Thus Councillor Salma Yaqoob observed that 'it was odd to warn of the perils of multiculturalism while visiting one of the most multicultural cities in Europe.' Birmingham (the venue for the 2008 Conservative conference), Yaqoob argued, 'is a diverse city, most people think of it as one of our strengths.' Don Lee, a former multicultural education adviser, objected that multicultural education was 'not intended to "create a melting-pot" or to deny the cultural identity of anyone who considers themselves British.' Rob Wheway of the Liberal Institute claimed that multiculturalism rather than integration was the way to unity. 'Respect for each other's culture is vital. Integration failed, multiculturalism works.' With regard to religious faiths Wheway asked, 'Since Christian denominations are multicultural rather than integrated, why should the Tories want a different standard from other faiths and cultures?' Tara Mukherjee, chairman of the European

Multicultural Foundation declared, 'Cultural diversity is a fact; multiculturalism is what we do with the fact' (letters to *The Guardian*, 28 September 2008).

Both Grieve and his critics regard culture and identity as important. The argument is over how best to deal with increasing cultural diversity. Grieve's critics think that wider social harmony is best promoted through multiculturalism rather than integration. Grieve wants to strengthen British culture and scrap multiculturalism, by implication encouraging integration and assimilation. (Both Blair and Brown have also talked of the need to define and strengthen British identity, but without scrapping multiculturalism.)

Conservative thinkers and politicians from Burke to Oakeshott have emphasised the role of cultural traditions in shaping people's values and behaviour. Parekh (and indeed modern communitarians) suggests that individuals are 'embedded' in their culture to an extent that both entails obligations to fellow members of their cultural community and constrains their own freedom of choice. Liberals (as we have seen in Chapter 2) place greater emphasis on individual freedom, and assume individual have greater autonomy in exercising that freedom. This leads on the very different criticisms that some liberals have made of aspects of multiculturalism.

The liberal critique of multiculturalism

With its long association with toleration, and religious toleration in particular, it might be expected that liberalism was fully compatible with multiculturalism, and, indeed, many liberals have no problems with either a multicultural society or some of the normative assumptions around multiculturalism. However, some liberals and socialists have issues with the concept of minority group rights associated with Kymlicka (himself regarded as a liberal), and the theoretical arguments for multiculturalism advanced by Parekh (see above). The gist of this liberal objection is that minority group rights may have adverse implications for universal human rights and the rights and interests of individuals.

Parekh is critical of some of the core assumptions of liberalism, and the notion that western liberal values have universal validity. He argues that such documents as the 1948 United Nations Declaration of Human Rights 'retains a distinctly liberal bias and includes rights which, though admirable, cannot claim universal validity' (Parekh, 2000a, p. 134). He maintains 'Leaders of almost all East Asian countries insist that some of the rights included in the United Nations and other western-inspired declarations of human rights are incompatible with their values, traditions and self-understanding' (Parekh, 2000a, pp. 136–7). He suggests these countries reject the liberal individualist ethos and largely cherish 'such "Asian" values as social harmony, respect for authority, orderly society, a united and extended family, and a sense of filial piety.'

His argument inspired a vigorous counter-attack by the British liberal philosopher Brian Barry (2001a and b). He claimed that Parekh's approach 'is liable to be harmful to women and children in minority communities, and to those within them who deviate from prevailing norms' (Barry, 2001b, p. 58). Thus, respecting the values embedded in a particular culture might entail accepting discrimination on grounds of gender or caste, and legitimising prejudices on sexual orientation. Thus, cultural norms may be employed to trump minimal universal norms expressed in declarations of human rights, including women's rights, gay rights and even rights to freedom of speech. Barry concedes that universal human rights have been only imperfectly implemented and upheld. However, he argues that the appeal to abstract universal principles has been the driving force behind the transformation of the legal rights of women in Britain and elsewhere, and behind the advance of the rights of American blacks. Deference to prevailing cultural norms would have justified the continuation of discrimination on grounds of race and gender. Barry's point is well made, although western academics and politicians might show rather more humility in castigating other cultures for being tardy in implementing rights and principles only recently accepted, and still very imperfectly implemented, in Britain and many other western states.

Although Parekh and Barry differ markedly both on principles and their wider political philosophy, they are not so far apart on practical issues arising from cultural disputes. Barry (2001b, p. 64) comments dismissively that Parekh's pragmatic compromises on these issues 'in every case broadly supports the status quo in Britain' but even so, Parekh's discussion and analysis of broad principles and contentious questions seems generally balanced and judicious. Thus, Parekh (2000a, p. 196) argues that a multicultural society 'cannot ignore the demands of diversity' but also 'should foster a strong sense of unity and common belonging among its citizens'. A multicultural society needs some common 'operative public values' (Parekh, 2000a, p. 267) which all should respect, but otherwise should allow diversity and relative autonomy to its various cultures. It is to some of the contentious issues around reconciling unity and diversity in practice that we now turn.

Language

One key issue is how far to accept and recognise minority languages. A distinction may perhaps be drawn here, following the arguments of Kymlicka (see above), between the treatment of indigenous minorities and voluntary immigrants. Thus, a strong case can be made for preserving and teaching Welsh and Gaelic, languages that are so closely bound up with the culture of these indigenous minorities. As for essentially voluntary immigrants, it is natural that Poles or Punjabis should continue (perhaps for some period of time) to communicate in their own language within their own communities. However, it is arguably in their interests, as well as the majority community, that immigrants who intend to stay indefinitely should learn to speak English, otherwise they may become severely disadvantaged both in employment and other respects. It is now widely conceded that the expenditure some public bodies incurred in providing translations (and sometimes translators) for a number of minority language groups, while necessary in some circumstances, was generally excessive and perhaps counter-productive, and that money would be better spent on providing more English language classes.

Food and dress

There are very few important issues in general over minorities eating and dressing according to their own cultural traditions. Sometimes, however, there are problems in schools over school uniforms, participation in sports and specific rules on dress and adornment, which particularly affect Muslim girls. Commonly, such issues are pragmatic-ally resolved. The wearing of the *hibab* (sometimes mistranslated as 'veil') by some Muslim girls has not aroused the same controversy in Britain as in France, where state education adheres to the principle of secularism, excluding all religious symbols and practices from state schools. There are sometimes issues of dress in employment and wider society, particularly where these involve issues of health and safety. Thus, there is a continuing issue over the refusal of Sikhs to wear helmets rather turbans when riding motor bikes. On diet, the insistence of some faith groups on only eating *halal* meat might cause some offence to animal rights groups, but generally speaking issues of diet are not particularly controversial. Schools and hospitals often provide a choice of food suitable for minorities where the numbers involved make it reasonably economic.

Faith schools

A contentious issue is over the extent to which the state should permit, and even fund, separate schools for particular faith groups. Unfortunately, a clear precedent has long been established. Arising from compromises in the nineteenth century and more recently in the 1944 Education Act, the state and the taxpayer has long funded religious schools for Anglicans and Catholics. In Northern Ireland in particular, school education has been segregated on religious lines, and critics suggest that this has had serious adverse consequences for the relations between the Protestant and Catholic communities. It is difficult on grounds of equity to deny Muslims and others the right to educate their own children in Muslim schools, although the consequences could be as unfortunate for inter-community relations as in Northern Ireland. The problem has been exacerbated by former Prime Minister Blair's enthusiasm for faith schools. While many liberals would prefer a system where state education and religion (of all varieties) were kept separate (as in France and the United States) this is not going to happen. Yet the maintenance and proliferation of faith schools is hardly likely to promote mutual understanding between faith communities, and difficulties could arise in the future.

Religion and free speech

To many liberals the right to free expression of opinion is paramount, and there are in Britain relatively few exceptions to its exercise (for example, laws on libel and slander and incitement to race hatred). Although blasphemy laws remain on the statute book, they are effectively a dead letter, a relic of a bygone age. The Church of England, and Christianity in general, is not protected from satire and hostile criticism. Some other cultures are not as tolerant of attacks on religion that offend the susceptibilities of believers. The furore aroused by the publication of Salman Rushdie's *The Satanic Verses* has already been discussed in the previous chapter. To many Muslims it appeared not only as an attack on their religion, but on their whole community, offending their identity and self-respect, as Parekh (2000a, pp. 298–304) argues. Yet he also concedes that the Muslim over-reaction, and particularly the *fatwa* declared on Rushdie, and the attacks on others connected with the publication of the book, did the community much damage and could not be justified.

The treatment of women

As we have seen (above), Brian Barry has argued that multiculturalism may have adverse implications for women, as some cultures continue to regard them and treat them as inferior, restricting their rights to education, work, and a free choice of partner. Moreover, some cultures appear to condone the physical ill-treatment of women, and even, on occasion, their murder in so-called honour killings. Yet minority cultures have no monopoly of male violence, exploitation and crime. Feminists have frequently drawn attention to the general and shocking extent of violence against women, and the rape and murder suffered by women at the hands of men of all creeds and colours.

However, there are specific issues for some minority cultures on women's rights. One such is arranged marriages, common in some Asian cultures. Much depends on whether coercion is involved. Western royalty and aristocracy have long arranged marriages, and 'matchmaking' has been a familiar feature of other levels of western society. A marriage 'arranged' in this way by family and friends in which both intended partners are free to say 'no' may prove more compatible and lasting than some 'love matches'. Forced marriage is another matter entirely and can have no place in a civilised society. Parekh (2000a, p. 275) accepts that it is 'crucial' that no-one should be 'coerced into marriages against their explicitly stated personal wishes.' However, he also argues that 'there is no justification for holding up personal autonomy and choice as universal values, especially in such culturally crucial matters as marriage'. The problem here, from a western liberal perspective, is that women may be culturally conditioned to accept an arranged marriage in which they have no personal choice, and which may prove disastrous for their health and happiness. Moreover, any subsequent attempt to escape from such an unfortunate marriage may involve horrendous obstacles.

Western liberal attitudes may often appear arrogant and patronising to those from other cultures. Indeed, the recent and still very imperfect nature of the conversion of the west to some universal principles, such as equality between the sexes, should be acknowledged with rather more humility. Moreover, the liberal principle of toleration has not always been extended to those from different cultural traditions, whose values have not always been appreciated. The west has much to learn from other cultures, for example with regard to the conservation of the environment, now belatedly promoted by western liberals.

Yet, despite these important caveats, Barry's argument that the appeal to universal human rights has been a major condition of past progress towards a more fair and equal society remains powerful. Such universal principles seem indispensable for future progress in all cultures, including our own, where much remains to be done. Multiculturalism should not be used as a cloak to condone attitudes and discriminatory practices unacceptable in a civilised society. Nor should minority rights, where these are conceded, entail any diminution of individual human rights.

Further reading

Recent statistics on the extent of national, ethnic and religious divisions in Britain can be obtained from various official sources, such as *Social Trends*. Solomos (2003) has a useful chapter on 'Race Culture and Identity Politics'. In Dunleavy *et al.* (2006, pp. 193–211) Gillian Peele discusses briefly both the practice and theory of multiculturalism. Modood (2005) explores the implications of multiculturalism for the British Muslim community. Ziauddin Sardar (2008) examines cultural diversity within the British Asian community briefly in an article in the *New Statesman* (29 September 2008) and more exhaustively in his book, *Balti Britain: a Journey Through the British Asian Experience*(2008).

Will Kymlicka (1989, 1995) has made significant contributions to the wider theoretical debate over minority rights in relation to multicultural societies. Huntington's apocalyptic *The Clash of Civilizations* (1996, 2002) involves a global overview of conflicts between (substantially faith-based) cultures, with negative implications for multiculturalism, made explicit on pages 304–7. Central to the debate over multiculturalism in Britain is the work of Bikhu Parekh, who chaired a major report on *The Future of Ethnic Britain* (2000b), and the same year published his own *Rethinking Multiculturalism* (2000a, 2nd edn, 2005). Parekh (2008) has since published another book on the allied topic of identity politics. Brian Barry responded robustly to Parekh's argument on multiculturalism in an article for *New Left Review* 'Multicultural Muddles' (2001b) and a book *Culture and Equality: An egalitarian critique of multiculturalism* (2001a).

8

Feminism

Introduction

Like other ideologies, feminism involves a critique, an ideal and a programme. The critique contains an analysis of the discrimination and injustices suffered by women in existing society; the ideal is justice for women, generally but not exclusively interpreted to mean sexual equality. The practical programme has included action to achieve political and legal rights, equality in the economic sphere, the elimination of sexual discrimination in education, the workplace and the home, and protection against physical and sexual violence. All political ideologies contain implications for political action, but feminism is markedly action-oriented.

Feminism clearly differs from most of the other political ideologies discussed in this book. It is not a party ideology. Moreover, many of its concerns are with the private sphere of family and interpersonal relations rather than the public sphere of government and conventional politics. Yet the definition of what is and what is not political is itself an essentially ideological question. While many conservatives or liberals would distinguish between state and civil society, and between a public and personal sphere, feminists have argued that 'the personal is political'. Thus, issues of identity and interpersonal relations, the exploitation of women within the family, or the sexual abuse of women are political questions, just as more conventionally political issues such as civil and political rights, and equal opportunities. Feminism involves a distinctive and radically different perspective that has important implications for politics in its broadest sense.

Analysis of feminism, as with other ideologies, has tended to involve distinctions and classifications into periods and sub-categories. Thus, the literature commonly refers to two main 'waves' of feminism – the first from the late eighteenth century until around 1920, and the second from the 1960s onwards. Largely, cutting across this time dimension there is also a conventional distinction between three main varieties of feminism – liberal feminism, socialist/Marxist feminism, and radical feminism – to which other sub-categories are now sometimes added, such as eco-feminism, or black feminism or post-modern feminism. Such classifications help to make sense of a complex range of feminist thinkers, ideas and issues, and some use is made of them here. However, categorisation always involves oversimplification and often distortion. There are strands of feminist thinking which cut across or lie outside the conventional categories.

While this chapter will draw on feminist thought from other countries, it will concentrate principally on British feminism, and the struggle of the women's movement to remedy discrimination and exploitation within the British economic, social, political and legal context (Carter, 1988; Lovenduski and Randall, 1993).

The origins and development of feminist thought – liberal feminism

Much early feminist writing involved the application of liberal assumptions and values to the position of women,. Although liberals initially were reluctant to extend the 'rights of man' to woman (Arblaster, 1984), a few men and rather more women, brought up within the liberal tradition, argued that women could and should compete on equal terms with men. These liberal feminists sought the same education for women as for men, and the same civil rights and economic opportunities (Tong, 1989, pp. 13–22). Among writers who contributed to the predominantly liberal 'first wave' of feminism were Mary Wollstonecraft, John Stuart Mill and Harriet Taylor, while modern liberal feminists include Betty Friedan, Susan Moller Okin and Janet Radcliffe Richards.

Mary Wollstonecraft's *A Vindication of the Rights of Women* (ed. Tauchert, 1995) is still widely regarded as the first key feminist text. It was written in 1792, soon after the outbreak of the French Revolution and the 'Declaration of the Rights of Man', and the appearance of Tom Paine's *Rights of Man*. Its fundamental assumptions were those of liberalism – the rights, freedom and equality of the individual – applied specifically to the position of women. Wollstonecraft argued that women were as capable of reason as men, and should be educated in the same way as men. They should be free to exercise their reason and choose their role in life. An equality of worth between men and women implied an equality of rights, including political rights.

John Stuart Mill as a young man championed women's political rights, and his feminist convictions were strengthened by his long intellectual partnership and subsequent marriage to Harriet Taylor, who was herself largely responsible for the essay *The Enfranchisement of Women* (ed. Pyle, 1995) published in 1851. Mill's own *The Subjection of Women* (ed. Okin, 1988) is still widely regarded as 'one of the landmarks of British feminism' (Pyle, 1995, p. ix). Although not published until 1869, it was actually written in 1861, the year of the beginning of the American Civil War in which slavery was a central issue. Many women who joined the eventually successful campaign for the abolition of slavery in the United States came to appreciate the irony of their own exclusion from political rights and privileges. Writing as an English opponent of slavery, Mill provocatively claimed that 'no slave is a slave to the same lengths and in so full a sense of the word, as a wife is' (ed. Okin, 1988, p. 33), detailing the extent of a woman's legal subjugation to her husband. While admitting that most women were treated better than the law permitted, Mill also wrote of the physical abuse some women suffered at the hands of men. Mill's remedies involved principally political and legal equality for women, which he hoped would lead to a partnership of equals between the sexes, to their mutual benefit.

Mill also demanded women's 'admissibility to all the functions and occupations hitherto retained as a monopoly of the stronger sex', although he still assumed a choice between career and marriage, and that most women would prefer the latter. Here he differed not only from modern feminists but also from his wife. Her expectation that women could and should combine marriage and career, however, depended on 'a panoply of domestic servants', 'presumably', as one historian of feminist thought tartly observes, 'working class females' (Tong, 1989, p. 19).

The second wave of feminism produced some notable additions to liberal feminist literature. Betty Friedan's work (1963, 1977, 1982) appealed to a generation of American and British women who wanted careers and fulfilment outside the home, without necessarily wishing to reject the traditional values of motherhood and family. Janet Radcliffe Richards' *The Sceptical Feminist* (1982), involved a reaffirmation of the traditional liberal feminist appeal to reason, equality and social justice in the face of modern radical feminist criticism of liberalism. Susan Moller Okin (1990) has extended the theory of justice of John Rawls to the family, and has also incidentally edited a modern edition of *The Subjection of Women* (1988), supplying a vigorous defence of Mill's work.

Before we proceed to a more critical analysis of liberal feminism generally, it is important to record that its achievements were far from negligible. In feminism's 'first wave', educational advances and legal reforms of benefit to women were secured, new careers were opened up and votes for women finally won (in 1918 in Britain). It was the perceived shortcomings of some of the achievements of 'first-wave' feminism – continued inequality at work and women's under-representation in management and the professions – which further helped to drive essentially liberal reforms in the second wave of feminism from the 1960s. An Equal Pay Act was passed in 1970, and a Sex Discrimination Act in 1975. A new body, the Equal Opportunities Commission, was established to monitor implementation of both Acts and to investigate allegations of discrimination. While such changes in the law did not ensure equal pay or equal opportunities, it did entail some significant advances, particularly for middle-class career women.

Modern feminist criticism of liberal feminism

Modern feminism is not predominantly liberal, and many second-wave feminists have regarded the 'whole liberal approach' as 'flawed and inappropriate for feminist purposes.' This was because it accepted 'without criticism a set of values that are essentially male', particularly 'the importance that liberalism attaches to rationality, self-determination and equal competition' as opposed to the qualities of 'empathy, nurturing and cooperation' associated with women (Bryson, 1999, p. 12). Liberal feminists are criticised for assuming that women's nature is much the same as man's, while radical feminists today are more concerned to emphasise female difference.

Liberal feminists are also criticised for failing to provide an adequate explanation for the injustices so universally inflicted on women. If the case for women's emancipation was as clear as the liberals suggested, how could their subjection for so long and in so many parts of the globe be explained? Liberal feminists assumed that rights for women would be secured by rational persuasion and specific legal reforms, and were not drawn to analyse the prevailing power relations which denied those rights in practice (Coole, 1988, ch. 6; Bryson, 1992, pp. 58–64). Many radical feminists today would argue that men enjoy too much the fruits of their power over women to surrender it without a struggle.

To critics, this central failure to explain women's inequality meant that the liberal strategy for tackling it was inadequate. Legal reforms were insufficient, and the evidence of continued discrimination in Britain after the achievement of formal legal equality was extensive and damning. Thus, women remained considerably under-represented in Parliament and local government long after their formal political enfranchisement (Lovenduski and Randall, 1993, 165–6). While women's representation in parliament and government has improved under Labour, men still dominate British politics (Childs, 2004). Similarly, even after the passing of an Equal Pay Act in 1970, average earnings for women in full-time employment remain only 80 per cent of male earnings (Bruley, 1999, p. 165). Despite the outlawing of discrimination on grounds of sex, and the establishment of the Equal Opportunities Commission, only relatively few women have reached the highest levels in the civil service, the judiciary (Lovenduski and Randall, 1993, pp. 166–9), the professions and company boardrooms. Neither rational persuasion nor legal compulsion seemed adequate to secure justice for women.

Particularly glaring were the continuing and perhaps increasing differences among women themselves. While a minority of largely white middle-class women signally gained from the changes in the legal and cultural climate, the majority of women hardly profited. Indeed, the opportunities opened up for a minority of professional career women were often dependent on the provision of child care, catering and cleaning services, performed by other women, commonly among the most exploited in terms of pay and conditions of employment. The majority of women were still largely confined to low status and low-pay jobs in manufacturing, retailing, catering, cleaning and that ubiquitous category, caring. Increasingly, economic necessity forced many women to combine the dual role of low-paid wage earner and unpaid domestic worker.

Finally, some modern feminists criticise liberals for concentrating on discrimination and injustice in the public sphere of the law, politics, school and work, and neglecting women's role in the private world of home and family, to many feminists the very centre of women's exploitation and subordination. As a consequence of the liberal separation of public and private spheres, of state and civil society, behaviour within the private world of the home and family was not regarded as a legitimate field for state intervention.

Socialist and Marxist feminism

Socialists and liberals start from different assumptions. For the liberal, society is the sum of its individual parts, and social change is the cumulative consequence of free choices made by individuals. For the socialist, individual men and women are severely constrained by economic and social pressures outside their control. While the liberal relates the position of women to fundamental underlying assumptions about individual liberty and formal equality, the socialist naturally attempts to explain women's exploitation in terms of broader social processes.

For Marxists this entails an analysis involving inevitable conflict between economic classes, shaped by the dominant mode of production – capitalism in the modern western world. Thus, the position of women can only be understood in terms of capitalism and class. The exploitation of women in modern society is a consequence of the exploitation of the industrial working class under capitalism; the unpaid domestic labour largely performed by women in modern western societies is related to the requirements of capitalism. Women may also be exploited in the labour force – used as part of the industrial reserve army of labour to swell the ranks of workers in times of boom and to undercut the wages of male workers more generally. It follows that liberal remedies are at best mere palliatives and that the emancipation of women can only be truly achieved by abolishing capitalism and those bourgeois social relations associated with capitalism.

By no means all socialist feminists are Marxists. There were pre-Marxist socialist thinkers who addressed the position of women, such as, notably, William Thompson (1775–1844) in Britain (Coole, 1988, pp. 158–65). Subsequently, there were many other writers and active socialists and social democrat politicians who put forward arguments and practical proposals to advance the position of women. These included both Keir Hardie and Ramsay MacDonald in the British Labour Party, the indefatigable campaigner for family allowances Eleanor Rathbone, and more recent mainstream Labour socialists such as Barbara Castle. Yet, while some writers distinguish between Marxist feminism and other socialist feminism, the line between them is in practice blurred, and it is difficult to construct a distinctive socialist or social democratic feminism which comprehends all the various feminists who were socialists but not Marxists.

However, socialist feminists of all kinds differ from liberal feminists in the importance they attach to class. Most women, it is argued, suffer from a double exploitation, belonging both to a subordinate class and disadvantaged by their sex. The link between class and gender is more problematic. Marxist analysis suggests that the exploitation of women both in the workplace and the home is the consequence of the class conflict associated with capitalism. Thus it is assumed that it is class conflict rather than gender conflict which is ultimately fundamental (Coole, 1988, p. 193).

Laying aside problems of analysis and classification, all socialist feminists share a practical concern for the condition of ordinary women, and specifically for women in paid employment, particularly those in low-paid casual and part-time employment who lack even the more basic legal protection afforded to most full-time workers. Socialist feminists not only seek to extend rights to part-time and casual workers, but also to empower female workers themselves through organisation, unionisation and consciousness raising. A characteristic practical concern has been the provision of adequate childcare for ordinary women workers for whom the facilities commonly utilised by professional women are unavailable, unsuitable or simply too expensive. Thus, socialist feminists commonly demand the availability, as of right, of day nurseries, nursery schools and workplace creches.

Some socialist feminists would argue that the provision of childcare for women in paid employment does not assist those women who, either through circumstances or choice, are obliged to perform housework and childcare services unpaid in the home. This practical concern was linked with a long-running theoretical debate among Marxist feminists over domestic labour, which was seen as providing a crucial underpinning for the whole capitalist system. Some argued that the low dependent status of domestic labour could only be significantly improved by acknowledging the value of the services performed through regular payment – hence the demand for wages for housework. This campaign was not supported by all feminists, partly because it condoned and legitimised traditional gender roles within the family and the unfair burden of domestic tasks undertaken by women.

Marxist and socialist feminists played a leading role in the Women's Liberation Movement in Britain that did so much to raise women's consciousness and stimulate action, particularly in the early 1970s. The demands of the founding conference at Ruskin in 1970 in large part reflected the socialist feminist agenda: equal pay, equal education and opportunity, 24-hour nurseries, and free contraception and abortion on demand (Bruley, 1999, p. 149). British Marxist feminists also made a rich contribution to feminist theory. Yet their analysis and prescription increasingly diverged from some of the new radical feminists who prioritised gender relations over class relations. (Lovenduski and Randall, 1993, pp. 93–100).

Criticism of Marxist and socialist feminism

Socialism and feminism do not invariably go together. Some feminists have learned from bitter experience that male socialists and trade unionists can display as much male chauvinism as their counterparts on the right. However, many feminists are also socialists, and are thus often faced with a conflict of loyalties or priorities. Aware that the treatment of women is only one, and not always the most important, of the manifestations of 'man's inhumanity to man', they are sometimes accused by other feminists of not giving sufficient priority to women's issues.

This criticism is linked with a more fundamental questioning of the theoretical assumptions underpinning Marxist feminism. In so far as the injustices suffered by women are linked with capitalism, there is a tacit assumption that the end of capitalism would entail the end of women's subjection. Ultimately, it is implied, inequality of the sexes derives from the inequalities between different economic classes. Thus, issues of class are primary, and issues of gender secondary. This hardly provides an adequate explanation for the extensive evidence of women's oppression across time and cultures. As Coole (1988, p. 193) points out, although Marxism is relevant to women 'because of its general analysis of the dynamics of oppression', it is also 'problematic ... because it cannot account for a specifically sexual form of oppression except in so far as it is functional to private property and production'.

There has been some anguished reassessment of *The Unhappy Marriage of Marxism and Feminism* (Sargent, 1981). Many Marxist feminists themselves would today acknowledge that male domination and the exploitation of women is a feature of most known societies, which implies at least a need to extend Marxist analysis by borrowing from other approaches. Thus, Juliet Mitchell (1971, 1974, 1984) has combined a Marxist class analysis with insights drawn from psychology and psychoanalysis to explain the subordination of women within the family and domestic sphere. Through childhood socialisation, gender roles are learned which have an enduring significance. Other Marxist feminists have acknowledged a need to incorporate the radical feminists' theory of patriarchy into their analysis. Thus, women are exploited because of their class position within a capitalist society, but also because they are women and generally subject to male domination. This does raise the question of the connection, if any, between capitalism and patriarchy, and of the fundamental source of women's oppression. MacKinnon (1983) has argued that while Marxism focuses on work, feminism focuses on sexuality, which is the real basis of women's subordination according to those described as radical feminists.

Radical feminism

Marxist feminism involved a widening of the focus of the women's movement away from specific legal and political concerns of the liberals towards an analysis of the underlying economic and social causes of women's oppression. At first sight, the work of the radical feminists implied, by contrast, a drastic narrowing of horizons to sexual and personal relations between men and women. However, if the focus appeared to be narrow, the radicals argued it had a universal relevance. Moreover, their central concept of patriarchy, rule by the father or the male head of the household, provided feminism with a theory which was not essentially derivative, not just an application of theories like liberalism and Marxism. For radical feminists the nature of the problem is neither an inadequate political and legal framework, as liberal feminists imply, nor capitalism, as Marxist feminists suggest, but just men. Everywhere men exploit women. It is the sex war, not the class war, which is fundamental.

Who are the radical feminists? Several key texts first appeared around 1970: Kate Millett's *Sexual Politics*, Germaine Greer's *The Female Eunuch*, Eva Figes' *Patriarchal Attitudes* and Shulamith Firestone's *The Dialectic of Sex*. What these books had in common was a preoccupation with the biology and sexuality of women. Indeed, the term 'women's liberation' was closely linked with what was seen as a sexual revolution in the 1960s. These writers were all less concerned with the discrimination against women in the political and public sphere, and more concerned with the everyday relations between men and women in the home, family and bedroom. They illustrated their themes of feminine exploitation with examples from literature, journals and popular culture.

This radical focus on male–female relations in the home involved not so much a retreat from politics as a deliberate widening of the political sphere. The title of Kate Millett's book *Sexual Politics* was not accidental; the implication was that sexual relations involved power and were inherently political, hence the radical feminist slogan, 'The personal is political.'

Another characteristic of much radical feminism is its style: they freely use the language of revolution rather than reform; they challenge and set out to shock. The prevailing tone is anger and outrage, and there is a clear difference in approach from that of the liberals. The enemy was male power, embodied in the universal institution of patriarchy. Patriarchy may be variously defined, but is a term most usually employed by radical feminists to signify, simply, male dominance. The power of the husband over his wife, the power of the father over his children, and the power of the male head of the household over everyone within in it was seen as the ultimate symbol and source of male power in politics and society. Justice for women could thus never be achieved unless the institution of patriarchy was destroyed. In this context the absence of legal rights and privileges were beside the point. These were not the cause of injustice for women, only its visible manifestation. Likewise, a socialist revolution which ended the oppression of one class by another would not by itself end the oppression of women by men.

For radical feminists it was in the sexual relations between men and women that male domination and female subjugation were most evident. A prime practical concern of radical feminists was violence against women, and most particularly rape, which was not perceived as a rare and aberrational act of violence but as a widespread and typical aspect of male sexuality. Thus radical feminists drew attention to the extent of unreported rape, 'date rape' and rape within marriage (Brownmiller, 1977). Another target was pornography which involved degrading images of women, reinforced their role as sex-objects, and arguably incited sexual violence against women (Dworkin, 1981). Radical British feminists involved in Women Against Violence Against Women (WAVAW) argued that 'pornography is the theory and rape is the practice', and led direct action attacks against porn shops and cinemas (Bruley, 1999, p. 155), although other feminists opposed censorship (Lovenduski and Randall, 1993, 337–51).

Radical feminists revolutionised thinking on gender relations. Liberal feminists had sought, as far as possible, to eliminate the differences between men and women, and to enlist male aid in the emancipation of women. They aimed to open up the existing all-male bastions to women to allow free and equal competition, regardless of gender differences. Mill and others argued that the equality of women would ultimately be to the benefit of men and society generally (Mill [1869] 1983). Radical feminists assumed, by contrast, that the advantages men enjoyed by virtue of their power over women would not be readily surrendered. Thus the women's movement would have to depend on women. Indeed, it might entail the positive exclusion of men. Moreover, many radical feminists celebrated women's difference; they did not want to be like men.

A subject of debate among feminists was the extent to which male nature and behaviour might be modified. Thus a 'new man' could emerge to be a fitting equal partner to a liberated woman. Others suggested that the new man was a myth. For a few radical feminists the rejection of the whole male sex was a logical corollary – a factor in the emergence of the hostile caricature of the typical feminist as a lesbian man-hater. Lesbianism has been an issue for feminists and sometimes a source of division between them (Lovenduski and Randall, 1993, pp. 67–78). However, the rights of individuals, both male and female, to pursue their own sexual preferences, as long as these do not involve harm to others, is essentially a different issue from women's rights.

Another closely associated target for radical feminists was the conventional family, perceived as the centre of the inequitable burden of domestic work and childcare imposed on women. In contrast to the arguments of liberals like Betty Friedan, or of the Marxist feminists who sought wages for housework, many radicals denied that women would be able to achieve fulfilment outside the home while they were fettered by domesticity. A meaningful career could not realistically be combined with traditional institutions of motherhood and family. Thus, the emancipation of women appeared to some to entail the abolition of the family.

Faced with the diversity within radical feminism, it is difficult to sum up its achievements. Certainly, the style of the radicals has provoked a reaction. Arguably, the anger and shock tactics of some radical feminists has had a signal effect on the climate of opinion towards women, and the treatment of women. There is now a greater consciousness of the implicit, and often quite explicit, sexist assumptions behind many advertising and media images of women. This has led to some attempt to avoid old stereotypes and provide new more appropriate female role models. Similarly, the campaigns focusing on rape and the general issue of violence against women have contributed to a significant shift in public attitudes and some changes in practice. The issue has been forced onto the political agenda, recognised as a serious problem, and is now treated more sensitively by the police than hitherto, encouraging more women to report rape and physical abuse, although it remains very difficult to secure convictions. More support is provided for the victims of violence, both in terms of counselling and in the provision of refuges (Lovenduski and Randall, 1993, pp. 302–34).

Criticism of radical feminism

The main strength of radical feminism has perhaps always been in action rather than theory, although only radical feminism can lay claim to a really distinctive political ideology, liberal and Marxist feminism both being essentially derivative. However, radical feminism has perhaps been more impressive in exposing the shortcomings of alternative theoretical foundations than in developing new theory. While there have been attempts to explore the implications of the concept of 'patriarchy', it has more commonly been employed as a catch-all definition and explanation of male dominance. The involvement of some radicals with environmentalism on the one hand or post-modernism on the other (see below) clearly involves other theoretical connections, but these have contributed to some fragmentation of feminist theory rather than offering a body of ideas which might be generally acceptable to radical feminism.

Feminists from Wollstonecraft onwards have stimulated a hostile reaction from many men, and often also women, so the anti-feminist backlash provoked by the radicals is perhaps scarcely surprising. Yet criticism is not confined to anti-feminists. Thus, the liberal feminist Betty Friedan (1982) claims that the shock tactics of the radicals have also alienated support, not least from many women. In particular, she suggests that 'sexual politics has been a red herring', a diversion from the real issues of political and economic exploitation. Janet Radcliffe Richards (1982) argues that exaggeration of the feminist case and neglect of the traditional liberal ideals of reason, justice and fairness have spoiled the legitimate demands of women for fair and equal treatment. She provides a spirited defence of traditional liberal reason in the face of the deliberate rejection of 'male' logic in favour of feeling and intuition by some radical feminists. She denies that feminism is 'the primary struggle', as some radicals would assert, and rejects the claim of the Redstockings Manifesto that 'All other forms of exploitation and oppression (racism, capitalism, imperialism, etc.) are extensions of male supremacy.' Natasha Walter (1999) has urged that the new feminism should be 'less personal and more political', an explicit criticism of the central thrust of radical feminism.

Some of this is a criticism of style rather than substance, but there are more fundamental points which go to the heart of the universalist claims of the radical feminists. Thus, the preoccupations of some western upper-middle-class feminists, particularly their outright rejection of the institutions of marriage and the family, and even maternity, do sometimes appear remote from the lives and experience of the majority of women, particularly working-class women, black women and women from other cultures. The rejection of patriarchy need not necessarily entail the rejection of motherhood, but some feminist writing has involved a rejection of maternal values (Freely, 1995). Scorn for motherhood is often accompanied by an over-idealised perception of the liberating value of a career, which does not recognise that for most women (as for many men) work involves endured tedium, undertaken from financial need, with little prospect of releasing creative energies.

Radical feminists from a relatively privileged background have sometimes been accused of universalising their own highly specific and untypical circumstances, as if these were the problems of women everywhere. Yet women may experience very different forms of oppression and have very different needs in different social classes, communities and cultures. The preoccupations of white middle-class feminists do not necessarily coincide with those of black women (ed. Mirza, 1997). In some cultures, women are more exercised over the right to bear children, free from pressures towards family limitation, unsafe contraception, abortion or sterilisation, than they are over the right to abortion. Black and Asian women in Britain have pointed to the distinctive problems and injustices they suffer, leading to claims that 'the Women's Liberation Movement as a whole is irrelevant to the needs and demands of most black women' (quoted in Lovenduski and Randall, 1993, p. 81).

Eco-feminism

Some feminists have moved in quite a different direction from those radicals who rejected traditional roles associated with motherhood and the family. Traditional feminine attributes are celebrated rather than spurned. Thus child-rearing, far from being stigmatised as demeaning, is perceived as the most obvious manifestation of the caring co-operative nature of women, compared with the aggressive, competitive behaviour of men. Women should not compete with men, or seek to be like men, but should be themselves and maintain their own distinctive characteristics, values and priorities. This did not necessarily entail a retreat from the political sphere back to the privacy of domesticity, but the promotion of a distinctive alternative female politics of love, peace and care for the environment, sometimes referred to as eco-feminism (Plant, 1989; Mies and Shiva, 1993).

There is perhaps no logical reason why feminism should entail a concern for the environment. Indeed, some forms of environmentalism have involved a markedly conservative view of the relations between the sexes. The fundamentalist cry 'back to nature' might seem to entail a return to a 'natural' division of labour between the sexes, but the image of the earth mother, sometimes associated with eco-feminists, is not one which all feminists find helpful or appealing.

Even so, it is clear that women are prominently involved in the green movement, and for many there is a clear link between their feminist values and their green commitment. There is a strong female presence likewise in the associated animal rights and vegetarian movements. It may be that experience of pregnancy, giving birth and child nurture do give women a closer sense of kinship with the natural and animal world. Concern for the health of their children entails perhaps a greater awareness of the possible dangers in the environment and in the food chain. Women's nurturing role also gives them a greater felt stake in the future.

Yet, the involvement of some feminists in environmentalism has revealed some fissures within the woman's movement, as the issue of abortion demonstrates. For many radical feminists of the 1960s and 1970s, the demand for abortion on demand was central to female emancipation; women could not be free unless they had control over their own bodies. Yet for some eco-feminists, respect for the life in the unborn foetus was part of their respect for the life of all created things, aligning them (on this issue) with the pro-life 'moral majority' associated with the neo-conservative New Right.

The impact of the New Right – Conservative feminism?

This raises the more general question of the impact of New Right ideas on feminism, which has usually been associated predominantly with the left of the political spectrum. Mary Wollstonecraft mixed with French revolutionaries and married the anarchist William Godwin. Many nineteenth-century American feminist women were closely involved with the anti-slavery movement. Similarly, the second wave of feminism was bound up with civil rights and anti-war protest movements. Thus, feminism was associated with other progressive or socialist political causes.

By contrast, the right tended to ignore, scorn or completely reject the demands of feminists for justice and equality. This was most manifest on the extreme right. The Nazis persecuted feminists, outlawed birth control, condemned women's involvement in politics and recommended a return to the traditional female concerns of *kirche, kuche, kinder.* Conservatives were less overtly hostile, but generally showed little sympathy for demands for the vote, equal pay and equal opportunities until after they were formally achieved. More recently, some Conservatives have shown more sensitivity to feminism, and Cameron has sought to increase the number of Conservative women MPs from a low base (17 out of a total of 198 in 2005). However, the relationship between feminism and traditional conservatism remains uneasy.

The New Right had some more positive implications for the role of women. From a neo-liberal perspective, discrimination against women in the labour market appeared not so much unjust as downright inefficient, involving interference with free competition and the employment of less productive workers. Thus, neo-liberal economists applauded the marked growth of female employment. A small proportion of women, moreover, have spectacularly benefited from the new meritocratic competition for career advancement. The economic position of women generally has been transformed; their purchasing power in the economy is increasingly evident not only in the advertising of traditional female products, but in the promotion of cars, banks and insurance policies.

The neo-conservative aspects of the New Right have had other implications for women. The reaction against 'permissiveness' involved a reaffirmation of traditional family values. Thus, neo-conservatives deplored the breakdown of marriage and the traditional family. This was in marked contrast to the criticism of marriage and the traditional nuclear family by many radical feminists. However, many radical feminists have also vigorously denounced pornography and the sex trade, and here they find themselves aligned with neo-conservative opponents of sexual permissiveness, once commonly associated with women's liberation. Indeed, men were arguably the main beneficiaries of sexual liberation, while many women were literally left 'holding the baby', forced into the dual role of sole breadwinner and carer in lone-parent households. Some feminists, while seeking a broader, more inclusive and more tolerant definition of the family, have cautiously endorsed family values. Betty Friedan, who encouraged a generation of American women to careers outside the narrow confines of conventional domesticity has in a later book (1982) reaffirmed the values of the family and marriage.

For most feminists, any ideological fellow-travelling with the New Right is strictly limited. While some policy prescriptions may coincide, underlying assumptions remain very different. To many neo-conservatives, the institution of the family is valued for its presumed capacity to restore the authority and social order, which they see as lacking in society. It is a means of disciplining the young, and the restoration of paternal discipline is a key facet of this neo-conservative agenda. Hence it is urged that 'families need fathers'. At another level, support for the traditional two-parent family is a means to limiting the escalating social welfare budget. Family break-up and single parenting is perceived as a significant burden on the state and the taxpayer. By contrast, feminists seek increased support for lone parents. While they too advocate more help for families, that presupposes a broader conception of the family.

Thus, conservative feminism remains somewhat problematic. Although Natasha Walter (1999, p. 40) strenuously argues that feminists can be Conservative, she concedes that 'Individual women who are both Conservative and feminist feel isolated and misrepresented by a culture that denies the compatibility of the two creeds.'

Feminism and post-modernism

Feminism has always appeared as a particularly action-oriented ideology, with immediate practical concerns generally taking priority over the elaboration of feminist theory which, indeed, has sometimes been criticised as relatively thin or essentially derivative. Some feminists have found new theoretical insights in the ideas associated with post-modernism.

Post-modernism is difficult to pin down and define. Its major thrust is to question the whole search for meaning and purpose in art and life, and essentially it involves a reaction against the post-enlightenment faith in rationalism and progress. The enlightenment was sceptical in the sense that it rejected traditional authority, particularly the 'revealed truths' of religion. Yet it was not sceptical over the search for truth itself through the exercise of human reason and science. Postmodernism, by contrast, rejects all 'meta-narratives', or universal explanations, including those derived from post-enlightenment science and rational enquiry. Just as sceptical post-enlightenment rationalism was a critical weapon in the struggle against the received wisdom of the age, so postmodernism is a useful intellectual tool for anyone (including feminists, greens, and post-colonial opponents of cultural imperialism) who wishes to challenge prevailing mainstream (or 'malestream') thinking in the modern world.

It is, therefore, unsurprising that many feminists have been attracted to post-modernism. Women have not always conspicuously benefited from the progress entailed in industrialisation and modernisation. Some feminists have seen rationalism as 'male logic', antipathetic to feminine feeling and intuition. Moreover, well before post-modernism became fashionable, feminists spelled out in some detail the unfavourable image of women presented both in 'serious' literature and popular culture, while others pointed to a persistent male bias in conventional estimates of literary worth. Post-modernist literary criticism has provided feminists with a powerful conceptual framework to reveal the gender-bias in the use of language, to uncover new messages in and behind texts, and to attack traditional male-oriented canons of literary excellence.

Some feminists have undoubtedly found the debunking thrust of post-modernism stimulating and liberating (McRobbie, 1994). Women, they argue, can only benefit from the rejection of received intellectual authority, from the undermining of old assumptions and the breaking down of old barriers between disciplines. In this intellectual atmosphere new diverse ways of thinking can flourish. Yet others have been more cautious. The relativism implicit in postmodernism is ultimately, they argue, not only destructive of 'malestream' assumptions but of any alternative, including feminism itself, which may be perceived as just one other subjective perspective with no claim to universal validity. Thus feminists 'must be wary of throwing out reason and justice in their entirety' (Bryson, 1992, p. 229), although the same author has come to accept that 'handled carefully, post-modernist insights can be helpful to feminist analysis' (Bryson, 1999, p. 9).

Post-feminism or new feminism?

Today it may appear that women have achieved many of the goals sought by feminists. Most notably, the movement of women into the labour market has been massive and almost certainly irreversible. Formerly male-monopolised or male-dominated occupations have been increasingly opened up to women. Gender segregation in employment has been significantly reduced, and there has been some narrowing of the pay gap. Women are consequently more financially independent than ever before. Women also have increased control of their own fertility and increased choice over relationships and family commitments. They have also achieved more political power, with increased representation in elected bodies and government. All this has been accompanied by a significant shift in the media portrayal of women. The 'new woman' has seemingly arrived, although it is questionable how far there has been a commensurate emergence of the 'new man'. Indeed, there has been some agonising over male roles and male identity in this new world of gender equality.

Thus, it is sometimes claimed that we now live in a post-feminist era in which feminist aims have already been substantially achieved. Feminists would disagree. They concede that some of the gains for women have been real enough, and even acknowledge that some men now have legitimate grievances (for example on divorce, child custody and support). Yet they point to the extensive evidence of persistent discrimination and exploitation – inequalities in pay and opportunities, lasting gross inequalities in domestic and child-rearing responsibilities, and continuing violence against women. Women remain under-represented in government and parliament. Thus, there are still only 128 women out of 646 MPs in the House of Commons (roughly 20 per cent) after the 2005 election. Feminists still have much to achieve.

If the future of feminism now seems more problematic, this reflects differences among women themselves, which partly reflect crosscutting divisions of class, ethnicity and sexuality. The relationship between gender and class has long been problematic for socialist feminists. The gap between rich and poor women in Britain is now as marked as ever, with the high-profile success of a few professional career women contrasting with the limited opportunities and low pay which is the lot of most working-class women. Race and ethnicity clearly cut across the gender divide. For many black women the injustices they suffer have more to do with their colour than their gender, and thus the primary struggle involves standing alongside black males to combat racial discrimination and disadvantage. Lesbians similarly unite with gay men to assert their rights to pursue their own sexual orientation without facing discrimination and prejudice from the 'straight', and still often homophobic, majority of men and women.

Thus, for feminists 'an important starting-point must be a recognition of the diversity of women's experiences and the specificity of the oppressions that particular women face' (Bryson, 1999, p. 66). Connections and tactical alliances may be made between the victims of different forms of oppression. However, Bryson warns that 'solidarity between oppressed groups cannot be assumed' as 'those who are disadvantaged in one system do not automatically empathise with or support other oppressed groups' (Bryson, 1999, p. 68). Bryson urges engagement with 'the politics of solidarity', while arguing that 'this does not preclude separatist activity by particular groups of women'.

Above and beyond the issue of engagement with other oppressed groups remains 'the problem of men' (Bryson, 1999, pp. 195–216). While liberal feminists like Mill argued that men, too, would benefit from female emancipation, radical feminists saw men as the problem and insisted that women would have to rely on their own efforts to secure justice for women. Indeed, some have seemed to turn their backs on the whole male sex (for example the Leeds Revolutionary Feminist Group, in Evans, 1982, pp. 63–72). Thus 'the popular idea of feminism' is that 'to be a feminist you must believe that all men are irredeemably bad' (Walter, 1999, p. 145). Admittedly, the charge sheet against men is a long one. Besides exploitation, abuse and violence in the domestic sphere, in the wider community men are far more involved with crime and acts of violence (including rioting), and men bear the major responsibility for wars and their consequences. Yet if 'male nature' presents a problem, as the radicals have always pointed out, women have to engage with men if only to prevent them destroying the communities and ultimately the planet which women and men inhabit together. As Bruley (1999, p. 180) observes, 'Radical feminists who will not engage with men … cannot help to transform the gender system.'

Bryson argues feminists should acknowledge the diversity among men as well as women. Men too are divided by class, ethnicity and sexual orientation. Masculinity, like femininity, is socially constructed. Thus 'there may be competing models of masculinity in society.' Dominant forms of masculinity 'may be experienced as oppressive by some men'. Accordingly, feminists should 'welcome and strengthen non-oppressive forms of masculinity', and 'attempt to move beyond the binary divisions of a gendered society' (Bryson, 1999, 2003). While Bryson is well aware of the 'damaging effects of dominant forms of masculinity', she argues that feminists may be able to 'form alliances with some men in pursuit of egalitarian social goals'. There may, as Mill argued, be benefits for both sexes in a relationship based on a partnership of equals. However, for many men 'the alleged long term benefits of greater equality may be intangible, while the immediate threat to their own privileges feels very real and their loss of centrality deeply disturbing' (Bryson, 2000, p. 8). Thus, justice for women will still not be won without a fight in which women will have to continue to rely mainly on their own efforts.

Table 8.1 Varieties of feminism

	Liberal feminism	Marxist/socialist feminism	Radical feminism
Who	(First wave) M. Wollstonecraft J. S. Mill, H. Taylor Suffragettes (Second wave) B. Friedan J. R. Richards S. M. Okin	(First wave) W. Thompson F. Engels (Second wave) J. Mitchell M. Barrett	G. Greer K. Millett S. Firestone E. Figes S. Brownmiller A. Dworkin Eco-feminists
Ideas	Extension of liberal principles to women – emancipation, equality, civil and political rights	Application of Marxist/ socialist principles to women – economic exploitation, industrial reserve army, domestic labour, reproduction of labour force	Patriarchy and male dominance; 'The personal is political'; sexual politics; celebration of women's difference?

Table 8.1 Varieties of feminism *cont.*

	Liberal feminism	*Marxist/socialist feminism*	*Radical feminism*
Practical concerns	Votes for women; legal rights; outlawing of discrimination; equal opportunities; education for women; equal pay	Unionisation and politicisation of women; child care for working women; wages for housework? Positive discrimination?	Alternatives to traditional nuclear family; abortion; violence against women – rape, date rape, rape within marriage, pornography, lesbian rights, green issues
Problems	Endorsement of male values; limitations of legal remedies; failure to explain or remedy continuing sexual inequality; focus on middle-class, professional career women, neglect of working-class women?	Assumption that end of capitalism and class domination would entail end of exploitation of women Problematic link between gender and class Continued discrimination against women in 'socialist' societies	Insistence on primacy of gender differences over other forms of injustice Remoteness from concerns of 'ordinary' women? Neglect of concerns of black and third world women? Neglect of the 'problem of men'

Further reading

Good introductions to feminist politics in Britain are provided by Randall (1987), Carter (1988) Lovenduski and Randall (1993) and Bruley (1999). More recent works include Stokes (2005) and Lovenduski (2005). Childs (2004, 2005) should be consulted on women's political representation. For a lucid analysis of feminist political theory Bryson (1992, [second edition 2003], and 1999) is invaluable, while Tong (1989) offers an incisive (although American-oriented) thematic survey, and Caine (1997) concentrates on English feminism. Coole (1988) focuses on the treatment of women in traditional political theory, from Plato onwards. There are several readers which offer a sample of the range of feminist thinking, including those edited by Evans (1982), Lovell (1990), Humm (1992) Jackson *et al.* (1993) and Mirza (1997) – the last covering black British feminism.

Liberal feminism may be explored through the classic texts of Wollstonecraft and Mill, and the more recent work of Friedan (1977, 1982, 1986), Richards (1982) and Okin (1990). Aspects of Marxist feminism are examined by Mitchell (1971, 1974, 1984), who combines psychological analysis with a Marxist framework, and Barrett (1980). Sargent (1981) has edited a collection of essays on *The Unhappy Marriage of Marxism and Feminism.* The modern radical feminist classics by Millett, Greer, Firestone and Figes are all still readily available. Other important texts are Brownmiller (1977) on rape and sexual violence, and Dworkin (1981) on pornography.

The diversity of modern feminism is further demonstrated by the ecofeminism of Plant (1989) and Mies and Shiva (1993), Freely's (1995) defence of motherhood, and Walter's (1999) lively and provocative *New Feminism.* Ramazanoglu (1989) points to the different preoccupations of women from ethnic minorities and the third world, while Bacchi (1990) critically examines the debate over sexual equality and difference. The implications of post-modernism for feminism are explored critically by Bryson (1999, 2003) and Grant (1993), and more enthusiastically by McRobbie (in Perryman, 1994).

9

Green Ideology

Introduction

Any survey of modern ideologies would be incomplete without an examination of green thinking, which now clearly constitutes an important and distinctive political philosophy, presenting a profound challenge to longer established political creeds. While its roots can be traced back a long way, to pantheism, romanticism and the rediscovery of nature, Malthusianism, elements of anarchism, and even aspects of fascism, it is essentially a new ideology. It has brought together a number of more specific concerns – over, for example, conservation, pollution, energy, population growth and climate change – and woven these together into a coherent and distinctive political philosophy, which, in a comparatively brief period, has achieved a remarkable impact over much of the world.

Inevitably, as with other ideologies, there are problems of definition and terminology. The label 'green' is a broad one, and is not easily adapted into an 'ism'. Thus, some commentators have preferred the terms 'environmentalism' or 'ecologism' to describe the political ideology which is here simply described as 'green'. Yet these alternatives are not only awkward and less familiar, but also carry their own baggage of associations. The term 'green', by contrast, is freely adopted by pressure groups and political parties, and both the name and the colour have become powerfully associated in the public mind with specific environmental concerns and a more general political outlook. All familiar labels involve problems and ambiguities, but there seems no compelling reason to substitute another term for one that is so universally recognised. Here the term 'green' is applied not just to specific causes, groups or parties commonly described as 'green' but to the underlying political philosophy that relates humanity to its environment.

Political ideologies are expressed at various levels and involve sharp internal tensions and conflicts. The Greens are no exception, and there are considerable internal differences over analysis, prescription and strategy. Distinctions have been drawn between dark Greens and light Greens (for example, Porritt and Winner, 1984), deep and shallow Greens, ecologists and environmentalists (Dobson, 2007), radicals and reformists (Garner, 1995), ecocentrics and technocentrics (O'Riordan, 1976), fundamentalists and realists (among German Greens). The pairs of terms overlap, but each has particular connotations, and they are not necessarily interchangeable. Most are relative terms implying a spectrum of attitudes, not sharp distinctions. Some people have specific environmental concerns which gives their general political outlook a greenish tinge. At the other end, there are those who hold a coherent and distinctive green philosophy which determines their whole personal and political behaviour.

This green philosophy is clearly marked off from other political ideologies. All other political creeds focus on the presumed interests, needs or rights of humanity, or sections of human society – such as a particular race, nation, class or gender. The Greens effectively relegate all these interests (and most of the issues of traditional political theory) by focusing instead on the universe or the planet. Mainstream political ideologies are dismissed as anthropocentric – they assume that humankind is the centre of the universe, rather than one species among countless others. To Greens the overriding political issue is the relationship of the human species with its environment.

The green message is a stark one. It is that a continuation of unthinking and unlimited human exploitation of the natural environment spells disaster for the planet and for its human inhabitants. Impending disaster can only be averted by a sharp change of direction, preserving rather than destroying the environment, using renewable rather than non-renewable resources, and adopting sustainable rather than non-sustainable lifestyles. There are massive implications for all areas of public policy, but particularly industrial and agricultural policy, energy policy and transport policy.

Green and other ideologies

One way of classifying older or more established mainstream political ideologies is by locating them on the familiar left–right political spectrum, although, as has been seen, there are some difficulties in placing nationalism and feminism. The Greens are similarly awkward to place. Indeed, many Greens would argue that the old classifications are irrelevant; they are 'neither left nor right but forward'. Yet attempts to relate green ideas to other ideologies are unsurprising.

In the first place, no ideology can be wholly new. Ideas derive from somewhere, and in exploring the roots of green thinking, connections are inevitably made with thinkers, values and interests more familiarly associated with other ideologies or traditions of thought. Secondly, virtually all political creeds now proclaim some environmental concerns, which in turn require some analysis of their green credentials. Thirdly, even those who reject older ideologies and identify themselves as 'green' generally also have views on political issues which are not essentially or exclusively green, and associate them with the 'left' or the 'right'. Finally, in pursuit of practical political objectives Greens may form tactical alliances with other interests and parties, and are thus linked with the political company they keep.

Aspects of green thinking can be derived from a very diverse range of sources. A pantheistic concern for the universe can be found among Greek stoics. The revolt against rationalism, industrialism and modernism can be discerned in such thinkers as Rousseau, Carlyle, Ruskin or Disraeli. The notion of limits to growth was famously articulated by Malthus. A preference for the small scale and community values can be derived from Kropotkin or William Morris. Thus, some green ideas can be derived from conservative, liberal, socialist and anarchist thinkers and there are also links with some forms of national-ism and even fascism. More recently, there is a marked compatibility with a significant strand of feminism, sometimes called eco-feminism (Warren, 1994).

Greens and the right

Soon after becoming leader of the Conservatives in 2005, David Cameron identified his party and himself with green concerns. He demonstrated his personal green credentials by sometimes cycling to parliament, choos-ing a green car, and fixing a wind turbine on his roof. The transforma-tion of his party was symbolised by replacing the old freedom torch with a new green tree logo, and the adoption of the election slogan, 'Think Green, Vote Blue.' There was less by way of detailed policy commit-ments. Even so, all this was widely seen as a radical new departure for British conservatism by some commentators, who forgot that back in 1988 Mrs Thatcher had startled the Conservative party conference by proclaiming

> We Conservatives ... are not merely friends of the Earth, we are its guardians and trustees for generations to come. The core of the Tory philosophy and the case for protecting the environment are the same. No generation has a freehold on this Earth. All we have is a life tenancy, with a full repairing lease. (Quoted in McCormick, 1991, p. 60)

Yet the free-market strand of conservatism with which both Thatcher and Cameron have been particularly associated has generally seemed the political ideology least obviously compatible with green ideas (Hay, 1988). The freedom of market forces and profit maximisation does not sit easily with controls over pollution and environmental exploitation. Even so, it has been argued that private interest and ownership may be more conducive to environmental preservation than common ownership (Hardin, 1968), and some neo-liberal economists argue for free-market solutions to problems of resource depletion and pollution. Thus, market pressures will oblige entrepreneurs to find innovative alternatives to scarce resources, while experience has demonstrated the profit potential of environmentally friendly goods. Moreover, ways can be found of making polluters pay (Ashford, 1989). However, the free market does not provide easy answers to either long-term resource depletion and pollution issues (such as climate change), or sudden environmental disasters (for example floods, earthquakes and famine). Such problems commonly involve more interference with free-market forces than neo-liberals are generally prepared to countenance (Martell, 1994, pp. 63–72).

Traditional conservatism has rather more affinities with green thinking, as it involved a reaction against post-enlightenment rationalism, science, industrialism, modernism and faith in progress (see Chapter 3), much of which is shared by modern Greens. Almost by definition, conservation is a key value, and traditional conservatives have had a strong interest in the land and the preservation of the environment. In some cases this has taken the form of support for groups such as the Council for the Protection of Rural England, the National Trust or more recently the Countryside Alliance. Further to the right on the political spectrum, some extreme nationalists or fascists would proclaim an almost mystical association between race and environment, of 'blood and soil'.

There are indeed some Greens whose views are compatible with the traditional or even the fascist right. However, many Greens would argue that the conservative interest in the land is essentially self-interested and exploitative. The concern is for the rights of landowners, including their rights to exploit the land for their own profit and pleasure, conserving game, for example, so they can subsequently hunt or shoot, and restricting access to the countryside. Many Greens, moreover, would reject the assumptions of natural hierarchy and inequality associated with the right. In terms of practical politics, although Greens might sometimes enter tactical alliances with local right-wing preservation groups opposed to new roads, housing or retail developments, the grounds of Green concern are fundamentally different from those of self-interested NIMBYs (Not In My Back Yard). Thus, although Greens share some conservative values, they are not essentially defenders of the *status quo*, but radicals, seeking a very different future.

Greens and the left

In practice, Green activists are more commonly associated with the left rather than the right, with anarchists, socialists, social democrats and radical liberals. 'Red–greens' are a more familiar phenomenon than 'blue–greens', at almost every level of political activity. There are socialists with a strong green commitment; some Greens were previously members of left-wing parties or groups, and retain an affinity with their former political allegiance. Other Greens have worked closely with socialists of all kinds in the peace movement or the women's movement. In terms of analysis, green concerns with certain aspects of industrialism overlap with the fundamental socialist critique of capitalism. Some Marxists have argued that not only are Marx's ideas compatible with environmentalism, but that his analysis is highly relevant to modern green thinking (Pepper, 1993). In terms of prescription, both socialists and Greens seek radical change.

Yet some strands of socialism are clearly more compatible with green ideas than others. Greens tend to be individualist rather than collectivist, with a mistrust of large bureaucratic organisations, whether these are major industrial unions or government departments. Anarchism, and the bottom-up decentralised approach of Owen, William Morris or the guild socialists have more in common with Green thinking than the centralised state socialism or labourism dominant on the British left. Moreover, for all their critique of capitalism, most socialists (including Marx) belong firmly to the modernist, rationalist and essentially optimistic post-enlightenment tradition. Their objections to the private ownership of capital does not extend to the industrialisation associated with capitalism. On the contrary, they tend to be fervent believers in modernisation, progress and growth. Indeed, the leading

British socialist revisionist, Crosland (1956), hoped to promote greater equality, in large part through redistributing the product of economic growth. At a practical level, the interest of the labour movement in jobs and living standards is not easily compatible with green concerns.

Thus, the Labour government elected in 1997 initially promised a new commitment to the environment, but in practice concentrated on traditional Labour issues such as employment, health and education. Greens have been particularly critical of Labour's record on biotechnology and transport. While Blair favoured trials of genetically modified crops, many Greens feared the risks of irreversible damage to the environment. On transport, Labour's initial commitments to improve public transport and restrain the growth of car use were given insufficient priority, even before the fuel protests of autumn 2000 which dramatised the difficulty for any government in pursuing unpopular policies to restrict car use (Carter, 2001). More recently, the Brown government has aroused the ire of the pressure group, Plane Stupid, and Greens generally, by its support for aviation, and particularly plans for the expansion of Heathrow and Stansted airports. The renewed commitment of Labour to nuclear power and the construction of additional nuclear power stations has also dismayed many Greens.

For both conservatives and socialists, green issues have a lower priority than core ideological concerns, for private property and the free market on the one hand, and concerns over living standards and social welfare on the other. Thus, for Greens, the environmental concerns of other political creeds involve only relatively shallow and cosmetic 'greenspeak'. Only for the Greens are environmental issues central and fundamental rather than essentially peripheral. Only the Greens (or perhaps some Greens) articulate a coherent alternative ecological ideology.

Key elements of green thinking

It is now necessary to identify the core ingredients of this green ideology. Lists of core principles generally include the assumption that there are limits to growth, and the corollary of 'sustainability', an eco-centric rather than anthropocentric view of the relationship between humans and their environment, and a 'holistic' rather than piecemeal approach to the analysis of environmental issues and problems. Some would add a preference for small-scale and local organisation and activity. Other principles sometimes mentioned might be regarded as essentially derivative – thus, limits to population might be seen as an application of sustainability (Kenny in Eccleshall *et al.*, 1994; Garner, 1995, Dobson, 2007).

While all the above have been regarded as core green principles, they are principles of different kinds. The holistic approach is a fundamental methodological assumption that environmental problems cannot be tackled in isolation, but only in relation to each other, as parts of a whole. The notion of 'limits to growth' can be interpreted, by contrast, as a scientific hypothesis, in principle susceptible to empirical investigation. The ecocentric view, crudely expressed in the slogan 'Earth first', asserts a moral principle although it may also be interpreted as a means to the anthropocentric end of human survival. The emphasis on the small-scale and the local might be interpreted as a fundamental political principle or alternatively as a means to an end.

Green thinking is sometimes associated with post-modernism, naturally enough, as the targets of post-modernists are largely targets of greens also – post-enlightenment assumptions over science, reason and progress (Pepper, 1993, pp. 55–8). Yet post-modernism implies a moral relativism which is at odds with the Greens' essentially ethical message. Moreover, post-modernism rejects all 'meta-narratives' or universal explanations, and ecologism is above all a meta-narrative. While Greens reject current orthodoxies, they have their own truths to proclaim. It is now necessary to explore these truths in rather more detail.

Limits to growth – sustainability

Greens challenge the near universal modern assumption of the benefits to be derived from economic growth. The green notion that there are limits to growth can be derived from Malthus' *Essay on Population*, (1798, ed. Flew, 1970) and his theory of diminishing returns, which was particularly applicable to agricultural society. However, the experience of the industrialising western world in the nineteenth century suggested, by contrast, that virtually limitless improvements in growth and living standards were possible. Since then, high growth has become a tacit and often explicit objective of governments across the ideological spectrum, and a crucial component of a revisionist social democratic creed which sought to promote greater equality without making anyone worse off through distributing the products of growth.

Modern Greens have rediscovered the essentially Malthusian assumption that there are limits to the increases in productivity to be derived from the exploitation of finite natural resources. They have also identified significant costs associated with the pursuit of growth, in terms of damage to the environment and risks to health. The limits to growth have been vividly dramatised in some celebrated attempts to predict the consequences of present trends, such as the Club of Rome report (Meadows *et al.*, 1972). Greens would argue that the fundamental point remains unchallenged and unchallengeable – that non-renewable resources such as fossil fuels are finite and will ultimately be exhausted.

The green alternative to the pursuit of growth is the principle of sustainability. Humanity should only adopt those policies that can in the long run be sustained without irreversible damage to the resources on which the human species and other species depend. Energy resources are critical. For many Greens there must be a massive shift to renewable sources of energy, including wind power, water power (including wave power) and solar power to replace reliance on fossil fuels. Not only are these exhaustible, but also their carbon emissions have very damaging environmental consequences, including climate change causing more frequent episodic disasters and a cumulative catastrophic rise in sea levels. Some Greens, however, including James Lovelock (2006) have become convinced that an increase in the use of renewable energy cannot cope with the scale of the problem, and that only nuclear power can meet our future energy needs and secure the reduction in carbon emissions to prevent major climate change. This solution remains anathema to most Greens, concerned over the problems of disposing of toxic nuclear waste, and the risks of accidents to nuclear power plants. These issues have provoked a lively and sometimes acrimonious debate.

On the broader issue of economic growth in general, there is a school of thought known as 'ecological modernisation' which suggests that environmental protection and sustainability is compatible with real growth and improvements in living standards (Weale, 1992, ch. 3). One issue at stake here is what 'growth' actually involves, and how it should be measured. One argument suggests that western consumerism is ultimately not fulfilling for human beings, who increasingly prize a quality of life and post-material values (Inglehart, 1977) associated with environmental conservation. Indeed, the involvement in green parties and causes of a growing section of the middle classes in advanced industrial societies provides some supporting evidence for this assumption (Martell, 1994).

Yet if economic growth is measured in conventional economic terms, many Greens would concede that sustainability can only be achieved (for developed nations at least), with zero or negative growth, involving lower material living standards, and a reduction in population levels.

This is, needless to say, a difficult message to sell. Politicians have generally sought power by promising to make people better off in material terms. Greens are effectively promising to make people worse off (although they argue that a reduction in material consumption could involve a better quality of life). On the assumption, particularly by neo-liberals, that human beings are naturally self-seeking and acquisitive, it is difficult to see how they can be persuaded to forego current consumption in the interests of generations yet unborn, still less other species or the long-run survival of the planet.

Ecocentrism

Some would argue that an ecocentric rather than an anthropocentric approach is the defining characteristic of a distinctive green philosophy (Eckersley, 1992). An anthropocentric view puts humankind firmly at the centre of the universe. Green policies of pollution control and resource conservation are justified in terms of human interests – both present and future generations. An ecocentric view does not accord any priority to humanity, but emphasises the intrinsic value of the natural world, and the need of men and women to live in harmony with the universe. The distinction seems clear, but in practice, like other attempts to categorise Greens, involves a subtle gradation of positions. Further sub-divisions can be discerned within both anthropocentrism and ecocentrism (for example Eckersley, 1992, ch. 2) and, moreover, there are some Greens who would reject anthropocentrism without endorsing a pure ecocentric position. Supporters of animal rights (Singer, 1975) occupy an important intermediate position (Martell, 1994). As they argue animals should be valued for their own sake, they are clearly not anthropocentric. However, in confining their concerns to sentient beings which can experience pain and pleasure they fall far short of the ecocentric perspective which values the whole universe, including non-sentient nature (e.g. trees) and inanimate objects (e.g. rocks).

It can be argued that ecocentrism is ultimately a moral principle, requiring human beings to place the interests of the planet above their own self-interest. It is a moral principle which runs counter to mainstream thought which is anthropocentric. This focuses on humanity and human needs. It is implicitly and often explicitly assumed that the rest of the natural world exists to serve the needs of humankind, and it follows that men and women are free to exploit natural resources in whichever way they please to suit their own interests. Scientific advances have enabled humanity to overcome specific problems and exploit the resources of the natural world more effectively, and industrialisation and modernisation has involved the apparent taming of nature in the service of man.

In place of this anthropocentric approach, the ecocentric view places the human species in the context of its environment. 'Earth first' is a shorthand slogan that requires humans to consider first and foremost the future of the planet rather than their own immediate requirements. They have no claim to primacy over other species. Indeed, some Greens argue, it is the human species which has provided the main threat to the long-run survival of the planet. If the earth is to survive, human beings must learn to live in harmony with their natural environment, rather than seeking to exploit it.

One version of the ecocentric approach is the Gaia hypothesis, which suggests that the earth – personified as the Goddess Gaia – is a complex super-organism which requires other organisms to operate so as to keep the planet fit for life (Lovelock, 1979, 1988, 2006). Greens who oppose spiritual values to the materialist values they see embedded in modern society have sometimes tended to deify nature, providing a quasi-religious foundation for their ethical assumptions. Yet, defining exactly what is 'nature' or 'natural', and identifying right with nature involves familiar philosophical difficulties. Another militant interpretation of the injunction 'Earth First!' is provided by extremists within the American group of that name who have sometimes employed violent direct action techniques to protect the environment from man.

The notion of animal rights might be considered as either an important subsidiary application of the ecocentric principle, or a distinctive political perspective. While all Greens would share a concern for animal welfare, and support the aims of established pressure groups such as the RSPCA and the League Against Cruel Sports, not all would go further to endorse animal rights. Greens in practice adopt a variety of positions with regard to the treatment of animals (Singer, 1976; Regan, 1988; Garner, 1993, 1995; Martell, 1994). Thus many, but by no means all, Greens are vegetarians or vegans. For some this is a matter of simple preference or health or efficient resource utilisation. For others it is a critical ethical issue – 'meat is murder'; they view the rearing and killing of animals for human consumption as morally on the same level as the deliberate murder of fellow humans. Similarly, the use of animals in experiments to test new beauty treatments or medicines is regarded by some animal rights activists as akin to Nazi medical experiments on the Jews. A few who take this view have been prepared to indulge in acts of violence, including even murder, against those who are perceived to abuse animals.

Ultimately, 'Earth first' or 'Animal Rights' are fundamental moral principles not susceptible to scientific verification or falsification, to be held irrespective of their consequences. Yet such principles are not widely held, and it is difficult to see how the majority of humanity might be persuaded to adopt them, particularly in the absence of religious sanctions. In practice, despite their explicit rejection of the anthropocentric approach, in order to persuade others, and perhaps also to persuade themselves, many Greens tend to fall back on human-centred justifications for their injunctions. Thus, human beings should refrain from exploiting and polluting in their own long-term interests, or those of their children and grandchildren (Barry, 1977).

The holistic approach

The holistic approach requires that problems should not be analysed in isolation but related to the whole of which they are a part; the whole in question here is the universe or the ecosystem. Thus holism might be derived from the ecocentric perspective. Yet, although it has moral overtones, it is essentially a matter of methodology.

The need to analyse environmental problems in context is sometimes seen as the defining characteristic which marks off genuine ecologists, deep or dark Greens, from those who have particular and limited environmental concerns. Thus, light or shallow Greens are commonly associated with particular single issues, such as live calf exports, or new roads, or nuclear power. By contrast, deep or dark Greens have a holistic concern for the environment of which such specific issues are at best only a part, and at worst a dangerous diversion from more fundamental objectives.

This can be illustrated by reference to the campaign for lead-free petrol, which demonstrated and publicized the harm caused to children's health by lead additives to petrol. At one level, it was a textbook example of a successful single issue campaign, which ultimately persuaded government to encourage lead-free petrol through a tax incentive (Wilson, 1984). From a light green perspective the problem was virtually solved. Yet 'dark Greens' perceive the problem against the general context of resource conservation, waste and pollution. From this perspective, the removal of lead from petrol is at best a palliative which does not tackle the fundamental problem of resource depletion, waste and pollution associated with human dependence on the motor car. At worst it might be regarded as ecologically counterproductive, encouraging false assumptions about green fuels and green motoring.

In one sense, the need to see problems in context and relate issues to the wider whole is simply common sense, and may help to avoid counterproductive strategies. Yet taken to extremes, it might inhibit any action, because it would be impossible to calculate all the possible environmental implications and side-effects of any policy initiative compared with all the alternatives. Moreover, any personal or local initiative might be regarded as 'a drop in the ocean' and irrelevant to the real issue.

In practice, even those Greens most insistent on a holistic approach tend to become involved in single-issue campaigns, which can often be justified not only in terms of incremental reform but also for raising environmental consciousness. Thus, pure or dark Greens may become involved in tactical alliances with others whose commitment to a wider green agenda is vestigial. Indeed, any specific environmental issue, such as opposition to a new road, or new airport runway, tends to attract a coalition of interests. These may include NIMBYs with little or no general concern for the environment, those seeking to preserve particular areas of countryside or wildlife habitats, as well as committed Greens, for whom the specific issue is only an illustration of much wider issues of pollution and resource depletion. For Greens, such tactical alliances present awkward questions of political strategy that might be perceived as particularly problematic for the green movement generally.

Small is beautiful?

Sometimes regarded as a core principle, sometimes seen as an issue of strategy, is the widespread Green preference for the small-scale, decentralised and local. An influential text was Schumacher's (1973) *Small is Beautiful,* which challenged the then fashionable presumption in favour of large-scale enterprise. Since then, the mass production associated with Fordism has increasingly given way to the small-scale and flexible 'high-tech' and service enterprises considered characteristic of a post-Fordist economy. To that extent, the previously heretical assertion 'small is beautiful' has become the new orthodoxy.

Schumacher was an economist, and much of the argument can be couched in terms of economic theory. Conventional economic theory suggested that there were economies of scale to be gained from larger-scale production, although it was always recognised that beyond a certain point there might be diseconomies of scale. Theory seemed to be abundantly confirmed by the expansion of manufacturing industry through the mass production of standardised products, such as the family Ford car, which in western capitalist societies brought previously luxury items into the reach of those on average income, a phenomenon sometimes described as Fordism. Standardisation and large-scale operations also seemed to yield benefits in such areas as retailing and catering, and even in government where it was suggested that larger departments, larger local authorities and larger units for administering specific services such as education, health or police would likewise yield economies of scale.

There were always those who held a more sceptical or hostile perspective on this trend towards larger-scale production and organisation in the modern world. Burke spoke eloquently of the love of the little platoon. Toulmin Smith fulminated against the centralising tendencies of the Victorian era. William Morris reaffirmed the value of individual craftsmanship in an age of mass production. Anarchists rejected the growing power of the modern centralised nation-state.

These often appeared as minority voices vainly protesting against the onward march of progress and modernisation. Yet modern green preferences for the small-scale and local seem rather more consistent with prevailing trends. Thus the Fordist assumptions behind mass production, standardisation, specialisation and the division of labour have given place to a post-Fordist emphasis on innovation, flexibility and autonomy in the workplace. To an extent, small has become fashionable. Mainstream analysis accords a leading role to small or medium-sized enterprises in fostering economic development, and modern management theory suggests the need for flatter hierarchies which accord more autonomy to front-line staff. Some current political wisdom reaffirms the need for government close to the people through decentralisation.

All this would seem to abundantly justify the common Green preference for community-based action at the local level, and bottom-up rather than top-down political strategies. Indeed, Green political activity seems largely to fit neatly into a post-industrial, post-Fordist, postmodern world. Their own organisational structures tend to be decentralised, with few concessions to the conventional requirements for discipline, unity and leadership. Thus the British Green party has, until recently, shown a marked reluctance to recognise leaders, and a distaste for actual or potential political stars. Green activists generally follow the injunction to 'think global, act local'.

A possible corollary of decentralisation is greater self-sufficiency or autarky. Indeed, unless there is to be considerable co-operation among self-governing small-scale communities, an increased level of self-sufficiency is essential. Yet some Greens would also point to substantial positive benefits from greater self-sufficiency in terms of resource conservation. Less fuel and other resources would be needed to transport goods and people. One version of this approach is described as 'bio-regionalism' (Eckersley, 1992, pp. 167–70; Martell, 1994, pp. 51–3; Dobson, 1995, pp. 112–17) which seeks the integration of human communities within their distinctive regional environment. Thus, the inhabitants of a particular region would utilise the specific resources of the region at a sustainable level, rather than relying on international trade to fulfil their needs. Bioregionalism rejects the general assumptions of the benefits to be derived from specialisation and comparative advantage in conventional economic trade theory. It also, incidentally, involves a critique of mass travel and tourism.

Although many Greens seem to favour greater decentralisation and self-sufficiency, there are some who would deny that it is or should be an integral element of a Green ideology (Eckersley, 1992; Goodin, 1992; Martell, 1994). The preference for the small-scale, decentralised and local is reminiscent of anarchism and, indeed, there are close links in theory and practice between Greens and anarchists (Bookchin, 1971). Yet for anarchists the decentralisation of power is clearly their fundamental principle – it is what anarchism is essentially about. For Greens the ultimate objective is saving the planet, and 'small is beautiful' would seem an essentially subordinate principle to this overriding end.

Decentralisation, particularly if combined with increased self-sufficiency, has for some Greens uncomfortable implications for the distribution of resources between different regions and communities. Thus 'insisting too emphatically on decentralization, local political autonomy, and direct democracy can ... compromise the ecocentric goal of social justice' (Eckersley, 1992, p. 175). It is difficult to see how considerable inequalities between regions could be avoided; those from poorer underdeveloped regions of the world would be effectively prevented from benefiting from the only assets they could offer richer areas – cheap raw materials and cheap labour.

Moreover, it may be questioned whether decentralisation is a political strategy that is likely to further other, more fundamental Green objectives. It is at least arguable that if drastic and urgent action is needed to save the planet this may be more effectively achieved by centralised and even dictatorial methods. Most modern Greens seem temperamentally averse to such an approach. The issue does, however, raise in acute form the problem that has already been alluded to in the above analysis: what is an appropriate strategy for the Greens?

Green strategy

It has been suggested that all political ideologies contain (implicitly or explicitly) three main elements – a critique of existing society, a vision of the future, and a strategy for moving from the present to the desired future, what is often termed the problem of agency. The first two are very clearly evident in green thinking, but Green strategy often appears relatively weak and undertheorised (Dobson, 2007).

Strategy is particularly problematic for those ideologies that assume a need for radical change. For example, many socialists have envisaged a future society very different from the world in which they lived, which inevitably raises acute questions over the means of achieving objectives, the agency for change. Indeed, socialists have often been more bitterly divided over strategy rather than ultimate ends. Greens similarly seek a very different future. They seek massive economic and social change, and their political philosophy has far-reaching implications for industrial policy, agricultural policy, energy policy, transport policy and taxation policy. Virtually all Greens, apart from the most optimistic reformists, believe that radical changes in government policy and human lifestyles are urgently required. Indeed, many Greens would argue that the Green revolution they seek is more fundamental and far-reaching than a socialist revolution. Nor, if their analysis is correct, do Greens have time on their side. Those who subscribe to the Green ideology readily proclaim that change is urgent now if catastrophe is to be avoided in the future. This is scarcely compatible with gradualism.

Yet it is not just the radical and urgent nature of the change envisaged which makes strategy particularly problematic for Greens. The early socialists portrayed a potential future which was very different, but in many ways attractive to the mass audience at which it was directed, if threatening to established wealth and power holders. They were promising a better life. Greens, by contrast, seek a future that is widely perceived as involving a worse, rather than a better, life for the majority of humanity.

A variety of strategies, not necessarily mutually exclusive, are adopted in practice, including personal commitments to a green lifestyle, education and rational persuasion, grassroots community action, single-issue and broader pressure group campaigns, and involvement in party politics. Most of them neglect or skate round the problem of power; all of them raise awkward questions.

Green convictions may clearly involve some implications for personal behaviour. Just as high living seems inconsistent with socialist views, so Greens indulging in conspicuous consumption and environmental degradation invite charges of hypocrisy. Many Greens in practice agonise over the concessions and compromises that they make to modern consumerism. Others prefer to express their convictions almost entirely through their lifestyles, giving up their cars and reducing their consumption of non-renewable resources, becoming vegetarian and growing organic food. Some join communes of like-minded people. Like medieval monks or nuns, they have opted out of conventional values and materialistic lifestyles (Eckersley, 1992, pp. 163–7). However, their individual commitment, while affording some personal satisfaction, is unlikely by itself to promote any wider change beyond the limited influence of their example.

Broadly compatible with the politics of personal commitment is involvement in local initiatives within the immediate community. This sometimes involves a conscious rejection of conventional national politics for a bottom-up grassroots political strategy, much as some of the early socialists sought to fulfil their ideals through self-help friendly societies, co-operatives, and educational projects. The question here is the extent to which the cumulative impact of such local initiatives can possibly achieve the extent and pace of change required by green analysis. 'Think global, act local' is an appealing slogan, but if the scale of the problem is global rather than local, it seems unlikely that local initiatives can produce global solutions.

Another strategy, similar to that adopted by some early socialists, is to rely essentially on education and rational persuasion. While green thinking often appears antipathetic to the post-enlightenment rationalism, some Greens in practice place a heavy dependence on the power of reason, assuming that people will be convinced of the need for massive changes in their current materialist lifestyles if they can only be persuaded to grasp the facts. Yet of course the 'facts', however persuasive to Greens, involve assumptions and projections which are disputable. There are optimistic as well as pessimistic perspectives on the future, and most human beings may understandably be inclined to accept interpretations which have less uncomfortable implications for their own well-being. Thus, concerns that greenhouse gases were causing climate change, in particular global warming with increased risk of floods, led to the 1997 Kyoto agreement to reduce emissions in which the British Labour Government played a prominent role. However, it has proved difficult to persuade major countries, particularly the USA, to keep to the modest targets agreed. Although there is widespread agreement among scientists of the facts and consequences of climate change, some politicians and the wider public remain unconvinced of the need for action that might adversely affect industry, employment and existing lifestyles.

At the other extreme to the employment of rational persuasion is the use of direct, sometimes illegal and even violent action by a minority of Greens. Examples include the attacks on the Huntingdon Life Sciences laboratory designed to secure its closure, the trashing of trial GM crops, the occupation of tunnels and trees to prevent the building of new roads or airport runways, and the more general demonstrations against global capitalism. Such tactics are sometimes successful in delaying or halting developments or activities that are opposed. They may also serve to raise public consciousness of wider environmental issues, yet 'extremist' action may sometimes prove counterproductive by alienating public sympathy.

Pressure group politics involve some familiar dilemmas, whether, for example, to seek increased influence on government through securing insider status, involving some compromise of ideals and possible incorporation, or to maintain ideological purity at the expense of effective exclusion from the decision-making process. In Britain, the environmental organisations with most members are the highly respectable National Trust and the Royal Society for the Protection of Birds, and these are both influential within their limited conservationist spheres, in part because they rarely challenge established interests. More radical are Greenpeace and Friends of the Earth, which both operate at an international level. Their activities have certainly raised public consciousness of green issues, and have often seemed to influence both business practice and government policy. While Greenpeace has generally maintained its provocative radical outsider stance, and has sometimes operated outside the law, Friends of the Earth has become more involved in the consultative process. Only time will tell which is the more effective strategy in terms of changing policy.

Pressure group politics is almost by definition the politics of influence rather than the politics of power. Indeed, it could be argued that none of the approaches discussed above really address the problem of political power. Greens need some effective leverage on centres of power if they are to have any hope of forwarding their extensive and urgent agenda for change, perhaps some involvement in conventional electoral and parliamentary politics, either through existing political parties, or through the relatively new Green party.

The extent of the compatibility of Green ideas with older established political ideologies is a contentious issue, and the potential for working through existing parties will depend in part on the view taken. Indeed, there are Green (or greenish) groups operating in all major British parties, although the extent of their influence is contentious (Robinson, 1993). There are others of course who would argue that green convictions are fundamentally inconsistent with the established political parties and their underpinning ideological assumptions. The logical corollary for those who accept, nevertheless, the need for involvement in electoral and parliamentary politics, is a separate Green party.

Yet Green parties, unless they can win power on their own (which no Green party anywhere has remotely approached), can only have any effective influence if they combine with others. Thus the German Greens, after enjoying some electoral success in local, state and federal elections, finally entered a coalition with the Social Democrats under former Chancellor Gerhard Schröder, while Greens have also joined coalition governments in Belgium, Finland France and Italy (Carter, 2001, p. 121). Such relative success in conventional politics inevitably forces some hard choices and compromises that are not always palatable to Green purists. Indeed, the political record of the German Greens has not always won the approval of Greens inside and outside Germany. Yet such bargaining and compromise are a necessary party of electoral and parliamentary politics.

In Britain, familiar problems of competing with established parties are compounded by the first past the post electoral system that effectively penalises national parties without a strong regional base. However, the introduction of new voting systems for European, Scottish, Welsh and London elections have led to more elected Green representatives, including, briefly, seven members of the Scottish Parliament (2003 to 2007, when green representation was reduced to two). Yet, without electoral reform for Westminster and local elections the Green party will remain confined to the margins of British electoral politics.

Lack of success should not perhaps be blamed solely on the electoral system. The Green party's cause has scarcely been helped by their disregard for the conventional imperatives of party politics, for which some Greens have a marked distaste. While the party's past avoidance of hierarchical organisation, discipline and leadership is true to their

Table 9.1   Varieties of Green strategies

Strategy	Examples	Problems
Personal	Green lifestyle, no car, etc.	Monastic withdrawal?
	Grow food, make clothes, vegetarianism, join commune	Lack of impact on environmental problems
Local or community	'Think global, act local'. 'Small is beautiful', local initiatives, self-help anarchism	Difficulty in coordinating local initiatives
		Negligible impact on global environmental problems
Pressure group activity – orthodox	Rational persuasion, Education, Lobbying Parliament, Whitehall, parties, public, etc. Seek insider status for purposes of consultation	Unpalatable messages not believed or rejected. Short-term horizons of public, politicians, etc.
		Danger of incorporation
Pressure group activity – direct action	Demonstrations, obstruction, sabotage, damage to property, violence to people (e.g. those involved in experiments on animals)	May be counterproductive, alienate sympathy, etc. Gives cause a bad name
		Remedy worse than problem?
Regional strategy	Regional government? 'Bio-regionalism', autarky, limits on travel and trade, encourage close relationships between people and region, regional diversity	Cuts across conventional wisdom on free trade
		Challenges existing economic and political interests
		Would lead to unacceptable inequalities between regions
National strategy	Involvement in conventional electoral politics Either seek to convert major parties to green ideas, or to support Green Party	Strength of vested inteests in traditional parties – Green policies only cosmetic?
		Electoral system and other factors hinders Green party
International strategy	'Think global' – influence and involvement on international organisations and multinational corporations, international pressure groups. Protests against globalisation, WTO, etc.	Lack of political clout
		Problems of coordination
		Differences between rich and poor nations – western paternalism

decentralist philosophy, it scarcely assists their electoral appeal in an environment where politics is personalised and is increasingly about image and presentation. Indeed, the Green party has belatedly realised that they need a single elected leader.

However, the real problem for any Green party is that the message they seek to present is at odds with prevailing materialist values, with the immediate apparent interests of the bulk of the electorate, and with dominant assumptions about political motivation. For most people, it seems, the good life is about increased income and wealth, and the enjoyment of more and better consumer goods and services. Parties, it is assumed, win votes by appealing to the self-interest of individuals, groups and classes, promising to protect or raise living standards, reduce taxation, improve benefits and services. Even when politicians demand sacrifices in immediate consumption, this is usually on the expectation of some tangible benefit in the not too distant future, such as stable prices, increased employment, steady growth. The Greens, by contrast, are effectively promising to make people worse off in material terms. The sacrifices they call for are not for an immediate better future, but to avert a potential environmental catastrophe which might not affect current voters. It is not an easy political message.

Other political ideologies are linked to a particular social class or an identifiable sectional interest within society. Indeed, as has been noted, an influential interpretation is that political ideologies are essentially rationalisations of interest. Now there are some who would link environmentalist concerns with class interests. Some (mainly left-wing) critics have seen the Greens as selfish well-heeled people concerned to protect their own lifestyles against the poor or aspiring. On a global scale, it is sometimes alleged that western concern with destruction of the Amazonian rain forests, or pollution in the third world, reflect neo-colonial attitudes designed to keep other countries poor and underdeveloped. There is something in the allegation. Green politics would seem to appeal more to the haves than the have-nots, both within and between countries (see Inglehart, 1977, 1990, 1997, on post-material culture).

Yet, ostensibly, in so far as the green ideology serves an interest at all, it would appear to be an interest that transcends present society or even humanity itself. It is concerned with generations yet unborn, with other species, and with the future of the planet. While this is a noble and unselfish concern, it poses a problem for conventional politics; there is no mechanism for taking into account the interests of future generations, still less threatened fauna and flora, in either the economic or political marketplace. The radical Greens require a collective sacrifice of current consumption and immediate aspirations on the part of humanity in the interests of an unknown and unknowable future. Such heroic unselfishness does not fit easily with the assumptions about humankind which are implicit or explicit in mainstream western political ideology. Yet, unless these assumptions prove mistaken, it is difficult to see a realistic political strategy for the Greens.

Further reading

There are useful introductory short chapters on what is variously described as ecologism, environmentalism or green politics in Vincent (1995), Adams (1998), Eatwell and Wright (1999), Eccleshall *et al.* (2003) and Heywood (2007). There are a number of longer but accessible accounts of Green politics, including Porritt (1984), Porritt and Winner (1988), McCormick (1991), and Garner (1995). Garner has a particularly useful chapter on 'green thinking'. Green political theory is explored in more detail in Goodin (1992), Eckersley (1992) and particularly Dobson (2007). Other useful books include Weale's *The New Politics of Pollution* (1992), Pepper's *Eco-socialism* (1993), Robinson's *The Greening of British Party Politics* (1993) and Martell's *Ecology and Society* (1994). David Elliot (2007) has edited a volume on sustainable energy. *Green* by Jane Hoffman and Michael Hoffman (2008) explores renewable energy. James Lovelock's *The Revenge of Gaia* (2006) is both thoughtful and contentious, not least for his endorsement of nuclear power that many greens reject.

Among books which have almost acquired the status of modern green classics are Carson's *The Silent Spring* (1962), the Club of Rome's *The Limits to Growth* (Meadows *et al.*, 1972), Goldsmith's *A Blueprint for Survival* (1972), Schumacher's *Small is Beautiful* (1973), O'Riordan's *Environmentalism* (1976) and Lovelock's *Gaia: A New Look at Life on Earth* (1979). Extracts from most of these and much else besides can be found in *The Green Reader* edited by Dobson (1991).

10
Changing Ideologies

Continuity and change

Political ideologies are not static, but change and develop over time, as should be clear from earlier chapters. British conservatism and liberalism developed out of the old Tory and Whig traditions respectively. Subsequently, each of the major ideologies was subject to periodic renewal and reinvention, sometimes labelled 'new' to heighten the contrast with the past. Thus a 'New Liberalism' emerged in the early twentieth century, a 'New Right in the 1970s, and New Labour in the 1990s. Some commentators have discovered a new feminism, and even a new racism.

Yet (as should also be clear from the accounts provided here) although such developments emphasise the new, in each case there was significant continuity with the past. Indeed, those promoting change have often claimed inspiration and legitimation from history. Thus, the post-war 'One Nation' Conservatives consciously harked back to Benjamin Disraeli, while some of the New Right later sought inspiration from Lord Salisbury. Similarly, Blair cited the 'progressive alliance' between radical liberalism and Labour before the First World War to legitimise his party's co-operation and potential coalition with the Liberal Democrats. Such historical parallels reassure the party faithful that new initiatives are compatible with fundamental values and principles.

From class politics to identity politics?

Changes in political ideas may sometimes reflect long-term demographic, social and economic developments. In an oft-quoted verdict the political scientist Peter Pulzer (1967) once declared, 'Class is the basis of British politics; all else is embellishment and detail.'

Although this statement always involved considerable exaggeration and over-simplification, it contained a significant element of truth at the time of writing.

Yet the country has changed. Britain's population today is not only larger, but more ethnically and culturally diverse. It is also an ageing population; those over sixty-five outnumber those under sixteen. Patterns of employment have been transformed, with far fewer engaged in heavy industry and manufacturing generally, and far more in services. The manual working class and their families no longer constitute a majority of the population. Women constitute almost half the paid workforce. Ethnic minorities have become larger, more visible and more vocal. Gays are an increasingly accepted element of the British social scene. Thus, increasingly, other cross-cutting social cleavages overlay older class divisions. Some argue that class distinctions are far less important than they were. There is still a correlation between class and voting for the two major parties, but this is diminishing, while support for other parties appears to be drawn from across classes.

Indeed, the British party system has clearly changed. One obvious indicator is the decline in the combined two party vote for Labour and Conservative. These two parties secured between them 97 per cent of the vote in 1951. In more recent elections they have commonly secured around three-quarters of the vote, while in 2005, their combined percentage reached a post-war low of 68 per cent. Part of the change is that more people are voting for a third party, the Liberal Democrats, heirs to the old Liberals. Thus three parties, loosely associated with three mainstream ideologies, now compete for power (as they did in the 1920s). However, there is also increased support for other parties, such as nationalists in Wales and Scotland, the Green Party, the UK Independence Party, the British National Party, and most recently the party opposed to the Iraq war, Respect. The support for all these substantially cut across class divisions, and reflected new allegiances, often based on other felt identities, to nation, culture, or religion.

Thus, the old class-based politics appears to be giving ground to the politics of identity (Parekh, 2008), linked with political ideas less easily located on the familiar left–right spectrum. Identity politics is about who we think we are, rather than how we may be classified by statisticians, social scientists or government officials. Felt identities increasingly appear to have more implications for political attitudes and behaviour than seemingly more objective economic interests. Identity politics may prove more fluid than class politics, as who we think we are can change, sometimes considerably, over a lifetime. Identity politics also suggests more diversity and choice, but also may be perceived as a threat to national homogeneity and social unity. Indeed, separatist nationalism in Scotland and Wales threatens the existence of the United Kingdom.

A more fluid politics and a more volatile and diverse electorate provides opportunities for other parties, and a challenge for established parties who must reach out beyond their traditional class base. This explains much of the change in thinking that has taken place in both the Labour and Conservative parties. Some of this change has been essentially symbolic (new party logos, new statements of aims). However, there has also been a determined attempt, first by New Labour, then by Cameron's Conservatives, to recruit more women and ethnic minority candidates, and promote policies appealing to other communities beyond their traditional supporters.

A new political consensus?

Yet, paradoxically, one effect of increased diversity among voters has been more similarity between the policies of the three main parties. Although there remain some areas of considerable continuing disagreement between and within the parties, there has also been considerable ideological convergence. While New Labour adopted the free-market competition and privatisation policies of their Conservative predecessors, the Conservatives later felt obliged to accept much of New Labour's agenda, including not only constitutional reforms but the national minimum wage, and increased spending on public services (Beech and Lee, 2008). Successive Conservative leaders shied away from promising substantial cuts in public spending and tax (although they continued to maintain they could secure 'better value for money' through 'efficiency savings'). Thus, both major parties engaged in some ideological cross-dressing in pursuit of the 'centre ground', in a strategy that the American political scientist Anthony Downs (1957) had long ago argued should logically be pursued in a two party system to maximise votes. Yet this centre ground has been long claimed by Britain's third party, the Liberal Democrats and their Liberal predecessors.

After the 2005 election, the ideological differences between Britain's major parties have narrowed further, and the areas of agreement apparently grew, partly because of changes in the leadership of all three parties. One catalyst was certainly the election of David Cameron as Conservative leader, who distanced himself from Thatcher, insisting, 'There is such a thing as society' (Lynch, 2006). He signalled a change in direction for his party with his green agenda and 'compassionate conservatism', involving fairness, and tackling poverty, (Fraser, 2007). Just as Blair has sometimes been seen as Thatcher's heir, so Cameron has been perceived as Blair's heir, pursuing triangulation and even a new 'third way' (Kelly, 2008).

Meanwhile, the election of first Campbell and then Clegg as leader of the Liberal Democrats has involved a move away from the distinctive radical politics associated with Kennedy. Partly this was because of the reduced significance of the Iraq war, but also because of a shift away from public spending and redistribution towards free market economics and tax cuts, particularly under Clegg.

By contrast, the shift from Blair to Brown involved a change in style but less change in policy than some had anticipated. There was no return to Old Labour, as the Labour left and the Conservatives had hoped, for very different reasons. Instead, New Labour, now led by Brown, remained in the increasingly crowded centre ground which both Cameron's Conservatives and the Liberal Democrats sought to occupy. All the mainstream parties used a similar rhetoric, supporting free markets, light regulation, fairness, social justice, and a Green agenda, at least until the financial crisis of 2008 obliged some rethinking (see below).

Ideological consensus, at least between the three main parties, tends to strengthen the cynical conviction that all politicians and parties are the same, perhaps reducing the incentive to vote, or increasing the attraction of parties outside the consensus, such as the nationalists, the Greens, or even the BNP. To some critics the problem with modern British politics is that it is now about personalities rather than ideas or policies. Individual politicians such as Blair or Cameron are sold to the public on the basis of their personal qualities. The effective choice offered to the electorate is not so much between parties with distinctive ideologies and programmes but between rival leaders, and, to a much lesser extent, their team.

An allied criticism is that modern British politics is all about pragmatism rather than ideology. 'What matters is what works' or what appeals to focus groups, as interpreted by professional politicians and their advisers (McKibbin, 2008a). McKibbin's article was headed 'What Works Doesn't Work' (presumably McKibbin's own title) but was described alternatively as 'Politics without Ideas' on the journal's cover. To some critics Blair's (and now Brown's) New Labour and Cameron's Conservatism equally involve both personality politics and pragmatism, or 'politics without ideas'.

The 2008 financial crisis and its ideological implications

Some of the points on which all parties were apparently agreed have been blown apart by the credit crunch. It is not appropriate here to provide an analysis of the causes of the global financial crisis and associated economic problems of 2008 (Elliot and Atkinson, 2008). However, the immediate and potential longer-term consequences for political ideologies could be considerable. The banking crisis has drawn comparisons with the 'great crash' of 1929 onwards, which also originated in the United States, and spread to most of the western world. That earlier crisis spelt the end of free-trade liberalism and ushered in an era of protectionism. International co-operation was replaced by narrow nationalism. Moderate liberal and social democracy appeared discredited. Some were drawn to Soviet Communism, others to authoritarian conservatism or fascism – and the German Nazis profited markedly from the economic depression. In the longer term, subsequent analysis of the causes of the depression and the remedies that might have prevented it led to a wide acceptance of Keynesian economics which underpinned the social democratic consensus after the Second World War (Judt, 2005, p. 324).

The 2008 crisis may not have such extensive implications for political thinking. Even so, it has already involved some dramatic reversals in past commitments and underlying assumptions. In the United States, the government's rescue package for the financial system led to accusations of socialism against the outgoing Republican administration of George W. Bush. In Britain, there was surprisingly little opposition to the huge government loans that involved part-nationalisation of major banks, on top of the earlier nationalisation of Northern Rock. New Labour politicians, who had spent years dissociating themselves from the party's previous commitment to nationalisation, and extolling the virtues of the market, the city, and light touch regulation now found restoring confidence required the nationalisation of banks. Even more remarkably, the Conservatives and Liberal Democrats initially endorsed the Labour government's rescue package. The chief political correspondent of *The Guardian* suggested that it had turned 'political ideologies upside down', while George Galloway, the Respect (and former Labour) MP commented, 'the Liberals sound like Labour and the Conservatives like Communists' (Nicholas Watt, *The Guardian*, 9 October 2008). A new cross-party consensus castigated the city, reckless irresponsible greedy bankers, and inadequate regulation. Commentators had a field day comparing and contrasting what politicians from all parties had said only a few years or even a few months ago (see, for example, Rawnsley, *The Observer* 19 October 2008).

Yet although the name of Karl Marx was frequently invoked, few believed the collapse of capitalism was now at hand. As John Lanchester (2008, p. 5) observed, 'there is an ideological and theoretical vacuum where the challenge from the left used to be. Capitalism no longer has a global antagonist.' While it was clear that unregulated capitalism and free-market neo-liberal economics had taken a substantial battering, the major challenge to neo-liberal orthodoxy came not from the far left but from Keynesian economics, now back in fashion. Also, posthumously rehabilitated, was the American economist, John Kenneth Galbraith, who had advised US Presidents from Roosevelt to Kennedy and incidentally had written a best-selling account of *The Great Crash* ([1955], 1992).

The longer-term consequences may depend on the success of action taken internationally and domestically to restore confidence. One surprising immediate consequence in Britain has been to boost somewhat the standing of Brown's Labour government, whose fortunes had earlier plummeted. Some anticipate that the 'Brown bounce' will prove short-lived as the recession deepens and lengthens. Yet the crisis has played to his strengths and posed problems for the Conservatives, who have not found it easy to respond (McKibbin, 2008b). Although both parties once pursued Keynesian policies, it is less easy for the Conservatives to endorse them now following the Thatcher years. Labour, by contrast, has little now to lose by acting boldly. Thus, widening differences over policy to tackle recession and unemployment followed bipartisan support for the initial measures to restore financial confidence. Thus, Labour favoured tax cuts and public spending financed by increased borrowing, with the Conservatives proposing help for small businesses to stimulate the private sector, but otherwise opposing further borrowing in the interests of 'sound money'.

The financial crisis has had far-reaching effects beyond the arguments between and within the major parties. In restoring to centre stage the economy and old arguments about the respective role of the state and market, it has temporarily marginalised a whole range of other political concerns. These even include the 'war on terror', foreign and defence policy and international relations (except in so far as they affect the international financial system). Thus, the Labour government quietly dropped its legislation to extend the period of detention without trial for terror suspects from 28 to 42 days. Another by-product could involve winding down military operations sooner rather than later and avoiding further commitments. While this might be widely welcomed, it may also inhibit humanitarian intervention to save lives in parts of the world (such as Dafur and the Congo).

Greens fear that the concentration on the apparent priority to stimulate economic growth could have harmful consequences for the environment and climate change, particularly if capital projects brought forward include airport extensions, new roads and coal-fired or nuclear power stations. On the other hand, partly to help those in the building trade affected by the recession, more resources might be directed into grants for home insulation and fuel conservation. Feminists fear that pressure to reduce costs on business, especially small businesses, could halt or reverse some of the gains women have secured on maternity leave and flexible working. More short-time working and increased flexibility in labour markets could have a harmful impact on the wages, conditions and career prospects of working women. Recession could also damage race relations, if it leads to more competition for jobs between indigenous workers and more recent immigrants. There have been calls for further controls on immigration, although recession may effectively deter some prospective economic migrants, and prompt others to return to their country of origin or try elsewhere.

The financial crisis has also impacted on the arguments for separatist nationalism. Partly this is an argument over the perceived costs and benefits attached to scale. Would smaller states be better or worse off, facing global economic turbulence? Alex Salmond and the SNP have argued strongly that Scotland would prosper economically as an independent sovereign state within the European Union. They have pointed to the prosperity that other small states, such as the Irish Republic, Norway and Iceland have enjoyed. The failure of Icelandic banks and the dire position of the whole Icelandic economy damaged that argument, and Brown lost no time in arguing that the future of Scotland was more secure within the UK. The argument has been complicated by what has been happening to once prestigious Scottish financial institutions, whose shares had plummeted. If the reputation of the city of London as a financial centre has been bruised, so has Edinburgh, and the immediate consequences for the prosperity of Scotland's capital city could be more severe. Salmond and the SNP have countered that the problems of Scottish banks are the consequence of poor regulation and poor economic management by the UK government under Brown, and that an independent Scottish government would manage these affairs better. The argument seems set to run.

The impact of the 2008 US Presidential election

Both the earlier 1929 financial crash and the 2008 credit crunch provide a dramatic illustration of the impact of the United States on the economics and politics of other countries. American influence on Britain has long been apparent. British governments have long claimed a 'special relationship' with the United States, although the direction of influence has often appeared largely one way. Thus, Britain has imported ideas (neo-liberalism, neo-conservatism) and policies (including foreign policy, aspects of economic policy and penal policy and multiculturalism). There are also some reciprocal links between Republicans and Conservatives on the one hand, and the Democrats and Labour on the other. There has sometimes been a strong personal rapport between American Presidents and British Prime Ministers (Reagan and Thatcher, Clinton and Blair, Bush and Blair).

The long drawn out 2008 Presidential election raised interest and excitement not only in the United States, but other parts of the world, including Britain. An African-American family in the White House was once unimaginable. The clear victory of the Democrat candidate Barack Obama on a high turnout is of huge symbolic importance. It appears a triumphant vindication of the American dream, and a belated victory for all those, black and white, who have struggled over the centuries to validate the bold claim in the Declaration of Independence that all men were created equal.

Inevitably, the election of Obama has stirred expectations that it will be difficult or impossible to fulfil, yet it has transformed the American political climate. Political leaders around the world have been keen to link their own fortunes with Obama. In Britain, Brown has stressed he and Obama share the same progressive values. Cameron has welcomed Obama's election (despite his party's past links with the defeated Republicans) and claims that they both stand for change. Nick Clegg argues that Obama's proposals for tax cuts resemble those of the Liberal Democrats (Andrew Rawnsley, *The Observer*, 9 November 2008).

Yet there could be some important differences in policy, particularly in US foreign policy and the war on terror, in economic policy, and environmental policy. Much of this, particularly a stronger commitment to tackle climate change, would be welcomed outside the United States, not least by British politicians. However, there are also fears that rising US unemployment could lead to increased protectionism (as after the great slump), more particularly as Obama made some commitments to raising tariffs in the course of the election campaign.

Yet the big story remains the victory for the American dream and the specific dream of Martin Luther King. The United States has long been one of the most ethnically and culturally diverse countries in the world. It has also sometimes appeared in the past as one of the most divided, and indeed most racist, societies in the world, ridden with discrimination and prejudice. None of this will change overnight. Yet Obama's victory is not just a victory for African Americans and, indeed, Hispanic Americans, Asian Americans and the increasing number of mixed race Americans of whom Obama is one himself. It may one day be seen as a victory for all Americans, involving a multicultural society, drawing unity from the acceptance of diversity.

This has some obvious implications for other ethnically and culturally diverse societies like Britain. For those who have embraced multiculturalism, which has been pursued more extensively and for longer in the United States than in Britain, it demonstrates that this does not necessarily threaten the unity and coherence of society as a whole. Nor do more specific allegiances to different ethnic groups, cultures and religions necessarily preclude strong wider allegiances to the nation and indeed our common humanity.

Obama's victory also raises the possibility of more international co-operation between peoples. It has, perhaps briefly, restored the hope that those from different nations, ethnic groups and religious faiths can live together peaceably, both within states and globally. The optimism may prove short-lived, as so often in the past, yet in the shadow of international conflict, a global economic recession and a worsening environmental crisis, it provides a glimmer of light in the gloom.

Bibliography

Abrams, M., Rose, R. and Hinden, R. (1960) *Must Labour Lose?* (Harmondsworth: Penguin).

Adams, I. (1993) *Political Ideology Today* (Manchester: Manchester University Press).

Adams, I. (1998) *Ideology and Politics in Britain Today* (Manchester: Manchester University Press).

Adelman, P. (1970) *Gladstone, Disraeli and Later Victorian Politics* (Harlow: Longman).

Adelman, P. (1986) *The Rise of the Labour Party,* 2nd edn (London: Longman).

Adonis, A. and Hames, T. (1994) *A Conservative Revolution? The Thatcher–Reagan Decade in Perspective* (Manchester: Manchester University Press).

Alter, P. (1994) *Nationalism,* 2nd edn (London: Arnold).

Anderson, B. (1983) *Imagined Communities* (London: NLB/Verso).

Anderson, P. and Mann, N. (1997) *Safety First: The Making of New Labour* (London: Granta Books).

Arblaster, A. (1984) *The Rise and Decline of Western Liberalism* (Oxford: Blackwell).

Ashdown, P. (2000) *The Ashdown Diaries, volume 1, 1988–1997* (London: Allen Lane).

Ashford, N. (1989) 'Market Liberalism and the Environment: A Response to Hay', *Politics,* vol. 9, no. 1.

Astle, J., Laws, D., Marshall, P. and Murray, A. (eds) (2006) Britain *After Blair: A Liberal Agenda* (London: Profile Books).

Ayer, A. J. (1988) *Thomas Paine* (London: Faber & Faber).

Bacchi, C. L. (1990) *Same Difference: Feminism and Sexual Difference* (London: Allen & Unwin).

Back, L. and Solomos, J. (2000) *Theories of Race and Racism: A Reader* (London: Routledge).

Ballard, J. (2000) 'What is the Future of the Liberal Democrats?', *Talking Politics,* vol. 12, no. 2.

Barker, R. (1978) *Political Ideas in Modern Britain* (London: Methuen).

Barker, R. (1994) *Politics, Peoples and Government* (Basingstoke: Macmillan).

Barker, R. (2000) 'Hooks and Hands, Interests and Enemies: Political Thinking as Political Action', *Political Studies,* vol. 48, no. 2.

Barrett, M. (1980) *Women's Oppression Today: Problems in Marxist Feminist Analysis* (London: Verso).

Barrett, M. and Phillips, A. (eds) (1992) *Destabilizing Theory: Contemporary Feminist Debates* (Cambridge: Polity Press).

Barry, B. (2001a) *Culture and Equality: An egalitarian critique of multicultur- alism* (Cambridge: Polity Press).

Barry, B. (2001b) 'Multicultural Muddles', *New Left Review*, March/April 2001.

Barry, N. P. (1986) *On Classical Liberalism and Libertarianism* (London: Macmillan).

Beech, M. and Lee, S. (2008) *Ten Years of New Labour* (Basingstoke: Palgrave Macmillan).

Beer, S. H. (1982) *Modern British Politics* (London: Faber & Faber).

Behrens, R. (1989) 'Social Democracy and Liberalism', in L. Tivey and A. Wright (eds), *Party Ideology in Britain* (London: Routledge).

Bell, D. (1960) *The End of Ideology* (Free Press).

Benewick, R. (1972) *The Fascist Movement in Britain*, 2nd edn (London: Allen Lane).

Benn, T. (1979) *Arguments for Socialism* (London: Jonathan Cape).

Benn, T. (1989) *Office without Power: Diaries 1968–1972*, (London: Arrow).

Benn, T. (1990) *Conflicts of Interest: Diaries 1977–80*, (London: Arrow).

Benn, T. (1994) *The End of an Era: Diaries 1980–90*, (London: Arrow).

Bentley, M. (1984) *Politics without Democracy* (London: Fontana).

Bentley, M. (1987) *The Climax of Liberal Politics: British liberalism in theory and practice, 1869–1918* (London: Edward Arnold).

Berlin, I. (1969) 'Two Concepts of Liberty', in *Four Essays on Liberty* (Oxford: Oxford University Press).

Bernstein, G. L. (1986) *Liberalism and Liberal Politics in Edwardian England* (London: Allen & Unwin).

Bevir, M. (2000) 'New Labour: A Study in Ideology', *The British Journal of Politics and International Science*, vol. 2, no. 3.

Birch, A. H. (1977) *Political Integration and Disintegration in the British Isles* (London: Allen & Unwin).

Blair, T. (1996) *My Vision of a Young Country* (London: Fourth Estate).

Blake, R. (1966) *Disraeli* (London: Eyre & Spottiswoode).

Blake, R. (1997) *The Conservative Party from Peel to Major* (London: Heinemann).

Bookchin, M. (1982) *The Ecology of Freedom* (Palo Alto: Cheshire Books).

Bosanquet, N. (1983) *After the New Right* (London: Heinemann).

Bottomore, T. (1991) *A Dictionary of Marxist Thought* (Oxford: Blackwell).

Bower, T. (2004) *Gordon Brown* (London: Harper/Collins)

Bradley, I. (1981) *Breaking the Mould: the Birth and Prospects of the Social Democratic Party* (Oxford: Martin Robertson).

Bradley, I. (1985) *The Strange Rebirth of Liberal Britain* (London: Chatto & Windus).

Branson, N. (1979) *Poplarism 1919–1925* (London: Lawrence & Wishart).

Breuilly, J. (1993) *Nationalism & the State*, 2nd edn (Manchester: Manchester University Press).

Brittan, S. (1968) *Left or Right – the bogus dilemma* (London: Secker & Warburg).

Brockway, F. (1977) *Towards Tomorrow* (London: Hart-Davis MacGibbon).

Brownmiller, S. (1977) *Against Our Will* (Harmondsworth: Penguin).

Bruley, S. (1999) *Women in Britain since 1900* (Basingstoke: Macmillan).

Bryson, V. (1999) *Feminist Debates: Issues of Theory and Political Practice* (Basingstoke: Palgrave Macmillan).

Bryson, V. (2003) *Feminist Political Theory: an Introduction*, 2nd edn (Basingstoke: Palgrave Macmillan).

Bryson, V. (2000) 'Men and Sex Equality' *Politics*, vol. 20, no. 1.

Buck, P. W. (1975) *How Conservatives Think* (Harmondsworth: Penguin).

Bullock, A. and Stallybrass, O. (eds) (1977) *The Fontana Dictionary of Modern Thought* (London: Fontana/Collins).

Bulmer, M. & Solomos, J. (eds) (1999) *Racism* (Oxford: Oxford University Press).

Bulpitt, J. (1987) 'Thatcherism as Statecraft', in M. Burch and M. Moran (eds), *British Politics: A Reader* (Manchester: Manchester University Press).

Burke, E. (1790) *Reflections on the Revolution in France,* edited by Hill, B. W. (1975) (Fontana/Harvester Press).

Butler, D. & Butler, G. (1994) *British Political Facts 1900–1994*, 7th edn (London: Macmillan).

Butler, D. & Butler, G. (2006) *British Political Facts Since 1979* (Basingstoke: Palgrave Macmillan).

Butler, D. & Kavanagh, D. (1997) *The British General Election of 1997* (Basingstoke: Macmillan).

Caine, B. (1997) *English Feminism 1780–1980* (Oxford: Oxford University Press).

Calhoun, C. (1997) *Nationalism* (Buckingham: Open University Press).

Callaghan, J. (1987) *The Far Left in British Politics* (Oxford: Basil Blackwell).

Callaghan, J. (1990) *Socialism in Britain* (Oxford: Basil Blackwell).

Cameron, D. and Jones, D. (2008) *Cameron on Cameron: Conversations with Dylan Jones* (London: Fourth Estate).

Carson, R. (1965) *Silent Spring* (Harmondsworth: Penguin).

Carsten, F. L. (1967) *The Rise of Fascism* (London: Batsford).

Carter, A. (1988) *The Politics of Women's Rights* (Harlow: Longman).

Carter, N. (2001) 'The Environment', in *Developments in Politics* (ed. Lancaster) (Ormskirk: Causeway Press).

Chadwick, A. and Heffernan, R. (eds) (2003) *New Labour Reader* (Cambridge: Polity Press).

Challinor, R. (1977) *The Origins of British Bolshevism* (London: Croom Helm).

Childs, S. (2004) *New Labour's Women MPs* (London: Routledge).

Childs, S. (2005) 'Feminising politics: sex and gender in the election' in Geddes, A. and Tongue, J. (2005) *Britain Decides: the UK General Election 2005* (Basingstoke: Palgrave Macmillan).

Clarke, J., Cochrane, A. and Smart, C. (1987) *Ideologies of Welfare* (London: Hutchinson).

Clarke, P. F. (1971) *Lancashire and the New Liberalism* (Cambridge: Cambridge University Press).

Coates, D. (1980) *Labour in Power?* (Harlow: Longman).

Coates, D. (2005) *Prolonged Labour: The Slow Birth of New Labour Britain* (Basingstoke: Palgrave Macmillan).

Cole, J. (1995) *As It Seemed To Me: Political Memoirs* (London: Weidenfeld & Nicolson).

Coole, D. H. (1988) *Women in Political Theory* (London: Wheatsheaf Books).

Cornford, F. M. (1945) *The Republic of Plato* (Oxford: Oxford University Press).

Cosgrave, P. (1989) *The Lives of Enoch Powell* (London: Bodley Head).

Cowley, P. and Fisher, J. (2000) 'The Conservative Party', *Politics Review*, vol. 10, no. 2.

Cowling, M. (ed.) (1978) *Conservative Essays* (London: Cassell).

Crewe, I. and King, A. (1995) *SDP: The Birth, Life and Death of the Social Democratic Party* (Oxford: Oxford University Press).

Crick, B. (1987) *Socialism* (Buckingham: Open University Press).

Crick, B (ed.) (1991) *National Identities* (Oxford: Blackwell).

Crick, B. (1993) *In Defence of Politics*, 4th edn (Harmondsworth: Penguin).

Crosland, C. A. R. (1956) *The Future of Socialism* (London: Jonathan Cape).

Dahrendorf, R. (1990) *Reflections on the Revolution in Europe* (London: Chatto & Windus).

Dangerfield, G. (1966) *The Strange Death of Liberal England* (London: MacGibbon & Kee).

Dearlove, J. and Saunders, P. (2000) *Introduction to British Politics*, 3rd edn (Cambridge: Polity Press).

Davies, N. (1999) *The Isles: A History* (London: Macmillan).

Deutsch, K. W. (1966) *Nationalism and Social Communication* (New York: MIT Press).

Dicey, A. V. ([1885] 1959) *Introduction to the Study of the Law of the Consitution* (London: Macmillan)

Dicey, A. V. ([1905] 1914) *Lectures on the Relation between Law and Public Opinion in England during the Nineteenth Century* (London: Macmillan).

Dinwiddy, J. (1989) *Bentham* (Oxford: Oxford University Press).

Disraeli, B. (1844, 1983 ed.) *Coningsby* (Harmondsworth: Penguin).

Disraeli. B. (1845, 1980 ed.) *Sybil* (Harmondsworth: Penguin).

Dobson, A. (2007) *Green Political Thought*, 4th edn (London: Routledge).

Dobson, A. (ed.) (1991) *The Green Reader* (London: Andre Deutsch).

Donald, J. and Hall, S. (eds) (1986) *Politics and Ideology* (Buckingham: Open University Press).

Downs, A. (1957) *An Economic Theory of Democracy* (New York: Harper & Row).

Driver, S. and Martell, L. (1998) *New Labour: Politics after Thatcherism* (Cambridge: Polity Press).

Dunleavy, P., Heffernan, R., Cowley, P. and Hay, C. (2006) *Developments in British Politics 8*, (Basingstoke: Palgrave Macmillan).

Dunn, J. (1969) *The Political Thought of John Locke* (Cambridge: Cambridge University Press).

Dworkin, A. (1981) *Pornography* (London: Women's Press).

Eatwell, R. (1995) *Fascism: A History* (London: Chatto & Windus).

Eatwell, R. and Wright, A. (eds) (1999) *Contemporary Political Ideologies*, 2nd edn (London: Continuum).

Eccleshall, R. (1977) 'English Conservatism as Ideology', *Political Studies*, vol. xxv, no. 1.

Eccleshall, R. (1986) *British Liberalism: Liberal Thought from the 1640s to the 1980s* (Harlow: Longman).

Eccleshall, R. (1990) *English Conservatism since the Reformation: An introduction and anthology* (London: Unwin Hyman).

Eccleshall, R., Geoghegan, V., Jay, R., Kenny, M., MacKenzie, I. and Wilford, R. (2003) *Political Ideologies, an Introduction*, 2nd edn (London: Routledge).

Eckersley, R. (1992) *Environmentalism and Political Theory: Towards an Ecocentric Approach* (London: UCL Press).

Edgar, D. (1984) 'Bitter Harvest' in Curran, J. (ed.) *The Future of the Left* (London: Polity Press/New Socialist).

Elliot, D. (2007) *Sustainable Energy: Opportunities and Limitations* (Basingstoke: Palgrave Macmillan).

Elliott, L. and Atkinson, D. (2008) *The Gods that Failed: How Blind Faith in Markets Has Cost Us Our Future* (London: Bodley Head).

Etzioni, A. (1995) *The Spirit of Community* (London: Fontana Press).

Evans, B. (1984) 'Political ideology and its role in recent British politics' in Robins, L. (ed.), *Updating British Politics* (London: The Politics Association).

Evans, J. (1995) *Feminist Theory Today* (London: Sage).

Evans, J., Hills, J., Hunt, K., Meehan, E., Tuscher, T., Vogel, U. and Waylen, G. (1986) *Feminism and Political Theory* (London: Sage).

Evans, M. (1982) *The Woman Question* (London: Fontana).

Evans, M. (1997) *Introducing Contemporary Feminist Thought* (Cambridge: Polity Press).

Eysenck, H. J. (1957) *Sense and Nonsense in Psychology* (Harmondsworth: Penguin).

Figes, E. (1978) *Patriarchal Attitudes* (London: Virago).

Fielding, S. (2003) *The Labour Party: continuity and change in the making of 'New' Labour* (Basingstoke: Palgrave Macmillan).

Finer, S. E. (ed.) (1975) *Adversary Politics and Electoral Reform* (London: Wigram).

Firestone, S. (1979) *The Dialectic of Sex* (London: The Women's Press).

Flew, A. (ed.) (1979) *A Dictionary of Philosophy* (London: Pan/Macmillan).

Foot, M. and Kramnick, I. (eds) (1987) *The Thomas Paine Reader* (Harmondsworth: Penguin).

Foote, G. (1986) *The Labour Party's Political Thought* (London: Croom Helm).

Franklin, B. (1994) *Packaging Politics* (London: Edward Arnold).

Fraser, D. (1984) *The Evolution of the British Welfare State* (London: Macmillan).

Fraser, D. (2006) 'Adversary and Consensus Politics' *Talking Politics* vol. 19, no. 1.

Fraser, D. (2007) 'David Cameron: Modern Liberal or One-Nation Conservative' *Talking Politics,* vol. 19 no. 2.

Freeden, M. (1978) *The New Liberalism: An Ideology of Social Reform* (Oxford: Oxford University Press).

Freeden, M. (1986) *Liberalism Divided: A Study in British Political Thought 1914–1939* (Oxford: Oxford University Press).

Freeden, M. (1996) *Ideology and Political Theory* (Oxford: Clarendon Press).

Freeden, M. (1998) 'Is Nationalism a Distinct Ideology?', *Political Studies*, vol. 46, no. 4.

Freeden, M. (1999) 'The Ideology of New Labour', *The Political Quarterly*, vol. 70, no. 1.

Freeden, M. (2003) *Ideology: A Very Short Introduction* (Oxford: Oxford University Press).

Freely, M. (1995) *What About Us? An Open Letter to the Mothers Feminism Forgot* (London: Bloomsbury).

Friedan, B. (1965) *The Feminine Mystique* (Harmondsworth: Penguin).

Friedan, B. (1977) *It Changed my Life* (London: Victor Gollancz).

Friedan, B. (1982) *The Second Stage* (London: Michael Joseph).

Fukuyama, F. (1989) 'The End of History?' *The National Interest*, no. 16, summer.

Fukuyama, F. (1992) *The End of History and the Last Man* (London: Hamish Hamilton).

Galbraith, J. K. (1955, 1992) *The Great Crash* (Harmondsworth: Penguin).

Gamble, A. (1974) *The Conservative Nation* (London: Routledge & Kegan Paul).

Gamble, A. (1988) *The Free Economy and the Strong State* (London: Macmillan).

Gamble, A. (2003) *Between Europe and America: The Future of British Politics* (Basingstoke: Palgrave Macmillan).

Gamble, A. (2006) 'British Politics after Blair' in Dunleavy, P. *et al.* (2006) *Developments in British Politics 8* (Basingstoke: Palgrave Macmillan).

Garner, R. (1995) *Environmental Politics* (London: Harvester Wheatsheaf).

Geddes, A and Tonge, J. (eds) (2005) *Britain Decides: The UK General Election 2005*, (Basingstoke: Palgrave Macmillan)

Gellner, E. (1983) *Nations and Nationalism* (Oxford: Basil Blackwell).

George, V. and Wilding, P. (1985) *Ideology and Social Welfare* (London: Routledge & Kegan Paul).

Giddens, A. (1994) *Beyond Left and Right: the Future of Radical Politics* (Cambridge: Polity Press).

Giddens, A. (1998) *The Third Way: the Renewal of Social Democracy* (Cambridge: Polity).

Giddens, A. (2000) *The Third Way and its Critics* (Cambridge: Polity)

Giddens, A. (2007) *Over to You, Mr Brown* (Cambridge: Polity).

Gilmour, I. (1978) *Inside Right* (London: Quartet Books).

Gilmour, I. (1992) *Dancing with Dogma: Britain under Thatcherism* (London: Simon & Schuster).

Gilmour, I. and Garnett, M. (1997) *Whatever Happened to the Tories? The Conservatives since 1945* (London: Fourth Estate).

Goldsmith, E. (ed.) (1972) *A Blueprint for Survival* (Harmondsworth: Penguin).

Goodin, R. (1992) *Green Political Theory* (Cambridge: Polity Press).

Goodlad, G. D. (2005) 'Devolution in the United Kingdom: Where are we now?' *Talking Politics*, vol. 18, no. 1.

Goodwin, B. (1997) *Using Political Ideas*, 4th edn (Chichester: John Wiley & Sons).

Gould, P. (1998) *The Unfinished Revolution* (London: Abacus).

Graham, P. (2007) 'Nationalism in the UK: progressive or reactionary' *Politics Review*, vol. 17, no. 2.

Grant, J. (1993) *Fundamental Feminism* (London: Routledge).

Grant, M. (2004) 'Feminism in the 21st Century' *Talking Politics,* vol. 17, no. 1.

Gray, J. (1986) *Liberalism* (Buckingham: Open University Press).

Gray, J. and Willetts, D. (1997) *Is Conservatism* Dead? (London: Profile Books).

Gray, R. (1981) *The Aristocracy of Labour in Nineteenth-Century Britain c. 1850–1914* (London: Macmillan).

Green, D. G. (1987) *The New Right* (Brighton: Wheatsheaf).

Green, T. H. (1881) *Lectures on the Principles of Political Obligation* (ed. Harris, P. and Morrow, J., 1986) (Cambridge: Cambridge University Press).

Greenfeld, L. (1992) *Nationalism: Five Roads to Modernity* (Cambridge, MA.: Harvard University Press).

Greenleaf, W. H. (1973) 'The character of modern British conservatism' in Benewick, R., Berkhi, R. N. and Parekh, B. (eds), *Knowledge and Belief in Politics* (London: Allen & Unwin).

Greenleaf, W. H. (1983) *The British Political Tradition, Vol. 1, The Rise of Collectivism, Vol. 2, The Ideological Heritage* (London: Methuen).

Greer, G. (1970) *The Female Eunuch* (London: MacGibbon & Kee).

Greer, G. (1984) *Sex and Destiny: The politics of human fertility* (London: Secker & Warburg).

Hall, M. (2004) 'Nationalism in the UK' *Talking Politics*, vol. 16, no. 3.

Hall, S. and Jacques, M. (eds) (1983) *The Politics of Thatcherism* (London: Lawrence & Wishart).

Hamilton, M. B. (1987) 'The elements of the concept of ideology', *Political Studies*, vol. xxxv, no. 1, March.

Hampsher-Monk, I. (1992) *A History of Modern Political Thought: Major Political Thinkers from Hobbes to Marx* (Oxford: Blackwell).

Hardin, G. (1968) 'The tragedy of the commons', *Science*, vol. 162.

Harvie, C. (1994) *Scotland and Nationalism* (London: Routledge).

Hattersley, R. (1987) *Choose Freedom: The future of democratic socialism* (London: Michael Joseph).

Hattersley, R. (1995) *Who goes home?* (London: Little, Brown).

Hay, J. R. (1983) *The Origins of the Liberal Welfare Reforms*, 1906–1914 (London: Macmillan).

Hay, P. R. (1988) 'Ecological values and the western political traditions from anarchism to fascism', *Politics*, vol. 8, no. 1.

Hayek, F. (1975) 'The Principles of a Liberal Social Order', in Crespigny, A. and Cronin, J. (eds), *Ideologies of Politics* (Oxford: Oxford University Press).

Hayek, F. A. (1976) *The Road to Serfdom* (London: Routledge & Kegan Paul).

Healey, D. (1989) *The Time of My Life* (London: Michael Joseph).

Heywood, A. (2000) *Key Concepts in Politics* (Basingstoke: Palgrave Macmillan)

Heywood, A. (2007) *Political Ideologies: An Introduction*, 4th edition (Basingstoke: Palgrave Macmillan).

Heywood, A. (2008) 'Liberalism, Toleration and Diversity' *Politics Review*, vol. 18, no. 1.

Hindess, B. (1971) *The Decline of Working Class Politics* (London: MacGibbon & Kee).

Hobhouse, L. T. (1911, 1964) *Liberalism* (Oxford: Oxford University Press).

Hobsbawm, E. J. (1969) *Industry and Empire* (Harmondsworth: Penguin).

Hobsbawm, E. J. (1992) *The Age of Revolution 1789–1848* (London: Abacus).

Hobsbawm, E. J. (1988) *The Age of Capital 1848–1875* (London: Cardinal).

Hobsbawm, E. J. (1989) *Politics for a Rational Left* (London: Verso).

Hobsbawm, E. J. (1990) *Nations and Nationalism since 1780* (Cambridge: Cambridge University Press).

Hobsbawm, E. J. (1994) *The Age of Empire 1875–1914* (London: Abacus).

Hobsbawm, E. J. (1994) *Age of Extremes: The Short Twentieth Century 1914–1991* (London: Michael Joseph).

Hobsbawm, E. J. (1996) 'The Cult of Identity Politics', *New Left Review*, 217, May/June.

Hoffman, J. and Hoffman, M. (2008) *Green: Your Place in the New Energy Revolution* (Basingstoke: Palgrave Macmillan).

Hogg, Q. (1947) *The Case for Conservatism* (West Drayton: Penguin).

Holland, S. K. (1975) *The Socialist Challenge* (London: Quartet Books).

Honderich, T. (1990) *Conservatism* (London: Hamish Hamilton).

Hume, L. J. (1981) *Bentham and Bureaucracy* (Cambridge: Cambridge University Press).

Humm, M. (ed.) (1992) *Feminisms: A Reader* (London: Harvester Wheatsheaf).

Hungtington, S. P. (1996, 2002) *The Clash of Civilizations and the Remaking of World Order* (London: Free Press).

Hutchinson, J. (1994) *Modern Nationalism* (London: Fontana Press).

Hutchinson, J. and Smith, A. D. (eds) (1994) *Nationalism* (Oxford: Oxford University Press).

Hutton, W. (1995) *The State We're In* (London: Jonathan Cape).

Hutton, W. (1997) *The State to Come* (London: Vintage).

Jackson, S. *et al.* (eds) (1993) *Women's Studies: A Reader* (London: Harvester Wheatsheaf).

Jenkins, R. (1991) *A Life at the Centre* (London: Macmillan).

Jennings, I. (1941, 1966) *The British Constitution*, 5th edn (Cambridge: University Press).

Joll, J. (1979) *The Anarchists*, 2nd edn (London: Methuen).

Joseph, K. (1976) *Stranded on the Middle Ground* (London: Centre for Policy Studies).

Judt, T. (2005) *Postwar: A History of Europe since 1945* (London: William Heinemann).

Kampfner, J. (2004) *Blair's Wars* (London: Free Press).

Kavanagh, D. (ed.) (1982) *The Politics of the Labour Party* (London: Allen & Unwin).

Kavanagh, D. (1990) *Thatcherism and British Politics*, 2nd edn (Oxford: Oxford University Press).

Kavanagh, D. and Morris, P. (1994) *Consensus Politics*, 2nd edn (Oxford: Blackwell).

Kavanagh, D. and Seldon, A. (1994) *The Major Effect* (London: Macmillan).

Kedourie, E. (1993) *Nationalism*, 4th edn (Oxford: Blackwell).

Keating, M. (1998) *The New Regionalism in Western Europe* (Cheltenham: Edward Elgar).

Keegan, W. (1984) *Mrs Thatcher's Economic Experiment* (London: Allen Lane).

Kellas, J. G. (1991) *The Politics of Nationalism and Ethnicity* (Basingstoke: Macmillan).

Kelly, R. (2008) 'Conservatism under Cameron: the new 'Third Way'', *Politics Review,* vol. 17, no. 3.

Kershaw, I. (1993) *The Nazi Dictatorship: problems and perspectives in interpretation* (London: Edward Arnold).

King, D. S. (1987) *The New Right* (Basingstoke: Macmillan).

Kingdom, J. (1999) *Government and Politics in Britain* (Cambridge: Polity Press).

Kirk, R. (1982) *The Portable Conservative Reader* (Harmondsworth: Viking Penguin).

Kitchen, M. (1976) *Fascism* (London: Macmillan – now Palgrave Macmillan).

Kogan, D. and Kogan, M. (1982) *The Battle for the Labour Party* (London: Kogan Page).

Kymlicka, W. (1989) *Liberalism, Community and Culture* (Oxford: Clarendon Press).

Kymlicka, W. (1995) *Multicultural Citizenship* (Oxford: Oxford University Press).

Laqueur, W. (ed.) (1979) *Fascism: A Reader's Guide* (Harmondsworth: Penguin Books).

Lanchester, J. (2008) 'Cityphobia', *London Review of Books*, vol. 30, no. 20, pp. 3–5.

Lawson, N. (1992) *The View from No. 11: Memoirs of a Tory Radical* (London: Bantam).

Laybourn, K. (2000) *A Century of Labour* (Stroud: Sutton Publishing).

Le Grand, J. (1998) 'The Third Way begins with Cora', *New Statesman*, 6 March.

Levitas, R. (ed.) (1986) *The Ideology of the New Right* (London: Polity Press).

Lichtheim, G. (1970) *A Short History of Socialism* (London: Weidenfeld & Nicolson).

Locke, J (ed. Gough, 1966) *A Letter Concerning Toleration*, with *Second Treatise of Civil Government* (Oxford: Basil Blackwell).

Lovell, T. (ed.) (1990) *British Feminist Thought: A Reader* (Oxford: Basil Blackwell).

Lovelock, J. (1979) *Gaia: A new look at life on Earth* (Oxford: Oxford University Press).

Lovelock, J. (2007) *The Revenge of Gaia* (London: Penguin Books).

Lovenduski, J. (2005) *Feminizing Politics* (Cambridge: Polity Press).

Lovenduski, J. and Randall. V. (1993) *Contemporary Feminist Politics* (Oxford: Oxford University Press).

Ludlam, S. (2000) 'New Labour: what's published is what counts', *British Journal of Political Science*, vol, 2, no. 2, June.

Ludlam, S. and Smith, M. (eds) (1996) *Contemporary British Conservatism* (Basingstoke: Macmillan).

Ludlam, S. and Smith, M. (eds) (2001) *New Labour in Government* (Basingstoke: Macmillan).

Ludlam, S. and Smith, M. (eds) (2004) *Governing as New Labour* (Basingstoke: Palgrave Macmillan).

Lynch, P. (2006) 'The Challenges for Cameron' *Politics Review*, vol. 16, no. 1.

Mac an Ghaill, M. (1999) *Contemporary Racisms and Ethnicities* (Buckingham: Open University Press).

MacDonald, J. R. (1911) *The Socialist Movement* (London: Home University Library).

Mackenzie, J. M. (ed.) (1986) *Imperialism and Popular Culture* (Manchester: MUP).

MacKinnon, C. (1989) *Towards a Feminist Theory of the State* (London: Harvard University Press).

Macpherson, C. B. (1962) *The Political Theory of Possessive Individualism* (Oxford: Oxford University Press).

Macpherson, Sir W. (1999) *The Stephen Lawrence Inquiry* (Cm 4262) (London: The Stationery Office Ltd).

Maddox, J. (1972) *The Doomesday Syndrome* (London: Macmillan).

Major, J. (1999) *The Autobiography* (London: HarperCollins).

Malthus, T. (1798) *An Essay on the Principle of Population* (ed. Flew, 1970) (Harmondsworth: Penguin).

Mannheim, K. (1960) *Ideology and Utopia* (London: Routledge & Kegan Paul).

Manning, D. J. (1976) *Liberalism* (London: Dent).

Marquand, D. (1977) *Ramsay MacDonald* (London: Jonathan Cape).

Marquand, D. (1988) *The Unprincipled Society* (London: Fontana).

Marquand, D. (1999) *The Progressive Dilemma* (London: Phoenix).

Marquand, D. (2008) *Britain Since 1918: the Strange Career of British Democracy* (London: Weidenfeld & Nicolson).

Marr, A. (1992) *The Battle for Scotland* (Harmondsworth: Penguin Books).

Marr, A. (2007) *A History of Modern Britain* (London: Macmillan).

Marshall, P. and Laws, D. (eds) (2004) *The Orange Book: Reclaiming Liberalism* (London, Profile Books).

Martell, L. (1994) *Ecology and Society: An Introduction* (Cambridge: Polity Press).

Marx, K. (ed. McLellan, D., 1977) *Selected Writings* (Oxford: Oxford University Press).

Marx, K. and Engels, F. (1962) *Selected Works* (two vols.) (London: Lawrence & Wishart).

McCormick, J. (1991) *British Politics and the Environment* (London: Earthscan Publications Ltd).

McCrone, D. (1992) *Understanding Scotland* (London: Routledge).

McGarvey, N. and Cairney, P. (2008) *Scottish Politics: An Introduction* (Basingstoke: Palgrave Macmillan).

McKenzie, R. T. (1963) *British Political Parties*, 2nd edn (London: Heinemann).

McKenzie, R. T. and Silver, A. (1968) *Angels in Marble* (London: Heinemann).

McKibbin, R. (2008a) 'Politics without Ideas', *London Review of Books*, vol. 30, no. 17.

McKibbin, R. (2008b) 'What can Cameron do?', *London Review of Books*, vol. 30, no. 20.

McLean, I. and McMillan, A. (eds) (2003) *The Concise Oxford Dictionary of Politics* (Oxford: Oxford University Press).

McLellan, D. (1976) *Karl Marx* (London: Paladin, Granada Publishing).

McLellan, D. (1979) *Marxism after Marx* (London: Macmillan).

McLellan, D. (1995) *Ideology*, 2nd edn (Buckingham: Open University Press).

Meadows, D. H., Meadows, D. L., Randers, D. L. and Behrens III, W. (1974) *The Limits to Growth* (London: Pan).

Michels, R. (1962) *Political Parties* (Free Press).

Middlemas, K. (1979) *Politics in Industrial Society: the experience of the British system since 1911* (London: Deutsch).

Mies, M. and Shiva, V. (1993) *Ecofeminism* (London: Fernwood Publications/ Zed books).

Miles, R. (1989) *Racism* (London: Routledge).

Miles, R. (1993) *Racism after 'Race Relations'* (London: Routledge).

Miliband, D. (ed.) (1994) *Re-inventing the Left* (Cambridge: Polity Press).

Miliband, R. (1972) *Parliamentary Socialism*, 2nd edn (London: Merlin Press).

Miliband, R. (1994) *Socialism for a Sceptical Age* (Cambridge: Polity Press).

Mill, J. S. (ed. Warnock, 1962) *Utilitarianism, On Liberty*, with introduction by M. Warnock (1962) (London: Fontana/Collins).

Mill, J. S. (ed. Acton, H. B., 1972) *Utilitarianism, On Liberty, Representative Government* (London: J. M. Dent).

Mill. J. S. (ed. Okin, S., 1988) *The Subjection of Women* (Indianapolis, IN: Hackett Publishing Company).

Mill, J. S. and Bentham, J. (ed. Ryan, A., 1987) *Utilitarianism and Other Essays* (Harmondsworth: Penguin).

Miller, D. *et al.* (eds) (1991) *The Blackwell Encyclopaedia of Political Thought* (Oxford: Blackwell).

Millett, K. (1977) *Sexual Politics* (London: Virago).

Minkin, L. (1978) *The Labour Party Conference* (London: Allen Lane).

Minkin, L. (1991) *The Contentious Alliance: Trade Unions and the Labour Party* (Edinburgh: Edinburgh University Press).

Minogue, K. (1967) *Nationalism* (London: Batsford).

Minogue, K. (1985) *Alien Powers: The Pure Theory of Ideology* (London: Weidenfeld & Nicolson).

Mirza, H. S. (ed.) (1997) *Black British Feminism* (London: Routledge).

Mitchell, J. (1974) *Psychoanalysis and Feminism* (Harmondsworth: Penguin).

Mitchell, J. and Oakley, A. (1986) *What is Feminism?* (Oxford: Blackwell).

Morgan, K. R. (1997) *Callaghan: A Life* (Oxford: Oxford University Press).

Morris, W. (1962) *Selected Writings and Designs* (ed. Briggs, A.) (Harmondsworth: Penguin).

Nairn, T. (1981) *The Break-up of Britain* (London: NLB & Verso).

Nairn, T. (2000) *After Britain: New Labour and the Return of Scotland* (London: Granta Books).

Nairn, T. (2001) 'Post Ukania', *New Left Review*, 7, Jan/Feb..

Nisbet, R. (1986) *Conservatism* (Buckingham: Open University Press).

Nozick, R. (1974) *Anarchy, State and Utopia* (Oxford: Blackwell).

Oakeshott, M. (1962) *Rationalism in Politics and other Essays* (London: Methuen).

Okin, S. M. (1990) *Justice, Gender and the Family* (New York: Basic Books).

O'Riordan, T. (1976) *Environmentalism* (London: Pion Ltd).

O'Sullivan, N. (1976) *Conservatism* (London: Dent).

Owen, D. (1981) *Face the Future* (Oxford: Oxford University Press).

Owen, D. (1991) *Time to Declare* (London: Michael Joseph).

Owen, R. (1991) *A New View of Society and Other Writings*, edited by G. Claeys (Harmondsworth: Penguin).

Paine, T. (1791–2 ed. Collins, 1969) *The Rights of Man* (Harmondsworth: Penguin).

Parekh, B. (2000a) *Rethinking Multiculturalism: Cultural Diversity and Political Theory* (Basingstoke: Palgrave Macmillan).

Parekh, B. (Chair) (2000b) *The Future of Multi-Ethnic Britain: Report of the Commission on Multi-Ethnic Britain* (London: Profile Books in association with Runnymede Trust).

Parekh, B. (2005) *Rethinking Multiculturalism: Cultural Diversity and Political Theory,* 2nd edn (Basingstoke: Palgrave Macmillan).

Parekh, B. (2008) *A New Politics of Identity* (Basingstoke: Palgrave Macmillan).

Parkin, F. (1972) *Class, Inequality and Political Order* (London: Paladin).

Patten, J. (1995) *Things to Come: The Tories in the 21st Century* (London: Sinclair-Stevenson).

Paxman, J. (1998) *The English* (London: Michael Joseph).

Pearce, N. and Margo, J. (2007) *Politics for a New Generation: The Progressive Movement* (Basingstoke: IPPR/Palgrave Macmillan).

Pearson, R. and Williams, G. (1984) *Political Thought and Public Policy in the Nineteenth Century* (London: Longman).

Peele, G. (2006) 'The Politics of Multicultural Britain', in Dunleavy, P. *et al.* (2006) *Developments in British Politics 8* (Basingstoke: Palgrave Macmillan).

Pelling, H. (1965) *The Origins of the Labour Party* (Oxford: Oxford University Press).

Pepper, D. (1993) *Eco-Socialism: From Deep Ecology to Social Justice* (London: Routledge).

Perryman, M. (ed.) (1994) *Altered States: Postmodernism, Politics, Culture* (London: Lawrence & Wishart).

Phizacklea, A. and Miles, R. (1980) *Labour and Racism* (London: Routledge & Kegan Paul).

Pierre, J. and Peters, B. G. (2000) *Governance, Politics and the State* (Basingstoke: Palgrave Macmillan).

Pierson, S. (1973) *Marxism and the Origins of British Socialism* (Ithaca, NY: Cornell University Press).

Pimlott, B. (1977) *Labour and the Left in the 1930s* (Cambridge: Cambridge University Press).

Pimlott, B. (1992) *Harold Wilson* (London: HarperCollins).

Plamenatz, J. P. (1963) *Man and Society: a critical examination of some important social and political theories from Machiavelli to Marx,* two vols (London: Longmans).

Plant, J. (ed.) (1989) *Healing the Wounds: The Promise of Ecofeminism* (Green Print, The Merlin Press).

Plant, R. (2008) 'Blair's Liberal Interventionism' in Beech, M. and Lee, S. (2008) *Ten Years of New Labour* (Basingstoke: Palgrave Macmillan).

Plato (tr. Cornford, 1945) *The Republic*, (Oxford: Oxford University Press).

Pois, R. A. (1986) *National Socialism and the Religion of Nature* (London: Croom Helm).

Popper, K. R. (1962) *The Open Society and its Enemies*, 4th edn, 2 vols., (London: Routledge & Kegan Paul).

Porritt, J. and Winner, D. (1988) *The Coming of the Greens* (London: Fontana/ Collins).

Pulzer, P. (1967) *Representation and Elections in Britain* (London: Allen & Unwin).

Pyle, A. (1995) *The Subjection of Women: Contemporary Responses to John Stuart Mill* (Bristol: Thoemmes Press).

Quinton, A. (1978) *The Politics of Imperfection* (London: Faber & Faber).

Ramazanoglu, C. (1989) *Feminism and the Contradictions of Oppression* (London: Routledge).

Randall, V. (1987) *Women and Politics* (London: Macmillan).

Ranelagh, J. (1992) *Thatcher's People* (London: Fontana).

Rawls, J. (1971) *A Theory of Justice* (Oxford: Oxford University Press).

Rawls, J. (1993) *Political Liberalism* (New York: Columbia University Press).

Rawnsley, A. (2001) *Servants of the People: The Inside Story of New Labour* (Harmondsworth: Penguin).

Rawnsley, A. (2008) 'A golden age, and other things they wish they'd never said' *The Observer*, 19 October 2008.

Regan, T. (1988) *The Case for Animal Rights* (London: Routledge & Kegan Paul).

Rex, J. (1986) *Race and Ethnicity* (Buckingham: Open University Press).

Rhodes, R. A. W. (1997) *Understanding Governance* (Buckingham: Open University Press).

Richards, J. R. (1982) *The Sceptical Feminist* (Harmondsworth: Penguin).

Riddell, P. (1983) *The Thatcher Government* (Oxford: Martin Robertson).

Robertson, D. (1993) *The Dictionary of Politics* (Harmondsworth: Penguin).

Robinson, M. (1992) *The Greening of British Party Politics* (Manchester: Manchester University Press).

Rubinstein, D. (2000) 'A New Look at New Labour', *Politics*, vol. 20, no. 3.

Rushdie, S. (1998) *The Satanic Verses* (London: Viking).

Russell, C. (1999) *An Intelligent Person's Guide to Liberalism* (London: Duckworth).

Sardar, Z. (2008a) *Balti Britain: A Journey through the British Asian Experience* (Cambridge: Granta).

Sardar, Z. (2008b) 'Who are the British Asians?' *New Statesman*, 28 September 2008, pp. 32–3.

Saggar, S. (1992) *Race and Politics in Britain* (London: Harvester Wheatsheaf).

Said, E. (2003) *Orientalism* (Harmondsworth: Penguin).

St John-Stevas, N. (1982) 'Tory philosophy – a personal view', *Three Banks Review*, June, no. 134.

Sandbach, F. (1980) *Environment, Ideology and Policy* (Oxford: Basil Blackwell).

Sargent, L (ed.) (1981) *The Unhappy Marriage of Marxism and Feminism: a Debate on Class and Patriarchy* (London: Pluto Press).

Sassoon (1997) *One Hundred Years of Socialism* (London: Fontana Press).

Saville, J. (1988) *The Labour Movement in Britain* (London: Faber & Faber).

Scarman, Lord (1981) *The Brixton Disorders 10–12 April 1981: Special Report* (London: HMSO).

Scholte, J. A. (2005) *Globalization: A Critical Introduction* (Basingstoke: Palgrave Macmillan).

Schultz, H. J. (1972) *English Liberalism and the State: Individualism or Collectivism?* (Lexington, MA: Heath).

Schumacher, E. F. (1973) *Small is Beautiful* (London: Sphere Books).

Schumpeter, J. A. (1943) *Capitalism, Socialism and Democracy* (London: Allen & Unwin).

Schwarzmantel, J. (1991) *Socialism and the Idea of the Nation* (London: Harvester Wheatsheaf).

Scruton, R. (1980) *The Meaning of Conservatism* (London: Macmillan).

Scruton, R. (2007) A *Dictionary of Political Thought*, 3rd edition (Basingstoke: Palgrave Macmillan).

Seldon, A. (2001) *The Blair Effect: The Blair Government 1997–2001* (London: Little, Brown and Company).

Seldon, A. (2004) *Blair* (London: Free Press).

Seldon, A. (ed.) (2007) *Blair's Britain* (Cambridge: Cambridge University Press).

Seldon, A. & Ball, S. (1994) *Conservative Century: The Conservative Party since 1900* (Oxford: Oxford University Press).

Seldon, A. and Kavanagh, D. (eds) (2005) *The Blair Effect 2001–5* (Cambridge: Cambridge University Press).

Seliger, M. (1976) *Ideology and Politics* (London: Allen & Unwin).

Seyd, P. (1987) *The Rise and Fall of the Labour Left* (London: Macmillan).

Seymour-Ure, C. (1974) *The Political Impact of the Mass Media* (London: Constable).

Shaw, E. (1994) *The Labour Party since 1979: Crisis and Transformation* (London: Routledge).

Singer, P. (1990) *Animal Liberation* (London: Cape).

Skellington, R. (1996) *'Race' in Britain Today* (London: Sage).

Skidelsky, R. (1967) *Politicians and the Slump* (Harmondsworth: Penguin).

Skidelsky, R. (1990) *Oswald Mosley*, 3rd edn (London: Macmillan).

Skidelsky, R. (ed.) (1988) *Thatcherism* (London: Chatto & Windus).

Skidelsky, R. (2008) 'A Thinker for Our Times: Man of the Year, John Maynard Keynes' *New Statesman,* 22 December 2008.

Skinner, Q. (1978) *The Foundations of Modern Political Thought*, 2 vols. (Cambridge: Cambridge University Press).

Smith, A. (1776) *The Wealth of Nations* (edited with an introduction by E. Cannan, 1976) (Chicago, IL: University of Chicago Press).

Smith, A. D. (1991) *National Identity* (Harmondsworth: Penguin Books).

Smith, P. (1967) *Disraelian Conservatism and Social Reform* (London: Routledge).

Solomos, J. (2003) *Race and racism in Britain,* 3rd edn (Basingstoke: Palgrave Macmillan).

Solomos, J. & Back, L. (1995) *Race, Politics and Social Change* (London: Routledge).

Solomos, J. & Back, L. (1996) *Racism and Society* (Basingstoke: Macmillan).

Spencer, H. ([1884] ed. Mack, E., 1981) *The Man versus the State* (Indianapolis, IN: Liberty Classics).

Stephenson, H. (1982) *Claret and Chips: the rise of the SDP* (London: Michael Joseph).

Stokes, W. (2005) *Women in Contemporary Politics* (Cambridge: Polity Press).

Tawney, R. H. (1961) *The Acquisitive Society* (London: Fontana).

Tawney, R. H. (1964) *Equality* (London: Unwin).

Taylor, S. (1982) *The National Front in English Politics* (London: Macmillan).

Temple, M. (2000) 'New Labour's Third Way: pragmatism and governance', *The British Journal of Politics and International Relations*, vol. 2, no. 3, October.

Thatcher, M. (1977) *Let Our Children Grow Tall* (London: Centre for Policy Studies).

Thatcher, M. (1993) *The Downing Street Years* (London: HarperCollins).

Thompson, E. P. (1980) *The Making of the English Working Class* (Harmondsworth: Penguin).

Thompson, K. (1986) *Beliefs and Ideology* (London: Ellis Horwood & Tavistock Publications).

Thomson, D. (1966) *Political Ideas* (Harmondsworth: Penguin).

Thurlow, R. C. (1987) *Fascism in Britain: A History 1918–1985* (Oxford: Basil Blackwell).

Tivey, L. (ed.) (1981) *The Nation State* (Oxford: Martin Robertson).

Tivey, L. and Wright, A. (1989) *Party Ideology in Britain* (London: Routledge).

Tong, R. (1992) *Feminist Thought: A Comprehensive Introduction* (London: Routledge).

Toynbee, P. and Walker, D. (2005) *Better or Worse? Has Labour Delivered?* (London: Bloomsbury).

Vincent, A. (1995) *Modern Political Ideologies*, 2nd edn (Oxford: Blackwell).

Vincent, J. (1966) *The Formation of the Liberal Party, 1857–1868* (London: Constable).

Waldegrave, W. (1978) *The Binding of Leviathan* (London: Hamish Hamilton).

Walter, N. (1999) *The New Feminism* (London: Virago).

Walker, M. (1977) *The National Front* (London: Fontana).

Wallace, W. (1997) *Why vote Liberal Democrat?* (Harmondsworth: Penguin Books).

Warren, K. J. (ed.) (1994) *Ecological Feminism* (London: Routledge).

Watson, J. S. (1960) *The Reign of George III* (Oxford: Oxford University Press).

Weale, A. (1992) *The New Politics of Pollution* (Manchester: Manchester University Press).

Wendelkin, D. (2007) 'Nationalism', *Talking Politics,* vol. 19, no. 2.

Whiteley, P. (1983) *The Labour Party in Crisis* (London: Methuen).

Whiteley, P., Seyd, P. and Richardson, J. (1994) *True Blues: The Politics of Conservative Party Membership* (Oxford: Clarendon Press).

Willetts, D. (1997) *Why Vote Conservative?* (Harmondsworth: Penguin Books).

Williams, R. (1976) *Keywords: A Vocabulary of Culture and Society* (London: Fontana/Croom Helm).

Williams, S. (1981) *Politics is for People* (Harmondsworth: Penguin).

Wilson, D. (1984) *Pressure: The A to Z of Campaigning in Britain* (London: Heinemann).

Winder, R. (2004) *Bloody Foreigners: The Story of Immigration to Britain* (London: Little, Brown).

Wollstonecraft, M. (1792) *A Vindication of the Rights of Women* (ed. Tauchert, 1995) (London: Dent, Everyman).

Wright, A. (1983) *British Socialism* (London: Longman).

Wright, A. (1987) *Socialisms: Theories and Practices* (Oxford: Oxford University Press).

Wright, D. G. (1970) *Democracy and Reform, 1815–1885* (Harlow: Longman).

Wright, T. (1997) *Why vote Labour?* (Harmondsworth: Penguin Books).

Young, H. (1989) *One of Us* (London: Macmillan).

Young, H. (1998) *This Blessed Plot: Britain and Europe, from Churchill to Blair* (London: Macmillan).

Index